Small Claims Proce
A Practical Guic
Fourth Edition

by
Her Honour Judge Patricia Pearl M.A(Oxon)
and
Andrew Goodman, LL.B, MBA, FRSA
Barrister of the Inner Temple

Small Claims Procedure: A Practical Guide

Fourth Edition

xpl publishing

© Patricia Pearl and Andrew Goodman 2008

Published by
XPL Professional Publishing Ltd
99 Hatfield Road
St Albans
Herts
AL1 4JL
www.xplpublishing.com

ISBN 978 1 85811 394 4

Typeset by Jane Adams

Printed in the UK

Contents

A Small Claims Flowchart		*306*
Preface		*vii*
Glossary – some specialist legal terms explained		*ix*
Procedural Table: Overview of Small Claims Procedure		*xvi*

1	Preliminary topics	1
2	Step by Step Guide to Starting a Small Claims Case	15
3	Responding to the Claim (including obtaining judgment in default or on an admission)	45
4	Allocation Questionnaires and Allocation	61
5	Steps between Allocation and the Hearing (including checklist for preparation for the hearing)	83
6	The No Costs Rule	109
7	The Hearing	127
8	Appeals and Applications to Set Aside Judgment	155
9	Mediating Small Claims	173
10	Other Parts of the Civil Procedure Rules	191
11	Drafting Rules and precedents for Small Claims Cases	215
12	Enforcement of Small Claims Judgments in the County Court	243
	Appendices	
	Appendix 1 – Court Fees Payable in Small Claims Cases – Commencement to Hearing	255
	Appendix 2 – Court Fees Payable in Small Claims Cases – Applications and Appeals	257

Appendix 3 – Fixed Commencement Costs   259

Appendix 4 – Fixed Costs on entry of judgment   261

Appendix 5 – Forms   263

Appendix 6 – Part 1 of the Civil Procedure Rules   265

Appendix 7 – Part 27 of the Civil Procedure Rules
               and the Practice Direction   269

Table of Citations   289

Index   299

Preface

Welcome to the fourth edition of this practical guide to Small Claims litigation.

Legal professionals rarely receive any formal training or guidance on how to conduct or present Small Claims cases. A lack of understanding of the rules leads to confusion and mistakes, which in turn adds to expense and causes delay. Litigants often have to deal with Small Claims cases without legal representation. The purpose of this book is to equip all those who are involved with Small Claims cases with the know-how to avoid errors and to make the most of the procedures that are available.

This book contains all the basic materials to help with the procedural aspects of a Small Claims case. It is written from a practical point of view and contains numerous cross references and precedents. This is a handbook and guide for the busy practitioner, but has been written with the litigant in person and lay representative in mind. The non lawyer reader of this book will find that relevant legal terms are explained in the glossary at the front of the book. Chapter 12 is an outline of procedures available for the enforcement of any judgment which is obtained.

The book will be of use to those who do not expect their claims to be disputed. The early chapters of the book set out all the procedures to start the claim and the steps leading to a judgment in default.

The no costs rule was introduced to enable cases to be pursued without the worry of the loser being burdened by the victor's heavy legal costs. Both sides in a Small Claims case should be comforted by the fact that, if attempts to settle fail, the case should be disposed of with the minimum of fuss because the procedural steps before the hearing are as simple as possible. The final hearing will not only be earlier than in cases allocated to the fast track and multi-track, but will also be shorter and more relaxed than a formal trial. A full appeal procedure is now in place with identical grounds for appeal as in appeals from cases allocated to the fast track or multi-track; for Small Claims slightly fewer documents are needed to support the appeal and the fee payable for the appeal is reduced.

We remain firmly of the view that the key to effective Small Claims litigation is simplicity in approach. Part 27 provides a straightforward system to bring claims of limited financial value to a hearing. These can now even be brought online using the Moneyclaim website. If a case is burdened by unnecessary procedure of any kind, it will soon become cumbersome and this will result in delays and expense.

Small Claims procedure had its beginnings many years ago and was formerly termed 'arbitration'. New stages in the Small Claims procedure were introduced by the introduction of the Civil Procedure Rules but has survived as a low cost method of resolving disputes and continues to be attractive to litigants in person.

Over the lifetime of the third edition a variety of court-directed mediation schemes have been piloted across the country resulting in a National Mediation Helpline service in which all county courts will eventually participate. A number of courts are now creating the role of dedicated mediation officers. To that end a new chapter on mediating small claims appears in this edition for the first time at chapter 9.

The law, procedure and court fee scales are as up to date as we could make them as at April 2008.

Patricia Pearl and Andrew Goodman
London
April 2008

Glossary – some specialist legal terms explained

Allocation	The procedure by which a District Judge decides if a case qualifies for the Small Claims track or some other track
Allocation questionnaire	The form which both sides complete and send to the court to assist the District Judge when giving initial case management orders and when allocating the case to a track
Alternative Dispute Resolution	Collective description of methods of resolving disputes other than by the normal trial process
Arbitration	A method of settling disputes by which the parties agree to a determination by an umpire or arbitrator; commonly used in the settlement of commercial disputes. (The term previously denoted the Small Claims procedure in the county court)
Assessment	See Detailed assessment and Summary assessment
Barrister	A specialist professional advocate who has been called to the Bar by one of the Inns of Court and undertaken the required pupillage (practical training)
Boxwork	The work done by a District Judge on a court file where there is no hearing and the parties are not present
Case management	The process by which the District Judge controls the progress of a case by making orders and imposing sanctions

Circuit Judge	A County Court Judge senior in rank to a District Judge (Circuit Judges hear appeals of Small Claims cases)
Claimant	The party who starts the action by making a claim
Community Legal Service	The provider of legal services funded by the Legal Services Commission (which replaced the Legal Aid Board). Its website, http://www.justask.org.uk also gives contacts for other organisations that can be approached for free legal help
Community Legal Services Fund	The replacement for the Legal Aid Fund (in April 2000). Parties awarded funding are called "funded clients", but such funding is not available in Small Claims cases (http://www.legalservices.gov.uk)
Costs terminology	See Chapter 6 for definitions of "no order for costs"; "costs reserved" and "costs in the case"
Counterclaim	A claim by a defendant against a claimant
Court Service	The government service responsible for running all courts in England and Wales (http://www.courtservice.gov.uk)
CPR ("the rules")	The Civil Procedure Rules 1998 (http://www.justice.gov.uk/civil/procrules)
Damages	A sum of money awarded by the court as compensation for wrongdoing
Default judgment	A judgment entered because a defendant has not filed an acknowledgment or defence to a claim within the time specified by the rules
Defendant	The party against whom a claim is made
Deputy District Judge	Part time District Judge (see page 6)

Detailed assessment (of costs)	When the costs of a case are decided after the case has been completed: the process involves costs being detailed in a bill and a hearing if they are not agreed (the procedure is not used in Small Claims cases)
Directions	Orders made to govern the procedure in a case
Disclosure	The process of each party notifying the others of any documents they intend to use at a hearing
Disposal	A hearing after judgment when the amount due to the claimant is determined by the court
District Judge	A member of the judiciary appointed to conduct business in the County court including Small Claims cases
Evidence	Information given to the court to support a case. Evidence takes a number of forms including information on the claim form supported by a statement of truth, affidavits, verbal evidence given in court and documents.
Ex parte application	An application made without giving notice to the other side (*N.B.* this term is obsolete under the CPR and instead the term "without notice" should be used)
Fast track	Case management track for cases of up to £15,000 in value which can be heard in one day or less and which do not qualify for the Small Claims track
Filing	Sending or taking a court document to the court office – the court staff then put the document on the court file relevant to the case
Home court	The County court for the district in which the defendant's address for service, as shown on the defence, is situated (rule 2.3); (note that this is the solicitor's address if the defendant is legally represented)

Jurisdiction	The geographical area to which the Civil Procedure Rules apply – this is England, Wales and adjacent territorial waters. Note that Scotland and Ireland (including Northern Ireland) are not within the jurisdiction of the Rules (rule 2.3)
Lay representative	Someone other than a lawyer exercising the limited rights audience at a Small Claims hearing (see also McKenzie friend). (Lay representatives are not legal representatives (rule 2.3(1))
Legal executive	A professional qualified under the Rules of the Institute of Legal Executives (ILEX). Specially qualified legal executives – ILEX advocates – can appear as advocates in open court county court hearings, including Small Claims hearings.
Legal representative	A barrister or solicitor, solicitor's employee or other authorised litigator (as defined in the Courts and Legal Services Act 1990) who has been instructed to act for a party in relation to a case (rule 2.3(1))
Litigant in person	Someone who acts for themselves without using a lawyer or lay representative
Litigation friend	Someone authorised by the court to conduct a case on behalf of a person under 18 or a person under a mental disability. Full details are set out in rule 21.
McKenzie friend	Someone who assists a litigant in person in court but does not present the case to the judge (see also Lay representative)
Mediation	A voluntary, non-binding, and private dispute resolution process in which a neutral person helps the parties try to reach a negotiated settlement, the contents of which remain confidential and 'without prejudice' unless or until a settlement is achieved.

Multi-track	Case management regime applicable to cases of over £15,000 in value which do not qualify for the Fast Track
Overriding objective	The underlying principle of the Civil Procedure Rules which is to deal with cases justly taking in certain criteria as to even and open-handedness and proportionality (rule 1.1).
Part	The civil procedure rules are divided into 76 parts, each containing a rule and often a Practice Direction. (Part 27 contains rule 27 and a Practice Direction)
Part 20 claim	Claims made in an action other than by a claimant – third party proceedings and counterclaims are types of Part 20 claims
Part 36 offers and payments	Part 36 describes the rules which apply if a party wishes to make a formal offer to settle including the costs consequences. These procedures are of limited application in.
Particulars of claim/ defence	Details of a case – applies to a claim, defence, or counterclaim
Practice direction	The civil procedure rules are supported by formal guidance notes – in the case of Small Claims the practice direction includes the routine directions orders.
Pre-action protocol	This is to promote settlement before litigation/ legal practitioners and others have reached a formal understanding on the steps to be taken in certain types of cases before proceedings are issued. The protocols which exist today do not cover Small Claims cases
Procedural judge	Any judge who takes decisions about the procedure in a case; in the County court this can be the District Judge or Circuit Judge

Reply	The claimant's answer to a defence (generally unnecessary in Small Claims cases)
Right of audience	Being allowed to present a case in court on behalf of someone else or on one's own behalf
Rule	One of the 76 Civil Procedure rules
Small Claims court	A term used colloquially to mean the Small Claims procedure in the County court – a misnomer because there is no Small Claims court as such (see page 5)
Small Claims track	The special case management regime applicable to cases of limited financial value (see Chapter 4 for more detail of which cases qualify for the Small Claims track)
Solicitor	Someone who has passed the Law Society examinations and is on the Law Society's roll of solicitors (section 1 Solicitors Act 1974)
Specified claim	Cases where the amount of the claim is stated by the claimant as a fixed sum of money (see page 31)
Statement of Truth	Formal confirmation that the contents of a court document are true, for example a statement of case or a witness statement (see page 169)
Statements of case	Formal documents setting out the details of a case
States paid defence	A defence when the defendant claims that the sum claimed has already been paid
Stay	A court imposed halt on proceedings; a case can only continue if the stay is removed
Strike out	Striking out means either the court ordering an end to the case or that certain written material be deleted so that it may no longer be relied upon.

Summary assessment (of costs)	If the District Judge decides that any costs are payable in a Small Claims case, the amount will be decided there and then at the hearing and this process is called summary assessment
Summary judgment	Procedure under Part 24 for obtaining a judgment without a full hearing (see page 174)
Third party claim	A claim where the defendant wants to shift blame on to a party who was not brought into the action by the claimant (see also Part 20 claims)
Track	One of the special case management regimes under the Civil Procedure rules (see also Small Claims track, Fast track and Multi-track)
Unspecified claim	Cases where the claimant leaves the amount of the claim to be determined by the court (see page 32)
Without prejudice	Negotiations with a view to a settlement are usually conducted "without prejudice", which means that the circumstances in which the content of those negotiations may be revealed to the court are very restricted

Procedural Table; Overview of Small Claims procedure

Stage of action	Step to be taken	Notes
Before the start of the action	Claimant writes a letter before action	
Before the start of the action	Both parties try to negotiate a settlement	
At the start of the court action	Claimant completes form N1 and sends it to the County court with the court fee	
When the court receives the claimant's papers	Court staff give the case an action number (proceedings are issued)	The papers may be referred to the District Judge by the court staff for directions at any stage of the case
	Court serves the proceedings by sending to the defendant by first class post	
14 days after service	Last date for responding to the case by defence acknowledgment or admission	The table on page 44 gives more detail of the steps to be taken at the allocation stage
28 days after service	Last date for defence (if acknowledgment has been filed)	
After filing of defence	Court sends out allocation questionnaires	The case is transferred to the defendant's home court if the amount is specified and the defendant is an individual

Stage of action	Step to be taken	Notes
14 days after receiving allocation questionnaires	Both parties return questionnaire (claimant pays fee if amount claimed £1,000 or more)	
	District Judge considers allocation questionnaires – case is allocated to Small Claims track and directions are given	In a few cases the District Judge may direct that there be a preliminary hearing
Before the hearing	Parties send each other the documents that they will use at the hearing	This is usually 14 days before the hearing but may be at a different time if the District Judge so directs
	THE HEARING	It is usual for both sides to attend the hearing but the rules do allow the parties to make arrangements for the case to be heard in their absence
Within 21 days of the date of the decision	Loser can lodge an appeal; the decision must be wrong or there must be a serious procedural irregularity	Permission is required which can be requested at the hearing itself or later by application to a Circuit Judge

CHAPTER 1

Preliminary topics

The overriding objective   2

Speedy – effective – proportionate   2

The Small Claims track: history and overview   3

Electing to use the Small Claims track   4

Terminology   4

District Judges   6

Reference materials   6

Special features of Small Claims cases   7

Evaluating the case   7

The court's management powers   10

Alternatives to court action – mediation or litigation?   10

Enforcement   11

Settlement   11

Court fees   12

Letters before action   12

European Convention on Human Rights   12

Public funding of Small Claims cases   13

Using this book   14

Preliminary topics

The overriding objective

This book is about the procedural rules which apply to running a Small Claims case in the county court and the practical and effective ways in which these rules are applied to cases of limited financial value.

The Civil Procedure Rules (CPR) govern the procedure applicable to Small Claims. The overriding objective of the Rules is to enable the court to deal with cases justly. Part 1 of the Rules describes the ways in which the court seeks to achieve this objective, for example by active case management. Throughout the book, references are made to the considerable case management powers which enable the court to control the way in which the case is prepared for hearing. The parties cannot expect poorly prepared or hopeless cases to run to a hearing – such cases are likely to be identified by the District Judge and will be subject to rigorous case management.

> See Chapter 10 for a more detailed discussion of the overriding objective

Speedy – effective – proportionate

The procedure for dealing with Small Claims is set out in Part 27 of the Civil Procedure Rules. It provides a speedy, effective and proportionate method of dealing with disputes of limited financial value.

The procedure is ideally suited to litigants in person. Practitioners advising in Small Claims cases are faced with the challenge of providing a cost-effective service. The efficiency of the Small Claims procedure depends on all court users understanding the rules applicable to Small Claims cases and applying them in a practical way.

The Small Claims track; history and overview

The procedure has evolved over the years, initially limited to claims involving sums in dispute of not more than £100, the current financial limit is £5000 for money claims. Such a sum is not 'small' for most people, and neither are Small Claims insignificant in any way for the county courts. Every year, more than 100,000 cases which qualify for the Small Claims track are started. Going by the sheer number of hearings, most disputes that are decided by civil judges in England and Wales are dealt with by the Small Claims procedure.

The Small Claims procedure was an integral part of the reforms recommended by Lord Woolf.[1] The procedure of the Small Claims track was inspired by the so-called arbitration procedure which existed prior to the introduction of the Civil Procedure Rules in 1999.

Cases allocated to the Small Claims track are exempted from some procedures which would burden them with undue formality, for example the detailed rules about experts, witness statements and the need to complete pretrial checklists.

Court fees are payable at three stages namely when starting the claim, after the defence and when the court considers case management dirctions and lastly before the hearing. It should be noted that some people with limited financial means are exempted from paying court fees (see page 12).

The old 'arbitration' hearings were in private. These days Small Claims hearings are open to the public. In reality, this has not made much difference to the conduct of Small Claims hearings as strangers rarely stray into them, which are nearly always dealt with in an informal setting in the judge's room and without outside observers (see page 131).

The introduction of the Civil Procedure Rules create a consistent approach in different courts. County courts no longer develop 'local practices' and District Judges and Circuit Judges are conscious that they must work together to ensure a coherent interpretation of the rules.

---

1 **Access to Justice** by the Right Honourable Lord Woolf, Master of the Rolls, Final Report July 1996.

Prior to 2000 there was no appeal against the award in a Small Claims case, albeit there was a limited right to apply for an award to be 'set aside'. However, since October 2000 there has been a full appeal procedure which is the same as for other cases and governed by CPR Pt 52 appeal process.

Electing to use the Small Claims track

Rule 26.7(3) allows parties to consent to a claim being allocated to the Small Claims track where the financial value of the claim exceeds the usual qualifying amount. The parties then have the benefit of the reduced procedures of the Small Claims track and an informal hearing, and the small claims track costs provisions will apply unless the parties agree otherwise: (rule 27.14(2)).

See page 80 for more about electing to use the Small Claims track

Terminology

A definitions of legal terms and frequently used jargon are explained in a glossary which appears at the front of this book.

The unfortunate word 'arbitration' which was formerly used to describe cases determined under the old Small Claims procedure has now been abandoned. The Civil Prodecure Rules created a new vocabulary for litigation. The term 'plaintiff' was replaced by 'claimant', and the use of Latin is frowned upon. The Rules still include some jargon, but where this intrudes in this book the phrases are explained in the text or the glossary in the front of this book.

Virtually all Small Claims cases are dealt with by District Judges, save for the very few that are dealt with by Circuit Judges at the time of an appeal. The Civil Procedure Rules do not prohibit a Circuit Judge dealing with a Small Claims hearing at first instance but, since this rarely happens, this book is written on the assumption that the District Judge will deal with the case throughout. While the Rules often refer to 'the court' doing things, in this book it is made clear where decisions are taken by a District Judge and where steps are dealt with by the administration of the court staff.

All County courts deal with Small Claims cases and there is no separate building or court called a *'Small Claims court'*. Nearly all hearings are conducted in the normal county court buildings. There are no special rooms set aside for the hearings and the litigants will do their prehearing business at the usual court office. Very occasionally a District Judge might conduct a hearing in a person's home, perhaps because of a party or witness's infirmity, or to look at property which may be the subject of the dispute; on one occasion one lucky District Judge got to go to somewhere in the Mediterranean to inspect a hotel which had been the subject of numerous claims.

Mediations held under the auspices of the National Mediation Helpline are often held in local solicitors' offices, the parties' homes or offices, or other agreed venues away from court buildings, although some court-annexed schemes do take place in rooms within the court building.

Cases which do not qualify for the Small Claims track will be managed under the Fast Track or Multi-track. Any description of Fast Track or Multi-track procedures is outside the scope of this book.

References to "the Rules" in this book mean the Civil Procedure Rules 1998 which came into force on 26 April 1999. The Rules are set out in Parts – so all the rules about summary judgment, for example, are set out in Part 24. Most of the Rules are supported by Practice Directions which set out explanations and guidance on their operations. Note that a case allocated to the Small Claims track can only be heard by a Circuit Judge with his consent (PD 2 para. 11.2).

> Part 1 is set out in Appendix 6
> Part 27 is set out in Appendix 7
> The practice direction to part 27
> is set out in Appendix 7

District Judges

Suitably experienced and qualified solicitors and barristers may become District Judges. They come from a wide variety of professional backgrounds including high street firms, large commercially based practices, local authority and government employment; or they may have formerly worked as 'in-house' lawyers or law lecturers.

In their work as full time judges, they deal with a wide range of work including

- case management of cases on all tracks
- matrimonial matters
- cases involving children
- bankruptcy
- landlord and tenant cases and mortgage possession
- fast track trials
- assessment of costs
- deciding the amount of a judgment where a default judgment has been obtained
- small claims hearings.

When dealing with Small Claims cases, District Judges use their accumulated knowledge and experience. They also have a working knowledge of the law most often relevant in Small Claims cases, including

- consumer matters
- contract law
- agency law
- the law of negligence.

Deputy District Judges work full time as solicitors or barristers and also undertake between 20 and 50 'sitting' days a year in the County court. In Small Claims cases the powers and jurisdiction of Deputy District Judges is identical to that of full time District Judges. In this book the term 'District Judge' incorporates their deputies.

Reference materials

The rules, without commentary, can be accessed on the internet, for example by visiting the Ministry of Justice (formerly Department for

Constitutional Affairs) web site at http://www.justice.gov.uk/civil/procrules_fin/index.htm. A directory of County courts, including a map and index of the area covered by each court, by parish, can be found on the Court Service web site http://www.hmcourts-service.gov.uk, which also has downloadable versions of court forms and leaflets giving notes for guidance.

This book is a comprehensive handbook with sufficient extracts from the Rules to cover most procedural situations encountered in Small Claims cases. It contains the full text of Parts 1 and 27 of the *Civil Procedure Rules* and the accompanying practice directions. The text includes extracts of other rules relevant to Small Claims cases, plus copies of the forms used in Small Claims cases. There is an extensive index, plus tables of fees and fixed costs as they apply to the Small Claims track.

The major legal publishers each publish hefty volumes containing the Rules, commentary relevant statutes, lists of fees, and other material useful for conducting litigation at all levels. These are colloquially termed the 'White Book', 'Green Book' and 'Brown Book'.

Special features of Small Claims cases

Small Claims cases are subject to many, but not all, of the same rules as other County court cases. Comments in this book are tailored to Small Claims cases and cannot be considered as general guidance for any other type of court action. Other cases will involve greater sums of money and matters of greater complexity; they are subject to important rules concerning costs, strict court timetables and special rules concerning witness evidence, including expert evidence.

Evaluating the case

The parties must step back from the case and ask four basic questions

Question 1: Do I have a good chance of winning?
Question 2: If I win, will I be able to recover the money from the other side?
Question 3: Is the amount at stake worth the cost of the court case?
Question 4: Rather than going to court should the matter be resolved instead by mediation?

This evaluation must take place not only at the start of the case, but when the defence and any counterclaim is received, and in the light of all changing circumstances before the hearing – for example when the other side's documents are received before the hearing.

Each side should

- consider the strength of their evidence
- find out if the law is in their favour
- weigh the personal and financial cost of proceeding
- consider if the other side can afford to pay their claim and court fees if they win.

Evidence

The strict rules of evidence do not apply in Small Claims cases but the parties must always be able to discharge the civil burden of proof, namely to establish their case 'on balance' or whether it is 'likely' that their version of events is what actually occurred Original documents, for example invoices and records, must be available for the hearing; and the parties must be able to bring to court with them any witnesses who will support their case. See page 143 for a discussion of the use of evidence at a Small Claims hearing.

The court may give permission for an expert to assist at the hearing, but such evidence will usually be considered in writing rather than by the personal attendance of the expert. The parties should consider at the outset who may be approached to act as an independent expert and how the fees of that expert will be met. The cost of the expert could well be more than the £200 allowance which may be awarded for expert's fees in favour of the winner (see Chapter 5).

Applying the law

District Judges are keenly aware of the need to apply the law accurately in Small Claims cases. If a mistake in the law is made, the loser will have grounds for appeal (see Chapter 8).

The District Judge will not act as legal advisor to the parties. The overriding objective provides that the court will, so far as practicable, ensure that the parties are on an equal footing (rule 1.1(2)(a)). If a point of law is raised at the hearing which takes either party by surprise, then an adjournment may be necessary for each party to seek legal advice.

The parties and their legal advisors must therefore ensure that they check and research any legal points before a hearing to avoid the delay and expense of an adjournment.

The cost of proceeding (time and money)

The claimant must pay not only the starting fee but two further sets of fees before the case goes to a final hearing. The fees are set out in appendix 1 and see the paragraph below headed 'court fees'.

Litigation involves not only money, but also time. Litigants must be prepared to set aside adequate time to prepare the case for the hearing and to attend court on the day of the hearing itself. The hearing may be quite short, but the parties may have to wait some hours at court before the case is called for hearing.

The parties must consider that if they lose they will be ordered to pay the other side's court fees and witness expenses. If the court decides that either party has behaved unreasonably an award for costs may be made (see page 117).

Does the other side have funds?

Make an informed decision about whether the other side is likely to have funds to pay before you start any court action. Consider in advance if you are prepared to bear the expense and possible frustration of enforcement action if you win, and the defendant refuses to pay. There is no point in starting a case if the loser will never have the money to pay the judgment.

Chapter 12 considers methods of enforcement and how to find out about the defendant's assets before starting a court case.

The court's management powers

The overriding objective is for the court to deal with cases justly (rule 1.1(1)) and this is achieved, in part, by the court actively managing cases. Rule 1.4(2) sets out a non-exclusive list of twelve ways in which the district judge can manage cases. This includes 'identifying issues at an early stage' and 'deciding promptly which issues need full investigation and trial and accordingly disposing summarily of others'. The court will also encourage settlement and consider ways of disposing of the case without a court hearing, including mediation.

> See Chapter 10 in particular for more about the court's case management powers.

Alternatives to court action – mediation or litigation?

Rather than issue court proceedings why not take the case to mediation? You will be helped by a trained, impartial mediator, not a judge, to reach a settlement. The settlement is likely to be achieved sooner than waiting for a court hearing and may prevent a permanent falling out between you and your opponent. The proceedings are confidential and cannot affect any future court action if no settlement is reached. Both parties must agree to go to mediation – it cannot be imposed – and the result, unlike a court order is not binding unless or until the parties come to agreement. Some industries, for example the travel industry, have been offering mediation-type schemes for some years and every county court can offer literature and guidance on how to contact a mediator. Chapter 9 of this book sets out the pros and cons of mediation and how to find a mediator plus practical tips on how to prepare for the mediation meeting. The Ministry of Justice promotes and encourages people to go to mediation and some county courts have their own mediation schemes which run in conjunction with the National Mediation Helpline. The mediators are paid by both parties and the fees are set out in Chapter 9. If court proceedings are running alongside the mediation process and a settlement is reached before the final hearing then all or part of the hearing fee may be refunded by the court (see below under the headings of settlement and court fees).

Enforcement

Although a short chapter on enforcement appears at the end of this book it should arguably be here at the beginning. Why? Because there is no point in pursuing a case through the small claims procedure, securing a judgment, and then being frustrated because the defendant has insufficient funds to meet the judgment. A party embarking on litigation should find out in advance if the other side has funds to pay. Chapter 12 sets out a number of straight forward ways for a claimant to do so.

Settlement

Both parties should at all stages actively consider settlement and compromise as an alternative to litigation. The whole of the hearing fee is refunded if the case settles more than a week before the final hearing.

The allocation questionnaire prompts the parties to consider if the case should be stayed for a month or more for settlement discussions (see page 61).

Discussions can take place at any stage, including outside court on the day of the hearing – some District Judges regularly insist on the parties trying to talk through a settlement before the hearing starts. The message is, it is never to late to settle. Even if a hearing has started, the parties can still settle – the lunch adjournment is a good time to talk, and if the parties reach a settlement whilst they are waiting outside the hearing room for the District Judge to consider his or her decision they should send a message in via the usher to tell the judge that the case has been settled.

Letters which aim to reach a compromise should be marked 'without prejudice'. A letter or document which discusses settlement and is marked "without prejudice" cannot be shown to the judge until after the final decision; this rule means that settlement offers cannot be used against someone as a sign of weakness.

Court fees

Fees are payable to the court depending on the amount of the claim and whether the proceedings are issued on line or not. Fees are payable at 3 stages of the court action

- upon issue – which is the starting or issue fee
- when the allocation questionnaire is returned – which is the allocation fee
- when the court fixes a hearing date – this is the hearing fee

the hearing fee is refundable in full if the claimant notifies the court that the hearing date is vacated more than 7 days before the final hearing. The procedure for a refund of court fees is an incentive for the parties to settle and is attractive to parties who elect to go to mediation after the allocation stage as this may result in them not having to pay the mediators fees in addition to the court fees.

Full information about court fees can be found at www.hmcourts-service.gov.uk/infoabout/fees/county.htm.

Letters before action

A letter sent to the other side before the court action has a number of benefits.

- The letter may prompt an offer of settlement and make the court case unnecessary
- A well prepared letter before action may be used as the 'particulars of claim' in a Small Claims action
- Never forget that the costs of the case will be in the discretion of the District Judge, who may be reluctant to award even routine costs if the winner launched into a court case without first giving warning that proceedings would be started.

European Convention on Human Rights

The Human Rights Act 1998 (HRA) gives effect to the European Convention on Human Rights (ECHR). It is a legally enforceable charter of human rights and fundamental freedoms. HRA became part of United Kingdom Law on 2 October 2000, and it has shown its influence in Small Claims procedures. For example, the fact that Small Claims hearings are no longer in private is a reflection of Article 6 (Right to a fair and public hearing). It was also thought that the previous appeal procedure which gave the Circuit Judge the jurisdiction to strike out an appeal on paper without recourse was not compliant with Article 6. All courts and tribunals, including the County court and cases allocated to the Small Claims track, are able to consider arguments raised under ECHR.

Public funding of Small Claims cases

The Community Legal Services Fund replaced the Legal Aid Fund on 1 April 2000, and offers those on low incomes financial assistance to pursue and defend civil cases. The Funding Criteria are strict and specify that an application for funding will be refused if a case is, or is likely to be, referred to the Small Claims track (paragraph 5.4.6). The criterion is mandatory, and the Legal Services Commission has no power to issue a certificate for a case in the Small Claims track. However, individuals can sometimes receive Legal Help or Help at Court for a Small Claims case. The help will generally be limited to two hours work. Litigants must use a solicitor with a contract with the Legal Services Commission; visit the web site for more information: http://www.legalservices.gov.uk.

Fee exemption and remission

People in receipt of benefit or with low incomes should apply to the Court Manager who can agree to waive or reduce court fees.

Litigants are automatically entitled to fee exemption in a Small Claims case when in receipt of a prescribed means tested benefit e.g. income support or, failing that can demonstrate that their gross household income is below a threshold that probably entitles them to such benefit.

The decisions on fee exemption and remission are taken by senior court officers and the judiciary have no part in the process.

To apply for fee exemption or remission, ask the court staff for a copy of the combined booklet and form EX160A – 'Court Fees – do I have to pay them?' This is also available from any County court office, or from the website www.hmcourts-service.gov.uk. You will have to make a separate application for each fee that is payable.

Using this book

The next chapter is a step-by-step checklist of how to start a Small Claims case and the following chapters take the reader through the procedures of a Small Claims case. Chapter 11 covers guidance on drafting documents for use in the case. There are numerous cross-references and major links with other sections are shown in grey shaded boxes. The glossary at page ix explains any legal terms used in the book.

CHAPTER 2

Step by Step Guide to Starting a Small Claims Case

Overview	17
Issuing claims on-line www.moneyclaim.gov.uk	20
Step 1: Name the claimant	22
Step 2: State the claimant's address	23
Step 3: Give the claimant's address for sending documents and payments	24
Step 4: Identify the defendant	24
Step 5: Name the defendant	28
Step 6: State where the defendant is to be served	28
Step 7: Brief details of claim	30
Step 8: Particulars of claim	31
Step 9: Complete tick box about Human Rights Element	32
Step 10: Decide if the claim is to be specified or unspecified	32
Step 11: Calculate interest	34
Step 12: Statement of Truth	35
Step 13: Value – check that the case is within the Small Claims limit	38
Step 14: Amount claimed	38
Step 15: Calculate the court fee	39
Step 16: Calculate the solicitor's costs on the claim form	40
Step 17: Choose a County court to issue	40

Step 18: Ask the court to issue the claim form or submit
   on-line   41

Finally: make a diary note   42

The next steps   43

Overview of procedure between response and allocation   44

Step by Step Guide to Starting a Small Claims Case

Basics

- The court case is started by the claimant
  (a) filling out a court form and
  (b) setting out the claim in writing and
  (c) paying a court fee
- The defendant defends by sending a written defence to the court within 14 days of service or within 28 days if an acknowledgment is filed
- A counterclaim is started by the defendant
  (a) setting out the counterclaim in writing and
  (b) paying a court fee
- Any claim, counterclaim or defence must be verified by a statement of truth

---

Overview

Thoughtful preparation of the claim may be the difference between success and disaster – if a claim is poorly drafted, issued in the wrong court or the parties are wrongly described the matter may become unnecessarily complicated. The essence of a Small Claims case is its simplicity, and this benefit will be lost if mistakes are made at the outset.

The headings below cover the main topics to be thought through by the claimant at the outset of the case. This is a checklist of how to commence a Small Claims case. The step numbers of that checklist are referred to in the various topics that follow.

The claim form must be served within 4 months of issue otherwise it expires (rule 7.5). An application can be made to extend the life of the claim form (Applications generally – Chapter 10).

Note that although mediation can occur after the issue of proceedings it makes sense to consider mediation as an option before you issue proceedings – see chapter 9 for more information about the mediation alternative.

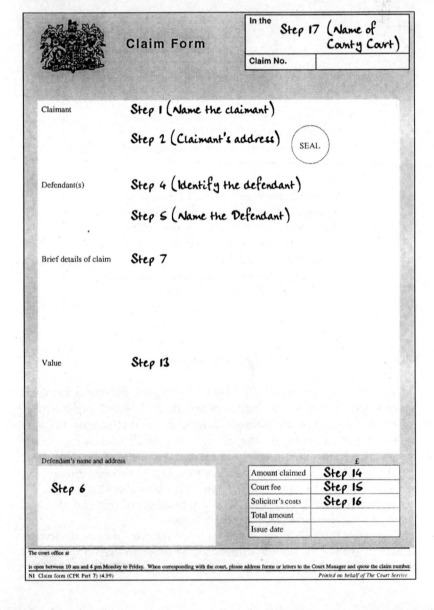

Claim Form

In the   Step 17 (Name of
                        County Court)

Claim No.

Claimant   Step 1 (Name the claimant)

Step 2 (Claimant's address)   SEAL

Defendant(s)   Step 4 (Identify the defendant)

Step 5 (Name the Defendant)

Brief details of claim   Step 7

Value   Step 13

Defendant's name and address   £

Step 6

Amount claimed	Step 14
Court fee	Step 15
Solicitor's costs	Step 16
Total amount	
Issue date	

The court office at

is open between 10 am and 4 pm Monday to Friday. When corresponding with the court, please address forms or letters to the Court Manager and quote the claim number.
N1 Claim form (CPR Part 7) (4.99)   *Printed on behalf of The Court Service*

	Claim No.

Does, or will, your claim include any issues under the Human Rights Act 1998? ☐ Yes ☐ No

Particulars of Claim (attached)(to follow) **Step 9**

        Step 8 (Particulars of claim)

        Step 9 (Specified or unspecified?)

        Step 11 (Interest)

Statement of Truth
*(I believe)(The Claimant believes) that the facts stated in these particulars of claim are true.
* I am duly authorised by the claimant to sign this statement

Full name **Step 12**

Name of claimant's solicitor's firm

signed _____ position or office held _____
*(Claimant)(Litigation friend)(Claimant's solicitor) (if signing on behalf of firm or company)
*delete as appropriate

Step 3

Claimant's or claimant's solicitor's address to which documents or payments should be sent if different from overleaf including (if appropriate) details of DX, fax or e-mail.

Issuing claims on-line www.moneyclaim.gov.uk

Litigants can use the money claims on line procedure for straightforward claims and this makes it ideal for many small claims cases. It is popular with litigants in person and also used by solicitors. The password procedure can appear somewhat cumbersome, but otherwise the website is easy to use and supported by a telephone helpline As well as enabling proceedings to be issued on line the customer can keep track of the case on line. Where proceedings are issued on line the defendant can also put in a defence on line using a password sent out with the information pack. There is a modest reduction in the court fees for money claims issued on line.

Issuing claims on line is

- ideal for simple debt cases
- quick, easy to use and convenient
- slightly cheaper than over the counter or by post

but think twice about using this procedure if

- if the case cannot be fully described in a couple of short paragraphs because there is a strict number of characters that can be entered in the on-line form

When issuing on line the proceedings are posted within 48 hours which makes it quick relative to the over the counter performance of many local County courts. The claimant needs a credit or debit card to pay the fee and a computer with internet access. The site gives links for the necessary Adobe software which can be installed on-line if necessary.

The site cannot be used if there are more than two defendants or the claimant has a postal address outside England and Wales and can only be used for fixed amount claims (specified claims). The site helpfully helps with calculating the court fee and adds everything up for you. There are prompts for claiming interest.

Claims issued on-line start their life in Northampton. If defended, the final hearing will be in the claimants home court or if the defendant is an individual the defendants home court. (The rules about this are set out in the practice direction to Part 7 which deals with money claims on-line).

Step by step checklist for starting a Small Claims case including information to help with completing the claim form on line

Step		check
1	Name the claimant	☐
2	State the claimant's address	☐
3	Give the claimant's address for sending documents and payments	☐
4	Identify the defendant	☐
5	Name the defendant	☐
6	State where the defendant is to be served	☐
7	Brief details of the claim	☐
8	Particulars of claim	☐
9	Complete the tick box about Human Rights Element	☐
10	Decide if the case is to be specified or unspecified	☐
11	Calculate interest	☐
12	Statement of Truth	☐
13	Value – check that the case is within the Small Claims limit	☐
14	Amount claimed	☐
15	Calculate the court fee	☐
16	Calculate the solicitor's costs on the claim form	☐
17	Choose the County court to issue	☐
18	Ask the court to issue the claim form or submit the claim on line	☐
finally	Make a diary note	☐

> ### Reminder
>
> The matters discussed in this chapter cover the mechanics of the case. The claimant's case must be carefully evaluated at all stages – not only at the outset but also when the defence has been received. This topic is discussed in more detail in Chapter 1.

The starting point is the Claim form – the 'N1'.[1] Rather than filling the form in from 'top to bottom', follow the steps in the order of the checklist and this should result in a perfect claim form every time! (See page 18 for an annotated version of the claim form). The form can be downloaded from the court service website on www.hmcourts-service.gov.uk.

Step 1: Name the claimant

The basic rules to be followed when naming the claimant are set out in Table 2.1.

Table 2.1 Rules for naming the claimant and defendant

Where the claimant or defendant is	Notes
An individual	Give full name
A sole trader carrying on business in a name other than his or her own	Must use personal name but should add trading name for clarity, e.g. John Smith trading as Smiths the Grocers
Partners (i.e. more than one individual carrying on business together)	Name of partnership or individual names of partners; see Note (a) on page 23

---

1   There is an alternative method of commencing proceedings, namely the 'Part 8 procedure'. This alternative method is used, for example, in claims for possession of land and in cases where there is unlikely to be substantial dispute of fact. The form that is used to start such cases is a N208 also for certain specialist claims as defined by Part 8. Note, however, that a case started by the alternative method may be allocated to the Small Claims track at the allocation stage.

Where the claimant or defendant is	Notes
Co-claimants	Where more than one person has a claim, then each must be named as a claimant; see note (b) below
A child or mentally disabled person	The claimant's name must be followed by the name of an adult 'litigation friend'; see note (c) below
A limited company	Give name of company and state whether it is 'limited' or 'plc'
More than one defendant	List the parties separately as 'first', 'second', etc defendant

Notes

(a) Partnerships, for example firms of solicitors or accountants, can sue either in their trading name or in the name of some or all of the individual partners.

(b) In cases involving a group in a holiday case, sometimes only the leader of the party need be named as claimant (Regulation 2(i) of the Package Travel, Package Holidays and Package Tours Regulations 1992).

(c) A child is anyone under the age of 18 at the date of the issue of the proceedings. (Rule 21.1(2)(a)). There are special procedures which must be followed before embarking on a case by a litigation friend, which are set out in Rule 21 and the accompanying practice direction (not discussed in detail in this book).

Step 2: State the claimant's address

If the claimant is an individual, the claim form requires the residential address to be given – in the case of an individual suing in a business capacity the business address can be used.

If the claimant is a limited company, the registered office must be shown; alternatively the place of business which is most closely connected with the claim.

The claim form must provide a residential or business address for the claimant in addition to any solicitor's address (PD 16 para 2.2).

Step 3: Give the claimant's address for sending documents and payments

This will be the claimant's "address for service" namely the address used by the court and by the other side for any correspondence about the case and the place where the defendant will send any money. This information is added on the back of the claim form in the box at the bottom.

The claimant must give an address for service in England or Wales (rule 6.5(2)).

The address of a solicitor can be used as the claimant's address for service.

If the claimant is a limited company, a business address will have already been inserted under step 2. However, a company's trading address is often different from the registered office. If the company is not using a solicitor, the business address of the actual person in the company who is running the case should be added here so that any papers from the court or the other side go to that person direct and not to the registered office.

There is no restriction on a litigant in person or a company conducting a case without a solicitor, but if the litigant has a non-solicitor to advise and assist the advisor cannot 'conduct' the proceedings.

The address for service can be the party's own address or that of a solicitor (rule 6.5(3)). A legal representative means solicitors and their employees but not general lay agents (rule 2.3(1)).

Step 4: Identify the defendant

Wrongly identifying the defendant is one of the most common errors in Small Claims cases. If the incorrect defendant is sued, the proceedings will be delayed and may become muddled.

Claims against shops

Every business is obliged to display a prominent notice at its premises which gives the names and addresses of the owners of the business (s.4 Business Names Act 1985).

If the name of the owner of the business is not known, then the defendant should be named as "[*Name of Business*]" followed by the words "a trading name".

If the owner of the business can be identified, for example from the Business Names Act sign in the shop, then the defendant should be shown as "[*Name of owner*]" followed by the words "trading as [*Name of Shop*]" CCR Order 5 rule 10.

Claims against "firms"

The use of the word "firm" in this chapter means a business which does not reveal on their notepaper, or otherwise, whether they are a limited company, partnership or sole trader.

If details of the owners of the business or firm cannot be found, then proceedings can be issued in the trading name of the business. The position then is the same as for claims against shops, see above.

A firm which does not reveal details of its ownership on its business paper or at its place of business is of course in breach of s.4 Business Names Act 1985.

Limited companies

If the firm's notepaper, website or the notice displayed at the shop reveals that the prospective defendant is a limited company, then that is the name which should be used on the claim form. Any individual director or employee should not be named as the defendant, as it is unlikely that they will be personally liable to meet the claim.

Directors of limited companies

The general rule is that where the claim is against a limited company then it is the company and not the directors or managers who are sued.

There are cases where a director can be liable for a debt incurred by a company. For example when a company director signs cheques knowing that the company does not have funds to honour them. However, remedies against directors in these circumstances are not available to litigants commencing County court proceedings. The claim or complaint should be referred immediately to the liquidator of the company, who will invite the claimant to "prove" in the liquidation. If there are circumstances that justify a claim against the directors personally, then such proceedings are brought by the liquidator, who will probably require a financial contribution towards legal costs from the claimant before starting proceedings.

Details of the liquidator will be found by making a search at Companies House (the address for which is in the table which is part of Chapter 12).

Claims against partnerships

Partners can be sued either in the trading name of the partnership, or in the individual names of the partners themselves, CCR Order 5 rule 9.

Principals and agents

This is a difficult area and will require careful thought before issuing proceedings. However, the following basic legal principles should be borne in mind.

- An agent does not deal on his or her own behalf but only on behalf of the principal
- Any court action must be against the principal and not the agent.

It is sometimes difficult to tell who is the principal and who is the agent. The situation is confused by the fact that some professionals call themselves "agents" when, in strict legal terms, they are not.

Travel agents may be giving advice in a professional capacity to clients as "travel consultants" or may be acting as an agent for a travel company. As a rule of thumb, a travel agent will be acting as a true agent (and as such should not be sued) if a booking has been made; the claim should then be against the tour operator who is the principal.

Estate agents usually act as agents for sellers, not buyers.

Letting agents usually act as agents for landlords.

Managing agents usually act for landlords, but may act on behalf of a residents' association or management company.

If there is any doubt or confusion about whether an individual or company is acting on its own behalf or on behalf of someone else, this should be resolved at the outset and before proceedings are issued. A litigant in person should certainly consider taking legal advice if there is any doubt at all about who should be sued.

If the confusion cannot be resolved, then an option is to sue both potential defendants. In the Small Claims procedure this is not particularly risky, as an order for costs cannot be made against the claimant unless it is shown that he acted "uneasonably" in joining a particular defendant as a party to the action. However if the situation is clarified by the defence, for example if one of the defendants admits to being the "principal", it may well then be unreasonable to pursue the case against both to the full hearing.

Companies in liquidation

Proceedings should not be issued against companies in liquidation and any claim must be referred to the liquidator – details of the liquidator will be found at Companies House (for the address see Chapter 12).

Claims against bankrupts

Proceedings cannot be issued against a bankrupt for any debt or claim which arose *before* the date of bankrupcty except with the permission of the court. Most claims against bankrupts should be referred to the Trustee in Bankruptcy. If the claim or debt arose *after* the date of bankruptcy then the bankrupt can be sued. However, if the claim involves the bankrupt obtaining credit after the date of bankruptcy then an offence may have been committed and the Trustee in Bankruptcy should be notified immediately. (See the table in Chapter 12 for how to find out if someone is bankrupt.)

Step 5: Name the defendant

Once the defendant has been identified, follow the guidance on naming which has already been set out in Table 2.1 (page 23).

Step 6: State where the defendant is to be served

Rule 6.5

Nature of party to be served	Place of service
Individual	• Usual or last known residence.
Proprietor of a business	• Usual or last known residence; or • Place of business or last known place of business.
Individual who is suing or being sued in the name of a firm	• Usual or last known residence; or • Principal or last known place of business of the firm.
Corporation incorporated in England and Wales other than a company	• Principal office of the corporation; or • Any place within the jurisdiction where the corporation carries on its activities and which has a real connection with the claim.
Company registered in England and Wales	• Principal office of the company; or • Any place of business of the company within the jurisdiction which has a real connection with the claim.
Any other company or corporation	• Any place within the jurisdiction where the corporation carries on its activities. • Any place of business of the company within the jurisdiction.

The Rules do not make it clear whether service by post to a defendant's last known address at which he no longer resides, and the defendant does not in fact receive the claim, is good service. But in a number of cases the courts have said that if the claimant opts to effect service (rather than the court doing so) the answer depends upon whether the claimant has taken reasonable steps to locate the defendant. In *Smith* v *Hughes* (reported under *Cranfield & Anor* v *Bridgegrove Ltd* [2003] EWCA Civ 656) solicitors for the claimant had served the claim form at the defendant's last known address in a case where the defendant had disappeared and the MIB had advised the solicitors he was no longer at that address. Nonetheless this was held to be good service as "last known address" is not qualified in any way in the rules. But in *Mersey Docks Property Holdings* v *Kilgour* [2004] EWHC 1638 the High Court decided that where the claimant knows the defendant has moved he cannot simply serve at the old address without making reasonable enquiries. The defendant was an architect. The claimant knew he no longer practised at his 1998 business address. Internet searches of directory enquiries and of the Royal Institute of British Architects directory of architect's practices did not reveal a new address (because Mr Kilgour had changed his firm name to MKA.) The court decided that the claimant did not take reasonable steps as they left the checking of the address until the end of the limitation period, and did not search in the individual architects directory or Yellow Pages or contact the RIBA. The claim form was not validly served. *Chellaram* v *Chellaram (No. 2)* [2002] EWHC 632 (Ch) decided that a defendant who was not ordinarily resident or domiciled in England had not been validly served with a claim form which was posted to an address occasionally used by him in London, since it could not be described as his "last known residence" and at the time of service the claimant had been out of the jurisdiction.

Tread carefully! The address which the court will use when sending the court claim form is specified in the table and if an incorrect address is used the claim form may be returned to the court "undelivered". If a claim form is incorrectly addressed the defendant will not be able to put in a defence on time, so a judgment obtained in default may be set aside.

Note that a claim form has to be served within 4 months of issue otherwise it expires (rule 7.5(2)).

When providing information about a defendant's address to the court bear in mind the following:

1. **The address must include a post code or will not be served.** Details of postcodes can be obtained from www.royalmail.com.
2. The 'last known address' means a last known address that reasonable attempts to investigate have revealed.
3. If a letter is returned either to the court office or the sender (if served in person) while this does not mean that proceedings have been invalidly served, it may later raise a question about whether the claimant's attempts to ascertain a last known address were reasonable.

If the claim is specified (see Step 10) and against an individual and the claim is defended, the case will automatically be transferred to the court for the district in which the defendant resides or carries on business (see Step 6); this will usually be the address shown on the claim form but may be a different address specified by the defendant.

> Note – see also Chapter 10 for
>
> - rules about service of the claim form and other documents
> - extending the life of the claim form
> - service of proceedings
> - alternative methods of service
> - deemed date of service

The Rules for service outside the jurisdiction are beyond the scope of this book. You should note that Scotland and Northern Ireland are not within the jurisdiction of the courts in England and Wales.

Step 7: Brief details of claim

There is space on the front of the claim form to give a brief description of the case. This will provide anyone looking at the claim with an "at-a-glance view" of what it is about. Some suggested wordings appear in Chapter 11.

Step 8: Particulars of claim

> See Chapter 11 for guidance on how to draft the claim including precedents

The particulars must include a concise statement of the facts on which the claimant relies (rule 16.4(1)). In many Small Claims cases the space on the back of the claim form will be sufficient to set out the claim fully. The claim may be set out on a separate sheet in which case write "see attached" on the back of the form.

N.B. When issuing a claim online the space for the claim form is limited to 1080 characters and up to 24 lines. Examples of claims drafted to fit into the online requirements are set out in chapter 11. Given the requirement for the claim to be set out in full this space will be insufficient for any claims that are complex and the online procedure is not suitable in such cases.

Chapter 11 contains guidance on how to set out the claim in a clear and effective way and in accordance with the court rules, including precedents.

In Small Claims cases it is best to set out the claim in full at the time of issue as service of particulars later will only complicate matters. However, if the particulars of claim are to be served at a later date the words "to follow" should be written on the back of the form. (rule 16.2(2)). Where the proceedings are started online the particulars of claim must included in the online claim form and may not be filed separately (PD 7 para EPD 5.2(2)).

If the statement of case is served separately the following rules apply

- The statement must be served within 14 days of the claim form (rule 7.4(1)(b))
- The statement of case must be verified by a statement of truth (PD16 para 3.4)

- A copy of the statement and a certificate of service must be filed at the court within 7 days of service

If the claim involves a claim for personal injury then it is unlikely that the case will qualify for the Small Claims track because the maximum value of a personal injury claim in Small Claims case is £1,000 (see page 66). If there is a personal injury claim and the claimant relies on medical evidence, then a medical report should usually be attached to the statement of case. In cases involving minor injuries where the claimant can give direct evidence of the injuries, a medical report may be unnecessary.

Step 9: Complete tick box about Human Rights Element

The ticking (or ignoring) of this box has no effect at all on the claim even if, the claim includes any issues under the Human Rights Act 1998. The tick box has been introduced merely to help the Court Service to keep tabs on the issue of such claims. If the claim does rely on any provision or right under the Human Rights Act, the statement of case must set out all the information required by PD 16 para 16.1 (not covered in this book).

Step 10: Decide if the claim is to be specified or unspecified

A claim which is specified, for example a debt claim, is for a fixed amount of money. A claim is "unspecified" if the amount involved is not precisely known at the outset (for example 'damages for distress'). This is relevant to a number of practical matters, namely

- the choice of issue court and transfer between courts if the defendant is an individual (see step 17)
- checking that the value is within the small claims limit (see step 13)
- calculating the court fee (see step 15)
- entering judgment in default (see Chapter 3).

Specified claims

All claims for money alone, including all debt claims, are "specified". If a claimant states a fixed sum for the losses claimed (for example £50 for general inconvenience) this is also a specified claim.

The key features of a claim which is specified is that

1. if the defendant does not file a defence in time the claimant enters judgment in default for the amount claimed and the judgment can be enforced straight away (see Chapter 3 page 55);
2. if the defendant is an individual and defends a specified claim then, upon receipt of the defence, the case will be automatically transferred to the defendant's court (see step 17);
3. the court fee is calculated on the basis of the sum specified.

Unspecified claims

Any claim where the amount is left to the court to decide is "unspecified". This includes all claims which are described as "damages" claims.

The key features of a claim which is 'unspecified' are

1. if the defendant does not file a defence in time the damages have to be decided by the court (see page 55) so the judgment cannot be enforced straight away;
2. there is no automatic transfer to the defendant's home court on filing of a defence;
3. to qualify for the Small Claims track, the claim should be limited to "a sum not exceeding £5,000" (or any amount under £5,000) (but note that if the amount can be limited to a lower amount this will reduce the court fee payable).

Step 11: Calculate interest

> See Chapter 11 for a method of calculating statutory interest. The Money Claims online website also provides a prompt for claiming interest and explains how to calculate it.

If the claimant is seeking interest then the claim must be fully set out on the claim form (rule 16.4(2)). Failure to set out a claim for interest on the claim form is likely to prevent the claimant from being awarded interest at the hearing.

Contractual interest

This only applies if it was in the *original agreement* between the claimant and defendant. For example

- interest on a **credit card, loan** or **bank overdraft**;
- interest on **unpaid professional fees**, but only where the professional has made it plain from the outset that interest will be charged at a specific rate on unpaid invoices; (accountants and solicitors often have a provision for interest in their terms of business);
- interest specified in the **small print of the contract**, e.g. for goods sold and delivered;
- interest on **unpaid rent and service charges** where interest is set out in a lease or tenancy agreement.

Statutory interest

This applies in debt claims where the rate of interest was not set out in the contract. The award of interest is discretionary, but, if claimed, is routinely made in most cases. The award of interest is not a penalty but recognition that the defendant, and not the claimant, has had the use of the money. The rate has been 8% since 1 April 1993.

Failure to set out a claim for interest on the claim form is likely to prevent the claimant from being awarded interest at the hearing.

Interest in other cases

Other interest, including interest on sums awarded for "damages", is discretionary and there are special rules covering interest in personal injury cases.

Late payment of commercial debts

The Late Payment of Commercial Debts (Interest) Act 1998 allows small business to claim enhanced interest (base rate plus 8%) against all large businesses and the public sector. The Act defines a small business as one which has on average employed 50 or fewer staff in the previous financial year. The interest can only be claimed on commercial debts. Further information on the Act can be obtained from the Better Payment Practice group (www.payontime.co.uk) and the court service leaflet EX351 The Late Payment of Commercial Debts.

Step 12: Statement of Truth

> - Various documents filed at court must be supported by a "Statement of Truth"
> - The statement is signed by the person filing the document or his or her solicitor
> - If the person signing the statement does not believe the statement is true then this can amount to contempt of court (rule 32.14)
> - Failure to sign the statement will restrict the use of the document in evidence

A Statement of Truth should be signed to support the claim form, plus any defence, witness statement and expert's report.

Wording of the statement of truth

> **Statement of Truth**
>
> *(I believe)*(the Claimant believes) that the facts stated in these particulars of claim are true. *(I am duly authorised by the claimant to sign this statement).
>
> *delete as appropriate

When issuing online the claimant is invited to confirm the statement of truth by adding their name; this fulfils the requirement to sign the statement of truth (PD 7 para EPD 12.1).

Who can sign the Statement of Truth? (PD 22 para 3)

Where statement is made by	The statement can be signed by
An individual	The individual; A legal representative*
A limited company	Director; Treasurer; Company secretary; Chief executive; Manager; Other officer; A legal representative*
A partnership	Any of the partners; A person 'having control or management of the partnership business'; A legal representative*

Note – the person who signs a Statement of Truth must print his or her name clearly beneath the signature. Where the statement of truth is signed by a legal representative they must use their own name plus state the capacity in which they sign; the firm's name should also be stated.

* If the person making the statement is represented by a legal representative he or she will be taken by the court as having

- been authorised to sign the statement on behalf of the client
- explained to the client that, by signing it, he or she is confirming the client's belief the statement is true and
- explained to the client the possible consequences that the client does not have an honest belief in the truth of those facts.

PD 22 para 3.8

A **lay representative** cannot sign a Statement of Truth – the definition of a legal representative in rule 2.3(1) does not include a lay representative.

If the claimant is acting through a **litigation friend** then the litigation friend will sign the Statement of Truth, (rule 22.1.(6)).

Consequences of failure to sign the Statement of Truth

Although it is likely that the court staff will point out that a statement has not been signed, they will not refuse to issue the claim just because it is not. The proceedings are effective, even without a Statement of

Truth, unless it is struck out. However, if it is not signed, the claimant will not be able to rely on the particulars of case in evidence (rule 22.2(1)).

A defendant who receives a claim which has not been verified by a Statement of Truth can apply to the court for an order that the case be struck out (rule 22(2)(2)).

> See also Chapter 10 for more about Statements of Truth generally

Step 13: Value – check that the case is within the Small Claims limit

The value of the claim must be written on the front of the claim form beside the word "value".

In summary, the claim will only qualify for the Small Claims track if

- it is for £5,000 or less and
- it does not include a claim for possession of land or a claim for harassment or unlawful eviction and the claim includes a claim for personal injury or compensation against a landlord for repairs of £1,000 or less.

> How does a case qualify for the small claims track? See Chapter 4 for more details

If a case is outside the qualifying limit then consider

- electing to use the Small Claims track by agreement (see Chapter 4)
- reducing the amount claimed to £5,000 or less.

Step 14: Amount claimed

Insert the amount claimed in the box on the form.

Step 15: Calculate the court fee

> Court fees payable on issue are
> set out in Appendix 1 and 2

The court fee payable to commence a Small Claims case is calculated on a sliding scale depending on the amount of the claim.

If the claim is limited to £5,000 and "damages" in general are claimed, the court will require the maximum scale fee, namely £115.

If damages are likely to be limited, for example to the expected cost of repairs – say £550 – it is best to limit the damages to the sum expected. Then the fee will be charged at the rate relative to the maximum damages claimed.

Those on low incomes may obtain a part reduction of the court fee (or even a total exemption) at the discretion of the court manager. Application for a fee exemption or remission of fees should be made to the court manager. The applicant will be asked to fill out a form so that the reduction can be assessed (County Court Fees Order 1982, as amended).

You can pay the fee in cash or by cheque in favour of H M Paymaster General (the court will also accept cheques in favour of "the [give name of court] County court").

Interest is not taken into account when deciding if the case qualifies for the small track but interest is taken into account when calculating the court fee.

> Remember that if the claim is for more than £1,500 then a further fee is payable at the allocation stage – see Appendix 1

Step 16: Calculate the solicitor's costs on the claim form

> The scale of charges is set out in Appendix 3

If a solicitor has issued the proceedings, fixed charges should be calculated and can be included on the County court claim form.

If the claim is for an unspecified amount then write "to be assessed" in the box – see Step 10.

Step 17: Choose a County court to issue (postal and personal issue only)

> See also the topic "venue of the final hearing" in Chapter 5

- The claimant gets the "first choice" of court
- The claimant can issue in any court in England and Wales
- If the claim is for a specified sum *and* the defendant is an individual, the case will automatically be transferred to the defendant's home court when a defence is filed
- The District Judge will make the final decision on the venue for a case if the parties cannot agree.

Note

Claims issued on line start their life in Northampton. If defended, the final hearing will be in the claimants home court or if the defendant is an individual the defendants home court. (The rules about this are set out in the practice direction to Part 7 which deals with money claims on line)

Claimant's or defendant's court?

The claimant's own local court will be convenient to issue the proceedings in person, and would be ideal for the claimant if the case were eventually to be heard at that court. This may, at first blush, be the obvious choice, but think again!

The problem is that, where the claim is for a debt, or specified sum, the claim – if defended – will automatically be transferred to the individual defendant's "home" court; (this automatic transfer does not happen if the defendant is a limited company). The case will also have to be transferred to the defendant's home court to enforce any judgment, or if a defendant applies for a judgment in default to be set aside.

Every time a case moves court, there will be a delay of at least a week, probably longer. Therefore the "obvious" choice, of the claimant's local court, may not be the best; it may be more logical to start the case in the defendant's home court.

Bear in mind that the court can deal with the application to issue proceedings by post, and you can always attend your local County court in person to ask questions about practical points. There should be no difference in procedure or practice between your local court and one several miles away – courts cannot create their own special procedures.

Address details for all the County courts in England and Wales can be found in one of the professional publications or the Court Service website, http://www.hmcourts-service.gov.uk.

Step 18: Ask the court to issue the claim form or submit the claim online

The claim form should now be fully completed.

If you have proceeded logically through all the previous steps the exercise of issuing the claim form should be trouble free.

You will need for the court

- the completed form N1 plus at least two copies (one for the court and one for the defendant)
- a further copy of the N1 for each *additional* defendant
- the court fee; in cash, or a cheque in favour of "H M Paymaster General" or "name of County court".

Note

The court does not return a copy of the form N1 to the claimant after the proceedings have been issued, so make a copy to keep before posting the original to the court.

The claim form can be issued by attending the court in person or by sending the documents to the court by post. A simple letter to send to the court when issuing the claim form will be found in Chapter 11.

Normally the proceedings will be served by the court by first class post, but if you want to serve the proceedings yourself then ask the court to return the papers to you for service (see Step 3 for more about service of proceedings).

Finally: make a diary note

When the claim form and court fee are lodged at the court, the staff will check through the papers and "issue" the claim. The process of issuing involves giving the case a number and sending the papers to the defendant. The action number starts with two letters, which identify the court of issue; for example, cases started in Watford County court start with WD. The case number, including the letters at the start, remain with the case throughout, and should be used to identify the case whenever letters are sent to the court about the case, and the case number should appear on any pleadings.

The cheque will be paid in immediately upon receipt, but it could be a few days before the issuing process is complete. The Courts Charter promises that proceedings will be issued within ten working days of the papers being received, but in practice proceedings are usually issued quicker than that, often on the day of receipt. Check with the court you are using to see when they can expect to serve the papers and notify you of the case number.

Make a diary note, for a couple of days after the date the court tells you to expect the case number, to check that it has actually been received. If you have not heard by then you can chase the court to make sure that they have your papers and that they are in order.

When the court notifies you of the case number you will also be told the date of service. Make a note in your diary of the date when the defence is due so you can apply for judgment in default if none is received. The defence or an acknowledgment will be due 14 days after service; see page 50 for further details.

The next steps

The following chapters explain all the steps to be taken by both parties and the court up to and including the allocation of the case to the Small Claims track. The steps must all be taken within a strict timetable. Practitioners and litigants must carefully note all relevant time limits in their diaries and make sure that deadlines are met.

Overview of procedure between response and allocation

14 days after service	Last date for responding to the case by defence acknowledgment or admission	See page 47
28 days after service if an acknowledgment has been filed	Last date for defence or admission	See page 48
	Last date for contesting the jurisdiction of the court	See page 53
Court sends out allocation questionnaires to both parties once a defence has been received		
14 days after receipt of allocation questionnaires	Both parties must complete and return allocation questionnaires to the court	See Chapter 4
	Claimant must pay the allocation fee if payable	See Chapter 4
	Claimant should file defence to counterclaim and any reply. Note: Failure to file a defence to counterclaim may result in judgment in default	See page 56 (defence to counterclaim) and see page 59 (Reply)
As soon as possible after receipt of allocation questionnaires	If either party wishes to make an application for summary judgment this should be done now	See Chapter 10
District Judge considers the allocation questionnaires, allocates the case and gives directions		

CHAPTER 3

Responding to the claim
(including obtaining judgment in default or on an admission)

Time for response	47
Admitting the claim (including summary table)	48
Acknowledging the claim	52
Dispute of jurisdiction	53
Defending the claim	53
Defence to counterclaim	56
When the defendant wants to pass the claim on to someone else	56
Judgment in default – the consequence of not responding to the claim in time	57
Deciding the value without a hearing	58
Disposal hearings	58
Amount to be decided by the court – upon allocation to the Small Claims track	59
Reply to defence	59

Responding to the claim
(including obtaining judgment in default or on an admission)

This chapter covers the steps to be taken by the defendant by way of acknowledgement, defence, counterclaim and admission. It also deals with matters relating to default judgments and disposal hearings.

Basics

- The defendant must respond to the claim within 14 days of service by acknowledgment, admission or defence
- The defendant must give reasons for defending the claim
- Any counterclaim should be set out at the same time as the defence
- The claimant can enter judgment on certain types of admissions
- In some cases where liability has been admitted, the amount payable can be decided at a "disposal hearing" and a full Small Claims hearing will not be necessary

---

The court sends the defendant a "response pack", which includes notes and guidance to the defendant on how to proceed.

The response pack contains

- the claim form and the particulars of claim plus "notes for the defendant on replying to the claim form"
- an acknowledgement of service form
- an admission form
- a form for a defence and counterclaim.

The court sends out different types of response pack, depending on whether the claim is "specified" or "not specified".

Where a claim has been issued on line the response can be done on line – the response pack issued by the claims issue centre provides the defendant with a instructions on how to proceed including a unique access code for each claim.

Reminder

The matters discussed in this chapter cover the mechanics of the case. The defendant's case must be carefully evaluated before a defence is prepared, see page 54. At the outset the defendant should be concerned about the viability, including the cost effectiveness, of fighting the case, and should give careful thought to using mediation, see page 174.

Time for response

The response can be an acknowledgment, admission, defence or counterclaim. In default of a response the claimant is entitled to a judgment in default (see page 57).

The time for responding does not start to run until the particulars of claim have been received. If the claim form states that the particulars of case are to follow then they should follow within 14 days of the claim form (rule 7.4(1)).

The first thing that the defendant or legal advisor should do on the receipt of the papers is to make a careful note of the date that the papers were received and make a diary note of the last date for responding. If the response to the court is to be made by post make sure that plenty of time is allowed for postal delays. The diary note should be at least three working days before the court's deadline.

The time for response depends on whether the defendant is an individual or a limited company, and on the method of service.

See the table on page 202 for deemed date of service

The basic rule is that the court must receive the defence or acknowledgment 14 days after the defendant receives the particulars of claim. The court will assume that the papers were received two days after the postmark if they were sent by first class post. If there has been personal service, the 14 days is calculated from the actual date of service.

See also

- methods of service, Chapter 2 Step 3
- calculating time limits, Chapter 10
- judgment in default, page 57.

Admitting the claim

> See Chapter 11 [4(f)] for guidance on drafting an admission

The steps to be taken depend on whether the claim is specified or unspecified, and whether the defendant admits all or part of the claim.

If the defendant admits all or part of the claim the claimant may

1. accept the sums offered or paid and take the matter no further or
2. apply for a judgment on admission or
3. apply for a discretionary judgment.

Judgment on admission

This is a judgment which the claimant is entitled to as of right under rule 14.1(4). The court staff enter the judgment without any judicial intervention, although where the claim is unspecified, the papers will be passed to the District Judge after judgment for directions, including directions for disposal. Upon receiving an admission of part of a specified amount, or an admission of an unspecified amount the court staff will send the claimant a standard form which prompts the claimant to apply for judgment (N225A and N226).

Judgment on admission is only available where

- the claim is for payment of money and
- there is an admission of a **whole** claim for a **specified** sum (rule 14.4) or

- there is an admission of a **part** of a claim for a **specified** sum (rule 14.5) – if the claimant accepts the amount admitted or
- there is an admission of the **whole** of the claim for an **unspecified** sum (rule 14.6) – the court will then determine the amount payable or
- the defendant **offers** a sum in payment of an **unspecified** claim (rule 14.7) – if the claimant does not accept the sum offered, a judgment on admission can be obtained with the amount to be decided by the court (rule 14.7(10)).

No court fee is payable on a judgment on admission (County Court's Fees Order Schedule 1 para 2.5).

Discretionary judgment

The claimant can ask the court for judgment in cases which do not fall neatly into the categories set out in rule 14.1(4) (see previous paragraph) by making an application under rule 14.3. The application can be an application on notice under part 23 (see Chapter 10) or an application for summary judgment under part 24 (see Chapter 10). A court fee will be payable on the application.

Judgment of the court's own initiative

The court's management powers under part 3 of the rules give the District Judge the discretion to enter judgment in appropriate cases. For example, if the terms of the defence amount to an admission, the District Judge may order judgment on his or her own initiative. In suitable cases, a claimant could write to the court to prompt the District Judge to review the defence and enter judgment. The defendant will be entitled to apply for such a judgment to be set aside within a specified number of days (usually seven).

See also the topic Orders made of the court's own initiative, page 196

Request for time to pay

The usual procedure is for a senior member of court staff to look at the admission form and financial information and to determine the rate of payment as a paper exercise; the figures are based on set criteria balancing income against various standard allowances. Once the determination has been made, the parties are notified and can choose to accept or reject the determination. Either side can apply for a hearing before a District Judge to change the determination. The application for a re-determination hearing must be made within 14 days and the case will be transferred to the individual defendants home court for the re-determination hearing (rules 14.9 to 14.3).

Admitting a claim – summary table		
Defendant wishes to	**Steps to be taken within 14 days after receipt of the statement of case**[note 5]	**Consequence**
Admit and pay the whole claim (rule 14.4)	Pay[note 1] full amount (including court fee and costs on summons) to the claimant direct. It is not strictly necessary to return the response form to the court	Provided the claim has been paid in full and the payment safely received, the action will be over[note 9]
Admit the whole claim but request time to pay[note 6] (rule 14.4)	Fill out the admission form including the income details	Court will send a copy of the admission form to the claimant who is entitled to enter a judgment on admission[note 8] – the rate of payment can then be agreed between the parties or will be set by the court
Admit and pay part of the claim (a part admission)[note 2]	Pay the amount admitted to the claimant direct and file a defence as to the balance	Court will send the defence to the claimant together with allocation questionnaires to both parties. Claimant can either accept the sum paid and take the matter no further or return the completed allocation questionnaire to the court and request a hearing date to determine the balance due

SPECIFIED CLAIMS

	Defendant wishes to	Steps to be taken within 14 days after receipt of the statement of case[note 5]	Consequence
		(continued from previous page)	
SPECIFIED CLAIMS	Admit some of the claim (a part admission) but request time to pay or defend the balance[note 6] (rule 14.5)	Fill out the admission form including the income details and file a defence as to the balance	Apply to the court for judgment on admission on Form N225A. Or apply for a judgment on admission[note 8] of the amount admitted and do not pursue the balance
	Have more time to consider a response	Return the acknowledgment	This gives a further 14 days (28 days in total) to respond
UNSPECIFIED CLAIMS	Admit the whole claim (rule 14.6)	State on the defence form that the claim is admitted, subject to the court determining the amount due[notes 3 and 4]	Claimant will be sent a copy of the admission form and is entitled to a judgment on admission[note 8] for damages to be decided by the court[note 3] Claimant applies for judgment on form N226
	Make an offer to settle (rule 14.7)	The defendant should say how much the he or she offers to pay[note 4]. Also, if time is required to pay[note 6], complete the financial information on the admission form	If the claimant accepts the offer then he or she can enter a judgment on admission[note 8] for the amount admitted. If the claimant does not accept the offer then the claimant can apply for a judgment on form N226 with the amount to be decided by the court (rule 14.7(9) and (10))
	Have more time to consider a response	Return the acknowledgment	This gives a further 14 days (28 days in total) to respond

Notes
1. The payment must be made to the claimant direct and not to the court. It makes sense to insist on a receipt if paying by cash.
2. A defendant will often want to admit the "claim" (or part of the claim) but may wish to dispute the court fee, interest, and solicitor's costs on the summons. As a general rule the claimant who has been forced to issue proceedings to recover money due will be entitled to recover these sums. In some cases, however, the proceedings may not have been justified. In such cases the "part admission procedure" should be followed.
3. The defendant will be given a chance to be heard when the court decides what the defendant has to pay (see page 58 – disposal hearings).
4. Make an offer to settle – there is no facility to pay the money into court.
5. The defendant can take any of the steps mentioned after 14 days provided the claimant has not in the meantime entered judgment in default (Rule 14.2(3)).
6. Request for time to pay – see topic on page 50.
7. Discretionary judgment – see topic on page 49.
8. Judgment on admission – see topic on page 48.
9. If the defendant pays the whole amount of the claim before judgment is entered then the defendant is entitled to have the judgment set aside (rule 13.2(c)).

Acknowledging the claim

There are two possible reasons for returning the acknowledgment form, rather than just sending in a defence straight away

1. returning the acknowledgment form automatically gives the defendant a further 14 days to file and serve a defence
2. to give the defendant time to make an application to the court to dispute the jurisdiction of the court.

Although the 14 days extra time sounds useful, bear in mind that the case cannot be allocated to the Small Claims track until after the defence has been filed. The defendant will not be protected by the "no costs" rule until allocation.

The claimant can apply for summary judgment once an acknowledgment has been filed (rule 24.4(1)(a)) (see also Chapter 10 – summary judgment).

Rules about acknowledging the claim are in Part 10.

Dispute of jurisdiction

A dispute of jurisdiction means challenging whether the court has the right to determine the dispute. Often a dispute on jurisdiction may have an international flavour, though such disputes are rare in small claims cases. Sometimes in small claims causes a dispute of jurisdiction arises when the parties have agreed in advance that any dispute will not go to court but will be dealt with by private arbitration; this frequently happens when parties have signed a formal building contract.

To dispute jurisdiction, the defendant must make an application either before acknowledgement or before the time for filing a defence has expired. The application should be supported by evidence (for example documents, or reasons on the application form supported by a Statement of Truth). A defendant can dispute jurisdiction even though an acknowledgement has been filed, but not usually after a defence has been filed. It is therefore important to apply to dispute jurisdiction before filing a defence.

Rules about disputing jurisdiction are in Part 11 of the CPR.

Defending the claim

- See Chapter 11 for guidance on how to draft the defence and the matters which a defence must include
- Each separate defendant must file and serve their own defence

Four types of defence will be considered.

Type 1:   The bland denial (or holding defence)
Type 2:   The "states paid" defence
Type 3:   The full defence
Type 4:   The defence by way of set off or counterclaim.

Reminder

The filing and serving of a defence by an individual in a claim for a specified sum automatically prompts the transfer of the case to the defendant's "home court".

Type 1: Denial

Sending a few lines (or just one) to the court to state that the claim will be contested and without giving reasons is not enough. The defendant must give the reasons for the defence (rule 16.5). See Chapter 11 for guidance on how to prepare a defence.

A District Judge can strike out a defence if it is flimsy and insubstantial – see Chapter 11 – orders made of the court's own initiative.

Type 2: States Paid Defence

The response form to a "specified" claim invites the defendant to state if the debt has already been paid, and if so when. If it has been paid, and the defendant says so, this is called a "states paid" defence.

A states paid defence is sent to the claimant when the court receives it, and the claimant is asked to comment before the matter proceeds further. If the claimant accepts that the debt has been paid, the case will be at an end.

Costs will ultimately be in the discretion of the District Judge but the defendant should not expect to pay the court fee and the costs on the summons if the claim was paid in full before the proceedings were issued. However, if the proceedings were issued before payment, even if they were served later, the defendant should expect to pay the costs on the summons, especially if the claimant sent a "letter before action".

Type 3: The full defence

> The rules for what a defence must include are set out in Chapter 11.

The defence must say

- what parts of the claim are disputed (and why)
- which parts of the claim the defendant does not know enough about to admit or dispute, but which the defendant wants the claimant to prove
- what parts of the defence are admitted (rule 16.5).

The defence can be written or typed on the response form or set out in a separate document.

Type 4: Defence by counterclaim

A counterclaim can *only* be made *without* obtaining permission from the court at the time of the defence. If a defendant wants to put in a counterclaim at a later date the court will have to give permission (rule 20.4 (2) and this permission must be obtained by making an application; see Chapter 11 for details on how to make an application.

The court will require a fee from the defendant based on the amount of the counterclaim. The fee is calculated on the scale of fees shown in Appendix 1 and is paid on the full amount of the counterclaim (Fee 1 Column 1 County Court Fees Order 1982 (as amended)).

If the amount of the counterclaim exceeds £5,000 this may prevent the claim from being allocated to the Small Claims track (rule 26.8(e)); however it is the amount of the claim which usually determines if the case qualifies for the Small Claims track (see Chapter 4 – how does a claim qualify for the Small claims track?).

A counterclaim is a statement of case (rule 20.2(1)). When preparing the counterclaim, follow the guidance for drafting a statement of case (see Chapter 11) and note that the counterclaim should be supported by a statement of truth.

The counterclaim and defence should be one document – the counterclaim usually runs on at the end of the defence (PD20, para 6.1).

A defendant who makes a claim against a claimant by way of counterclaim is technically a part 20 claimant. If the claimant withdraws a claim the counterclaim will remain unless that is also withdrawn.

Defence to counterclaim

A claimant must respond to the counterclaim within 14 days by serving and filing a defence or admission. There is no acknowledgment procedure.

The defendant can enter judgment in default of defence to counterclaim if none is filed (rule 12.3(2)).

Often a simple defence to counterclaim will suffice – a possible wording is set out in Chapter 11.

When the defendant wants to pass the claim on to someone else

These are called "third party proceedings". An example of this type of claim would be if the claimant's car was hit in the rear by the defendant and the defendant's defence is that he or she was shunted into the claimant by a driver at the back driving into his or her car. The defendant would then start third party proceedings against the driver at the back of the shunt.

The court must give permission for the defendant to add another party to the proceedings (rule 20.5(1)). See Chapter 10 for details of how to make an application.

A formal application is not needed if the defendant wishes to make a claim against an existing defendant and the claim is made at the time of the defence (rule 20.6).

Rules about claims against third parties are in Part 20.

Judgment in default – the consequence of not responding to the claim in time

If the defendant does not respond to the claim in time (see page 44 and 47), the claimant can apply for judgment in default by using the correct form (rule 12.4(1)). The form is supplied to the claimant when the court notifies the claimant that proceedings have been issued and served. If the claimant is represented by a solicitor, fixed costs will be allowed in addition to those set out on the claim form – these are set out in Appendix 4.

No court fee is payable on applying for a default judgment.

If the claim is for a specified amount (e.g. debt claims) the judgment is for the full claim plus interest to the date of judgment. If the claim is for an unspecified amount then the judgment is for "an amount to be decided by the court" (rule 12.4).

Judgment in default of defence cannot be obtained if the claimant has already made an application for summary judgment (see Chapter 10) or if the proceedings have been commenced by the alternative "Part 8" procedure (see footnote on page 22).

An application for judgment in default cannot be made until after the date for service of the defence or acknowledgement has expired but must be made within six months after the date for fiing the defence – if not the claim is stayed and the claimant has to apply to the court to progress the action (rule 15.11).

Judgments for unspecified sums – getting the court to determine the amount payable

If the amount is to be decided by the court then, immediately after judgment, the papers will be put before a District Judge who will decide how the amount is to be arrived at. The District Judge can

- decide the value without a hearing, or
- list for a "disposal" hearing, or
- direct that allocation questions be sent out with a view to allocating the case to the Small Claims track for disposal

Deciding the value without a hearing

This will only be done in the simplest of cases, the decision being made under the District Judge's case management powers (rule 3.1). In these circumstances the order will state that, because the decision has been made without a hearing, any party affected by the order can apply for the order to be set aside. The order will also state the time period within which the affected party may apply for the order to be set aside, often seven days. See Chapter 10 – Orders made of the court's initiative (PD 23 para. 11.1 and 11.2).

Disposal hearings

A disposal hearing offers a simplified method of determining a case where it is only being defended as to value, and is suitable in simple cases where a judgment has been obtained by default or through an admission. The case goes straight from the judgment stage to a final hearing without having to go through the process of allocation directions (PD26 para. 12.8). The District Judge who orders an allocation hearing will give simple directions, usually limited to the claimant serving a witness statement and documents to support the claim.

The disposal hearing will not normally last for more than 30 minutes during which the court will not usually hear oral evidence (PD26 para 12.4). The defendant will be notified of a disposal hearing and can argue with the amount being claimed by the claimant. The defendant can comment on any issue affecting the amount of the claim, including commenting on the claimant's evidence, raising issues of contributory negligence, mitigation and causation, so far as these are not inconsistent with any matter determined by the judgment (see *Lunnan v Hari Singh and others* Times 1 July 1999 and *Maes Finance and Mac No.1 Ltd v Al Philips & Co (a Firm)* Times 25 March 1997).

Both the District Judge who lists the case for a disposal hearing and the District Judge on that hearing can if they wish allocate the case to the small claims track and have the case proceed, in which case the rules about small claims costs will apply.

Amount to be decided by the court – upon allocation to the Small Claims track

If the District Judge decides to allocate a case to the Small Claims track, the action will then take on the structure of Small Claims case. Examples of cases which will be allocated after judgment would include "holiday cases", or others where the amount of the judgment can only be determined after considering detailed evidence. Chapter 5 deals with preparation for a Small Claims hearing.

Reply to defence

A claimant does not usually need to file a reply to defence because, by not doing so, the claimant will not be taken as having admitted any part of the defence (rule 16.7(1)). If the claimant wants to make a reply to the defence then the reply must be filed and served with the allocation questionnaire (rule 15.8) and should usually follow on as the same document (PD15 para 3.2). In Small Claims cases, the aim will be to limit procedural matters and it will rarely be necessary or proportionate to serve a reply to defence.

> Chapter 8 covers applications to set aside default judgments

CHAPTER 4

Allocation questionnaires and allocation

Introduction	63
What does allocation mean?	64
What is a track?	64
How does a case qualify for the Small Claims track?	65
Principles of allocation – the court is in charge	65
A value in dispute not exceeding £5,000	66
The allocation questionnaire	70
How and when to complete the allocation questionnaire	71
A – Settlement	73
B – Location of hearing	73
C – Track	73
D – Witnesses	73
E – Experts	74
F – Hearing	74
G – Other information	75
H – Fee	76
I – Signature	76
Consequences of failure to return or complete the allocation questionnaire or pay the fee	76
What happens when the court receives the questionnaires?	77

Decisions can be taken without a hearing 77

Orders of the court's own initiative 78

The allocation hearing 78

Can the court dispense with allocation questionnaires? 79

Can the allocated track be changed or challenged? 79

Can the parties elect for the case to be allocated to the
Small Claims track even if the case does not qualify on
financial grounds? 80

Hearings in Welsh 81

Allocation – what next? 81

Allocation questionnaires and allocation

Introduction

Some courts which run a mediation scheme and which may, after the defence has been received, actively encourage the parties to take the case to an out of court mediation. Courts which run such schemes include Exeter and Central London. Please refer to chapter 9 for discussion about mediation.

When mediation fails, or if it does not occur, all courts will then try and move the case to a final hearing as swiftly and efficiently as possible. The parties should have tried to settle the case before issue. There is one "last chance" at the allocation stage for the proceedings to be stopped for settlement discussions to take place. Otherwise, the impetus of the case is maintained and the parties must continue to be vigilant about time limits and following court directions otherwise the claim, defence or counterclaim may be struck out. The court is in charge.

Look back at the schedule at the end of Chapter 2 on page 44 for an overview of the steps to be taken at this stage of the case.

Basics

- The case can be allocated to the Small Claims track if it meets the financial qualifications of the track
- The parties are all required to return completed allocation questionnaires to the court before the District Judge can make an allocation decision
- Some cases may require an allocation hearing
- An allocation fee is payable on cases of over £1,500 in value

---

What does allocation mean?

The Civil Procedure Rules provide a code of practice applicable to all civil courts in England and Wales. All the procedures described in the book to this point will be followed in every case, even large money claims issued in the High Court. However, the rules recognise that all cases do not need the same treatment in preparation for a hearing and not all cases need a formal or lengthy trial. To cater for this diversity, and to ensure that procedures are proportionate to the value of the claim, the rules create three distinct categories of case. Once the District Judge knows what the claim and defence involves, he or she can assign, or allocate, the case to the category most suited to that case. This process is termed "allocation".

What is a track?

The three case management categories are termed 'tracks'. They are shown in the following table.

Small Claims track Part 27	Cases up to £5,000 in value except: • Cases which include a claim for personal injury up to £1,000 in value only • Housing cases – limited to where the claim against the landlord for repair/damages is no more than £1000 each
Fast track Part 28	Cases above the Small Claims limit (see above) but of not more than £15,000 in value and where the case can be heard in one day or less
Multi-track Part 29	Cases which do not qualify for the Small Claims or fast track including all cases of over £15,000 in value

Once a case has been allocated to a track, the management of the case and the hearing are in accordance with the rules of that track. The track which the case is suited to by the rules is termed its "normal track".

How does a case qualify for the Small Claims track?

The Small Claims track is the normal track for

- *any claim which has a financial value of not more than £5,000 subject to the special provisions about claims for personal injuries and housing disrepair claims;*
- *any claim for personal injuries which has a financial value of not more than £5,000 where the claim for damages or personal injuries is not more than £1,000; and*
- *any claim which includes a claim by a tenant of residential premises against his landlord for repairs or other work to the premises where the estimated cost of repairs or other work is not more than £1,000 (and the financial value of the claim for damages in respect of those repairs is not more than £1,000)*

(rule 27.1(2))

Principles of allocation – the court is in charge

(1) When deciding the track for a claim, the matters to which the court shall have regard include
(a) the financial value of the claim, if any;
(b) the nature of the remedy sought;
(c) the likely complexity of the facts, law or evidence;
(d) the number of parties or likely parties;
(e) the value of any counterclaim or other Part 20 claim and the complexity of any matters relating to it;
(f) the amount of oral evidence which may be required;
(g) the importance of the claim to persons who are not parties to the proceedings;
(h) the views expressed by the parties; and
(i) the circumstances of the parties
(2) It is for the court to assess the financial value of a claim, and in doing so it will disregard
(a) any amount not in dispute;

(b) any claim for interest;
(c) costs; and
(d) any contributory negligence

rule 26.8 (1) and (2)

As well as the list of points in rule 26 as quoted above, the District Judge will have the overriding objective firmly in mind (see page 170) including the need to achieve justice by dealing with the case in a manner which is "proportionate" (rule 1.1(1) (c). The experience of the District Judge will be that most types of case can be sensibly managed by Small Claims directions, even those which the parties find complex or difficult. It is the essence of the Small Claims procedure that a case can be kept in proportion by stripping the pre – hearing procedure to its bare essentials.

The District Judge will also recall that the Court of Appeal, in the past, when considering whether a case was suitable for the old-style arbitration procedure under CCR Order 19, took a robust view of the matter. It decided that even cases involving accidents at work were not to be excluded from the small claims process *Afzal and Others v Ford Motor Co Ltd and other appeals* CA (1994) 4 All ER.

Whereas previous versions of the court rules specified that interest should be excluded when considering the value of a claim this has been changed and the District Judge alone determines the value of the claim and will include interest on valuing the claim if that is an item in dispute. (Rule 26.7.3(1)).

A value in dispute not exceeding £5,000

The money in dispute is the factor primarily taken into account in deciding whether the case qualifies for the Small Claims track (Rule 26.8(1)).

The District Judge looks at the amount which the claimant states as the claim, but a different valuation may be put on the claim by the District Judge and this is determinative for allocation purposes. In making the allocation decision the claim and counterclaim are not added together, and the fact that the counterclaim may be in excess of £5,000 does not automatically disqualify the case from the Small

Claims track; *Berridge (Paul) (t/a EAB builders)* v *RM Bayliss* (1999) Lawtel 23 November.

It is the *disputed* amount which is considered for allocation purposes. So, if a claim starts out at, say £10,000 and the defendant pays £8,000 after the issue of proceedings and before allocation, the case will qualify for the Small Claims track (PD 26 para 7.4). In cases such as this see also the answer to Frequently Asked Questions about costs, on page 124 (question 4).

Housing claims

Cases for harassment or unlawful eviction will not be allocated to the Small Claims track (rule 26.7(4) and rule 27.1(2)).

Cases of housing disrepair where either the cost of the repair or the damages for non repair are expected to be £1,000 each do not qualify for the Small Claims track (Rule 27.1(2)). The expected cost of repair and damages each have a separate £1,000 limit making the total up to £2,000.

If the tenant claims only for the *cost* of the repair, for example if the tenant has done the repairs and claims a refund, then the case will qualify for the Small Claims track, if the amount claimed is not more than £5,000.

Personal injury claims

The Small Claims procedure can be used for personal injury cases, including claims arising from accidents at work. However, if the personal injury aspect of the claim is above £1,000 the case will not qualify for the Small Claims procedure (rule 26.6(1)(a)(ii)).

Some claims mix personal injury and non-personal injury aspects. If either the personal injury aspect exceeds £1,000, or the combined injury and non-personal injury aspect exceeds £5,000 in value the case will not qualify for the Small Claims track.

"Damages for personal injuries" means sums claimed as compensation for pain, suffering and loss of amenity (rule 26.6 (2)). Medical expenses, loss of earnings and damage to clothing do not count as "personal injury" elements of a claim when calculating whether the case qualifies for the Small Claims track.

In reality, few cases involving a claim for personal injury will qualify for the Small Claims track – only the most superficial of personal injuries are likely to merit an award of £1,000 or less.

It is the assessment of value put on the case by the District Judge which matters, and not assessment made by the claimant (rule 26.8(2)). The District Judge will assess the potential value of the claim on the basis of the injuries as described in the claim or supporting medical report and will disregard the claimant's own estimate if necessary.

Claims involving disputed allegations of dishonesty

If there is a disputed allegation of dishonesty this will make the case unsuitable for the Small Claims track (PD 26 para. 8.1(d)). For example in the case of *Geoffrey Arnold Wheen* v *Smithmann and another LTL* 25 September 2000 the Court of Appeal confirmed that a case involving allegations of fraud against estate agents was plainly not suitable for a Small Claims hearing. Bear in mind that the District Judge will decide if the allegation of dishonesty is sufficiently serious to merit the case not being allocated to the Small Claims track. If a party uses the words 'fraud' or 'dishonest' this will be assessed by the District Judge who will decide if the allegation is substantial or a mere insult.

Injunctions

The Small Claims procedure is not restricted to money claims and the District Judge may, at a Small Claims hearing, award an injunction or similar relief, for example ordering

- a shop to supply replacement goods
- a neighbour to replace a fence or boundary
- a claim for information under the Data Protection Act
- a case to stop a bank from closing a customer account.

Claims of no financial value

The court will allocate a claim which has no financial value to the track which is most suitable to the case having regard to the factors mentioned in rule 26.8 (1) (see page 63). The Small Claims track might well be the best track for such a case – and if the parties themselves tell the court that they want a Small Claims hearing this will certainly be taken into account.

The views of the parties

The court will consider what the parties have to say, but this is only one of the factors. The District Judge will, in accordance with the overriding case management responsibilities of the court, ultimately make the decision on allocation.

Even if the normal track is not the Small Claims track the parties can, by agreement, elect to use the Small Claims track (see page 80).

Claims which do not qualify on financial grounds

The court cannot allocate the case to the Small Claims track if the claim is greater than the Small Claims limit, except with the agreement of both parties (rule 26.7 (3)). The small claims track is an attractive way to determine matters where the issues are not complex and the parties do not have lawyers. Please refer to page 80 which discusses voluntary referral to the small claims track.

The allocation questionnaire

Basics

- The District Judge reads the allocation questionnaires submitted by all parties to make case management decisions about a case, including deciding to which track the case is to be allocated
- There is a special allocation form (N149) which is tailored to the needs of the Small Claims track
- Each side must complete an allocation questionnaire within 14 days of receipt
- The claimant must pay an allocation fee
- If the claim has been discontinued and the defendant wishes to pursue the counterclaim then the defendant pays the allocation fee
- The claim, or counterclaim, can be struck out if the allocation questionnaire is not returned
- The District Judge uses information on the questionnaire for case management, including allocation decisions

The allocation questionnaire is sent out to both sides by the court when the defence is received. The form is sent out with another form (the N152) which includes basic information on the date to return the questionnaire and the court it must be sent to.

The form N149 is sent to the parties in cases where it appears to the court staff that the case qualifies to be allocated to the Small Claims track. Another allocation questionnaire (form N150) is sent in respect of other claims but this contains a section which provides space for a party who wants the case allocated to Small Claims to explain why. Unrepresented parties who are sent a form N150 rather than a form N149 should complete and return the N150 using guidance notes provided and the guidance of this book.

In exceptional cases the court may deal with allocation without first asking the parties to complete an allocation questionnaire (for example with respect to "bank charges claims").

How and when to complete the allocation questionnaire

Court fee

The allocation fee is payable when the allocation questionnaire is returned. It is payable by the claimant except where the action is proceeding on the counterclaim alone, when it is payable by the defendant. If there is no allocation questionnare The allocation fee is payable 14 days after the despatch of the notice of allocation to track. There is no allocation fee for claims which do not exceed £1500.

> What happens if the allocation
> fee is not paid? See page 76

Time limit

The allocation questionnaire must be returned to the court within 14 days after receipt (rule 26.3(6)).

The court's computer prompts the court staff to put the file before the District Judge after 14 days. At that point, if the allocation questionnaires are in order, the District Judge will proceed with allocation and case management. If not, the District Judge will make orders which specify sanctions if the allocation questionnaires are not returned.

> What happens if the allocation
> questionnaire is not returned?
> See page 76

Co-operate!

The rules suggest that the parties co-operate when filling out the form: although they do not require completed allocation questionnaires to be sent to the other side it is helpful to do so. In particular it is sensible to agree in which court both parties want the case to be heard, also to consider together what expert evidence is needed.

Which court?

The allocation questionnaire is usually returned to the court of issue. Where proceedings have been automatically transferred to the defendant's home court under rule 26.2, however, the court in which the proceedings have been commenced will serve an allocation questionnaire *before* the proceedings are transferred. The allocation questionnaire must then be returned to the defendant's home court (the destination court) and not the court of issue.

Filling out the form

There are several sections to complete

- A Settlement
- B Location of hearing
- C Track
- D Witnesses
- E Experts
- F Hearing
- G Other Information
- H Fee
- I Signature

A – Settlement

The parties should have tried to settle before starting the case but, if there is still scope for discussion, there is one last chance to put the case on hold, or "stay" the proceedings, particularly pending an attempt at mediation.

If all parties request a stay the District Judge will direct that the proceedings are stayed for one month (rule 26.4(2)).

The District Judge can allow the stay to continue for more than one month but there must be a good reason, and the stay will be for a defined period of time only (rule 26.4(3)). If the parties stay the case for mediation to take place the court will probably require a report on the outcome.

The court must be told if the case settles during the period of "stay".

At the end of the stay the District Judge will review the file and give directions (rule 26.4(5)).

B – Location of hearing

This is the opportunity to tell the District Judge where you want the case to be heard. You should set out your reasons if the case is to be moved elsewhere. You should have tried to get the other side to agree the location of the hearing if you are asking the District Judge to move the case (see Chapter 5). Where the parties live at opposite ends of the country it may be rational to agree to the case being tried at a court between the two.

C – Track

This is explained on the form itself and in this book. Since the form is likely to be the form specially tailored for the small claims track just tick the 'yes' box.

D – Witnesses

A party who wishes to rely only on his or her own evidence will enter a zero in this box.

Potential witnesses are considered under two headings – witnesses of fact and expert witnesses.

Witnesses as to fact are non-expert witnesses, namely people who know about the facts of the case and can support your case in court.

For example

Witness name	Witness to which facts
Claimant (Brenda Lythe)	Driver of car – how the accident happened
John Lythe (husband)	Passenger – how the accident happened
Ashram Patel	Independent bystander – what the defendant said after the accident

E– Experts

Completing this section is self-explanatory. On pages 96 to 99 we explain about the appointment and use of experts in small claim cases. Please note that expert evidence is not allowed unless the court gives permission in advance.

F – Hearing

Completing this section is self-explanatory. The District Judge will be experienced in assessing how much time is required for the hearing (see page 98 for some guidance on what time estimates for the hearing are likely to be given by the District Judge). The task of estimating the hearing time is more difficult of course where the parties have not seen the other side's completed allocation questionnaire. However, the parties themselves must put some thought into whether there are unusual aspects of the case which will affect the time estimate. For example

- the number of documents to be considered by the District Judge (anything above about 20 pages would be quite a lot for a Small Claims case)
- more than one or two witnesses to give evidence on each side (including the parties themselves)
- if the witnesses themselves are likely to be slow in giving evidence (for example if any witness will be giving evidence through an interpreter)

A litigant in person is unlikely to be able to gauge how long a case will take and there is no harm in answering this question 'to be decided by the court', provided of course the questionnaire contains all relevant information about documents and witnesses to enable the District Judge to make a realistic time estimate.

It is important that you state any dates that any essential witness is unable to attend the final hearing. Although the court may list the case on 21 days' notice, it is far more likely that the hearing date will be several weeks in the future. It is suggested that you mention any important dates to avoid in the period from about 1 to 4 months after the return of the allocation questionnaire.

G – Other information

Use the box in this section to let the District Judge know about anything that will help with the management of the case. For example

- If there are to be a large number of documents for the District Judge to consider at the hearing.(Tell the District Judge if your documents are more than 20 pages)
- To ask the District Judge to make an order that the other side clarify aspects of their case or to provide copies of specific documents.
- To ask the District Judge to consider a site visit

- To notify the court that a video or DVD will be used as evidence at the hearing.
- If the proceedings are in Wales, to notify the court that the parties wish the hearing to be conducted in Welsh and if the witnesses can speak English or Welsh or both.

H – Fee

The fee is £100 but only for claims above £1500.

I– Signature

The questionnaire is usually signed by the litigant or his or her legal representative but can be signed by a litigation friend (see Glossary). A lay representative cannot sign this form.

Consequences of failure to return or complete the allocation questionnaire or pay the fee

If a party fails to file an allocation questionnaire the court may give any direction it considers appropriate

(rule 26.5(5))

The practice direction to Part 26 suggests that the District Judge is likely to make an order that, unless the missing allocation questionnaire is filed within seven days, the claim, defence or any counterclaim will be struck out; however, a different order can be made (PD 26 para. 2.5(1)).

The District Judge may decide to press on with allocation with one or both questionnaires missing, provided there is enough information on the file (see the topic on page 77 "Can the court dispense with allocation questionnaires?"). In practice, the District Judge will rarely deal with allocation without the claimant's questionnaire, but may well press ahead if it is only the defendant who is in default.

Alternatively, the District Judge may order an allocation hearing – see below under the heading "the allocation hearing".

Note that if allocation takes place without a questionnaire this does not save the claimant the court fee because this is payable in any event within 28 days of filing the defence (or filing the last defence if there is more than one defendant), or within 28 days of the expiry of the time permitted for filing all defences, if sooner (County Court fees order Para. 2.1).

If the allocation fee is not paid, the District Judge is likely to make an order that unless the fee is paid within a short period (often as short as three days) the claim will be struck out.

What happens when the court receives the questionnaires?

Assuming both questionnaires have been safely received, the file is given to the District Judge to review.

At this point, the District Judge will have the following information on the file

- the claim, defence and counterclaim (if any)
- any correspondence from the parties
- the completed allocation questionnaires (and any documents sent in with the allocation questionnaires).

The District Judge will then allocate the case there and then, or fix an allocation hearing.

The District Judge then as before goes on to give possible directions for the management of the case. The directions are discussed in the next chapter.

Decisions can be taken without a hearing

The District Judge can determine allocation of the case as a paperwork exercise without the attendance of the parties but only if both parties agree (rule 27.10); this is a method of disposal which cannot be used without consent and is not often used. If the parties wish the court to consider this procedure they should agree it, set out their agreement and the reasons for it in a joint letter to the court or in section G of their respective allocation questionnaires.

Orders of the court's own initiative

At this point, the District Judge may use the powers under the rules to strike out a claim or defence which is plainly hopeless, or an abuse of the process of the court.

> The topic "The court's case management powers" is in Chapter 10

The allocation hearing

In practice, in Small Claims cases these will be relatively rare. The rules make it plain that every case must be dealt with "proportionately" and where relatively small sums of money are at stake an allocation hearing will not often be justified. In a Small Claims case, possible reasons for an allocation hearing could be:

- where there is confusion as to the amount in dispute (especially if it is possible that the case may not qualify for the Small Claims track on financial grounds) or
- where there is an issue of dishonesty which might make the case unsuitable for the Small Claims track.

Both sides will be given at least seven days notice of the allocation hearing (PD26 6.2).

The practice direction to rule 26 sets out the general principles for allocation hearings and the orders which can be made. The allocation hearing is not a formality and must be attended by the parties themselves or, if represented, by someone who has authority to take decisions about the case.

NB Note the warning on the foot of the notice in form N153 (notice of allocation hearing) which states, "if you fail to attend the hearing, the court may order you to pay the costs of the other party, or parties, that do attend. Failure to pay those costs within the time limit stated may lead to your statement of case being struck out."

Can the court dispense with allocation questionnaires?

Yes, but this is not done often. Parties involved in the recent cases involving 'bank charges claims' will be aware that the judges have decided to dispense with allocation questionnaires in all of these cases and instead list the cases for a hearing under 'standard directions'. In other cases, the decision to dispense with allocation questionnaires will be taken on a case by case basis and only if the District Judge is sure that the case can be safely timetabled to a final hearing without the completion of the questionnaire. Note that if the allocation questionnaire is dispensed with the allocation fee is still payable – the court office will send out the fee demand to the claimant.

Can the allocated track be changed or challenged?

If either party is not happy with the allocation decision they can apply for reallocation (PD 26 Para. 11.1(1)).

A formal appeal is only made if the allocation was made at an allocation hearing or some other hearing of which the party was notified.

If there has been a change of circumstances since allocation, the parties should notify the court so that the District Judge can re-allocate (PD 26 para. 11.2). For example, this should happen if the case was allocated to the fast track and the amount in dispute was later reduced by the defendant admitting or paying part of the sum claimed.

Can the parties elect for the case to be allocated to the Small Claims track even if the case does not qualify on financial grounds?

Yes, this can happen under rules 26.7(3) and 27.14(5). This is sometimes termed 'voluntary referral'.

This option will be particularly attractive to litigants in person who have a fairly straightforward case that they wish to be heard promptly and with the minimum of fuss. By electing to use the Small Claims track the parties also avoid having to pay the fee of £275 which is payable on cases allocated to other tracks upon filing of the listing questionnaires. There is no listing fee for Small Claims cases. However all cases including Small Claims cases attract a "hearing fee" (see Chapter 5).

The District Judge must approve the voluntary election, which must be made by both parties, and he or she will only do so if satisfied that the case is suitable for the Small Claims track. The judge will not approve the election if it seems that the case is likely to take more than one day to be heard (PD26 para. 8.1 (2)(b) and (c)).

Where the parties elect to use the Small Claims track then the case will be subject to the streamlined Small Claims procedure in every way, and the procedural restrictions in Part 27 will apply. The practice direction to Part 26 does envisage that a case of higher value may need special directions and points out that the case management directions may reflect this (PD 26 para. 8.1(2)(d)). If a case is allocated to the Small Claims track by this voluntary method) then the "no costs" rule will apply (see page 112). As with all Small Claims cases there is a full appeals procedure.

Benefits of voluntary referral to the small claims track

- simplified steps to the final hearing
- relatively informal procedure at the final hearing
- the no costs rule applies
- no pre trial checklist and no listing fee payable
- depending on the court, possibly an earlier hearing date

Hearings in Welsh

The court service in Wales has adopted the principle that the English and Welsh languages must be treated equally; this is in line with Section 22(1) of the Welsh Language Act 1993. Those familiar with conducting court proceedings in Wales will know that many of the court forms, including the allocation questionnaire, are bilingual. All court hearings, including small claims, hearings may be conducted in Welsh if this is the choice of the parties and certain District Judges are able to conduct the hearings in Welsh. Arrangements for co-ordinating the Welsh speaking parties with a suitable District Judge are made by the county court. Welsh speakers are entitled to an interpreter at any hearing if this is needed for them to follow the proceedings.

Allocation – what next?

Once the District Judge has allocated the case to the Small Claims track, he or she will give directions to bring the case to a Small Claims hearing. The next chapter deals with those directions.

Once the case has been allocated, and directions given, both parties will be notified. A copy of the other side's allocation questionnaire is sent out by the court with the notice of allocation.

In addition the claimant will be notified of the requirement to pay a hearing fee whch must be paid withing 14 days of being notified of the hearing date. There is a system to refund all of the hearng fee if the court is notified more than 7 days before the hearing date that it can be vacated (see Chapter 5).

CHAPTER 5

Steps between Allocation and the Hearing

(Including Checklist for Preparation for the Hearing)

Introduction	84
Standard directions	85
In detail – the allocation directions explained	88
– Venue of the final hearing	88
– What documents are needed for the case	92
– Documents	92
– Request for additional information	93
– Witness Statements	94
– Experts' reports	96
– Lists of disputed items	99
– Photographs and sketch plans	100
– Inform the court if the case is settled before the hearing	100
– Time estimate	100
– Special directions	101
Preliminary hearing	102
Applications for directions by the parties	103
Checklist for preparing for a Small Claims hearing	103
Visiting the court before the hearing date	107

Steps between Allocation and the Hearing
(Including Checklist for Preparation for the Hearing)

Introduction

Once the District Judge has decided that the case is to be allocated to the Small Claims track he or she immediately sets out the exact steps each side must take to prepare the case for a hearing. The objective is to get the case to a hearing with the minimum of fuss and expense, and to ensure that both sides have prior warning of the details of the other sides case – no surprises!

Each party will each receive a notice which sets out

- the fact that the case has been allocated to the Small Claims track
- the date and place of the hearing
- any directions which the parties must follow
- the time estimate for the hearing.

The court will give the parties at least 21 days notice of the date of the hearing unless they agree to accept shorter notice (rule 27.4(2)(a)).

Basics

- The District Judge will give standard directions in a range of different types of cases but may give special directions
- In some cases there will be preliminary appointment

- The court will give both sides at least three weeks' notice of the date of the hearing of the case
- Both parties must send copies of their documents to the other side, usually 14 days before the hearing
- The District Judge may require a party to provide further information at any time but the parties themselves are not allowed to serve "Part 18" requests (see Chapter 10)

Standard directions

The practice direction to rule 27 sets out the standard directions in a Small Claims case plus standard directions for four of the most usual types of Small Claims disputes. The District Judge may also order 'special directions' which are in addition to or instead of the standard directions.

FORM A – The standard directions
FORM B – Claims arising out of road accidents
FORM C – Claims arising out of building disputes, vehicle repairs and similar contractual claims
FORM D – Tenants' claims for the return of deposits; landlords' claims for damage caused
FORM E – Holiday and wedding claims
FORM F – Some special directions

See the full text of the directions in Appendix 7 at page 269 and the overview table on page 6

Every case is reviewed by the District Judge at the time of allocation and every attempt will be made to tailor directions in a particular case.

Overview of preparation directions in Small Claims cases (taken from PD27)

	All cases	Road Traffic	Building disputes Vehicle repairs and similar contractual claims	Disputes between landlords and tenants about damage caused and deposits	Holiday and wedding claims
	Form A	Form B	Form C	Form D	Form E
Documents	Will include any: • letters • contracts • notes • photographs • witness statements	May include: • experts' reports • medical evidence • witness statements • invoices and estimates for repairs • documents which relate to other losses, such as loss of earnings • sketch plans and photographs	May include: • experts' reports • the contract • witness statements • experts reports • invoices for work done or goods • photographs • estimates of work to be done	May include: • tenancy agreement and any inventory • rent book/evidence of rent payments • photographs • witness statements • invoices or estimates for work or goods	May include: • any written contract, brochure or booking form • photographs • documents showing payments made • witness statements • letters
When documents are to be sent to the other side	[14 days] before the hearing	[14 days] before the hearing	[14 days] before the hearing	[14 days] before the hearing	[14 days] before the hearing
Bring original documents to the hearing?	Yes	Yes	Yes	Yes	Yes
		Parties to try and agree the cost of repairs and other losses subject to blame being decided at the hearing		Parties to try and agree the cost of repairs/replacements and other losses subject to the court's decision about any other decision in the case	

	Standard directions	Road Traffic	Building disputes Vehicle repairs and 'Similar contractual claims'	Disputes between landlords and tenants about damage caused and deposits	Holiday and wedding claims
	Form A	Form B	Form C	Form D	Form E
			Party who complains to provide a list of complaints [14 days] before the hearing	Party who complains to provide a list of complaints plus the cost of repair/replacement [14 days] before the hearing	
			A breakdown of the cost of remedial work must be filed at court		Any party wanting to rely on video evidence to tell the court in advance (because of equipment)
		Signed witness statements to be prepared (including witnesses who will not attend the hearing)	Signed witness statements to be prepared (including witnesses who will not attend the hearing)	Signed witness statements to be prepared (including witnesses who will not attend the hearing)	Signed witness statements to be prepared (including witnesses who will not attend the hearing)
		• Parties invited to prepare a sketch plan and photographs • Court may disregard evidence which is not served in advance of the hearing	• Parties invited to produce photographs of the work in question • Court may disregard evidence which is not served in advance of the hearing	• Parties invited to produce photographs of the condition of the property • Court may disregard evidence which is not served in advance of the hearing	Court may disregard evidence which is not served in advance of the hearing and may disregard video evidence if not warned about it in advance
The court must be informed immediately if the case is settled by agreement before the hearing date	Yes	Yes	Yes	Yes	Yes

The basic standard directions are

- Fourteen days before the hearing (or on such other date as the court directs) send copies of documents that are to be relied on to the other side.
- Original documents are to be brought to the hearing.
- The court must be informed immediately if the case is settled by agreement before the hearing date.
- The parties are told the date of the hearing and the time allowed by the court.

Appendix A to PD 27

In detail – the allocation directions explained

Venue of the final hearing

> **Basics**
>
> - A money claim can be started in any County court
> - The case is transferred automatically to the defendant's home court when a defence is served if
>   - the claim is for a specified amount of money *and*
>   - the defendant is an individual
> - The District Judge has the final say as to where a case is heard
>   - the defendant is an individual (Rule 26.2).

Overview

The operation of the transfer rules are of particular importance in Small Claims cases. Although in most Small Claims cases there will be no award for costs, the winner can expect to be awarded reasonable travel expenses plus the cost of overnight accommodation. Such expenses may be significant, especially when measured against what may be a relatively small sum of money in dispute. A litigant may think twice about pursuing or defending a case if attending the hearing will involve a lot of travelling. If proceedings are moved from court to court this may cause delay in an otherwise fairly speedy procedure. When a case is moved from court to court, there is always the chance that papers will get lost or mislaid.

The system of "automatic transfer" enables large scale court users pursuing debts, e.g. credit card companies and banks, to issue proceedings either at the Summons Production Centre in Northampton or at their own local County court, which may be more convenient for them. The claim, if disputed, will be transferred automatically to the court local to the defendant, so in this way debtors are not disadvantaged by the claimant's initial choice of court.

Each action has its own case number, which includes a code identifying the court where the proceedings commenced; this number, including the court code, is retained by the individual case even after transfer e.g. Aberdare AA.

Definitions

Every County court has its own geographical district or area. You can establish the court relevant to a post code or address by visiting www.courtservice.gov.uk and navigating to the 'court finder' part of the website. The court staff of a particular court will also be able to tell you if any particular address is within the area of that court.

The **defendant's home court** means the 'county court for the district in which the defendant resides or carries on business'.

A claim for a **specified sum** includes any claim where the claimant puts a fixed value on the claim. This will mean all debt claims and any claim for damages where the claimant specifies the amount which is claimed in advance.

It is important to note that the rules about automatic transfer only apply where the defendant is an **individual**, which excludes limited companies. If an individual is a trader, for example "Mike Smith trading as Aroofer" the case will be transferred to Mr Smith's home court. However a transfer will not automatically be prompted if the defendant is named simply as "Aroofer" or "Aroofer (a firm)".

Automatic transfer on defence

The rule about 'automatic transfer on defence' does not apply if

1. the case has already been moved to *another* defendant's home court, to set aside or vary a judgment or for the amount to be determined by the court (rule 26.2(1)(c)) *or*
2. the defendant files a "states paid" defence (see page 52) or a partial admission. In these circumstances the case is not transferred on the receipt of the defence but only when the claimant confirms that the case is to continue (rule 26.2(4)).

It has already been noted that the rule only applies where the claim is for a specified sum and the defendant is an individual.

The automatic transfer is to the home court of the defendant who first files a defence (rule 26.2(5)).

An application to transfer the case to another court after automatic transfer should be made to the receiving court (the defendant's home court), as that is the court which has all the papers.

Money claims on line

Claims issued on line start their life in Northampton. If defended, the final hearing will be in the claimants home court or if the defendant is an individual the defendants home court. (The rules about this are set out in the practice direction to Part 7 which deals with money claims on line.)

Transfer by court order

The District Judge has discretion to decide where a case should be managed or heard, irrespective of the automatic transfer rules. For example, a party who is disgruntled with the operation of the "automatic" transfer can apply to have the case transferred back to the court of issue or to another court. The parties may apply by agreement to have the case transferred by consent to another court, possibly one part way between the two of them.

For the preparation of the application, follow the guidelines about applications generally (see Chapter 10). The District Judge may feel able to make the order by consent or upon the application of one party without a hearing.

The matters which will be taken into account by the District Judge in deciding which court the case will be heard include:

- the financial value of the claim and the amount in dispute
- whether it would be more convenient or fair for hearings (including the trial) to be held in some other court
- the facilities available at the court where the claim is being dealt with and whether they may be inadequate because of any disabilities of a party or potential witness (rule 30.3).

In making an order to transfer a case to another court the District Judge will also have the overriding objective in mind including dealing with the case in a manner which is proportionate to the amount of money involved and the financial position of each party (rule 1.1(2)); and giving directions to ensure that the trial of the case proceeds quickly and efficiently (rule 1.4(l))

Once an order for transfer has been made, an application to set aside that order is to the same court which made the order (PD 30 para 6.1) – contrast the situation where the transfer is *automatic* (see above).

The best way to ensure that a case is heard in a suitable location is for the parties to co-operate and agree which is the best court for their particular case to be heard in. Although the District Judge is not bound by the recommendation of the parties, their views will certainly be taken fully into account.

Changing the hearing venue

County courts are organised into local "groups" and the court staff who organise hearings (listing officers) co-operate with each other and with their local District Judges to make the best use of court space and judicial time. It is therefore possible that any case may be transferred from the court of issue to another nearby court in the same "group" for the hearing. The court should warn the parties well in advance that there is to be a change of venue and the parties should feel free to ask the court for an explanation if this happens. Reasons for such a transfer may be

- to give the parties an earlier hearing date if the District Judge's lists are overloaded in the court of issue
- to make use of specific facilities needed for the case (for example video/DVD equipment)
- to provide specific facilities for disabled parties or witnesses.

What documents are needed for the case

The definition of "documents" in a Small Claims is wide and includes contract documents, letters photographs and witness statements. The directions in any particular case will set out what documents should usually be included (see the table opposite).

The formal rules about disclosure do not apply to cases allocated to the Small Claims track – no list of documents is required. (Rule 31.1(2) and rule 27.2(1)(b)).

The standard direction is that copies of documents must be sent to the other side at least 14 days before the hearing, although a different time may be specified. The parties do not have to make a list of documents, but are required to send to the opposite party copies of documents that they intend to rely upon at the hearing.

One reason frequently given for disregarding this direction is that "they have the documents anyway, so I didn't send them again". This is a perverse interpretation of the direction, which requires the documents to be sent again, even if they have been sent to the other side before the court case started.

Documents

There is no point in withholding documents and producing them for the first time at the hearing. The element of surprise will not impress the District Judge. Litigants who are 'ambushed' by the other side producing documents at the final hearing should consider asking for an adjournment (see Chapter 7).

Documents which should be excluded from the papers sent to the court are

- those which are not relevant to the dispute and

- without prejudice letters; namely letters which include offers to settle and make admission with a view to settlement (these letters should be headed "without prejudice").

There will be two bundles of documents – one prepared by each side. This may result in duplication, but that doesn't matter. The most important thing is that all the documents should have been seen by both sides before the hearing and that all the documents are available for the District Judge at the hearing.

It makes sense to keep a record of the documents sent, and this may be done by preparing a schedule. Whether or not a copy of that schedule is sent to the opposite party is purely a matter of choice. The obvious advantage of sending a schedule is that the other party can check that the copies are complete and will not be able to complain at the hearing that vital documents are missing.

Make sure that the copies are legible, and that the reverse of a document is copied especially if it includes any terms and conditions – the District Judge is bound to want to see the terms and conditions. It is helpful to put the documents in date order and to add page numbering.

The standard directions require the documents to be sent to the court before the hearing.

A direction to bring original documents to the hearing is made in all cases.

If a video or sound recording is to be used at the hearing make sure that the court knows in advance – this will ensure that equipment is available to show the video/DVD or to give the court staff a chance to transfer the case to a court with suitable equipment if necessary.

Request for additional information

It is worth noting here that the parties are not allowed to serve on each other requests for additional information – this is the Part 18 procedure and is excluded from the procedures available under the small claims track; please see chapter 10 for more detail. The District Judge should give full directions for disclosure of relevant information at the allocation stage (see Chapter 5) and if this is not sufficient then the request for further information must be dealt with informally by letter or, if this does not work, by making an application to the District Judge for an order; not by the serving of a 'Part 18' request.

Frequently asked questions about documents for a small claims	
Do I need to prepare a formal list of documents in the form required by rule 31?	No
The other side has already seen my documents before the case started – do I still need to send copies to them 14 days before the hearing?	Yes
Do the normal rules about disclosure apply to my Small Claims case?	No – list of documents is needed
What happens if I send copies to the other side in advance and at a later date I get extra papers which I want to use at the hearing?	You must send them to the other side and to the court at once – you may not be able to rely on them at the hearing otherwise.
Shall I make an extra copy of my documents for use by the District Judge at the hearing?	Yes
Should I bring the original documents to court?	Definitely!
Would it help the District Judge at the hearing if my documents were in date order and given page numbers?	Yes
Should documents marked "without prejudice" be shown to the judge and included in the bundle?	No – not until the District Judge has given the judgment

Witness statements

A witness is anyone who can help the court with the evidence, which includes the parties themselves. There are two types of witnesses, namely:

1. expert witnesses (see below)
2. non-expert or 'lay witnesses'.

This section deals with 'lay' witnesses, and includes the parties themselves. Directions about expert witnesses are considered on page 94.

The general rule is that any fact which needs to be proved by the evidence of a witness at a trial (including a Small Claims hearing) is given verbally (rule 32.2). Most litigants write down their evidence before coming to court and the common use of computers means that it is rarely a burden for a party to have to produce a typed statement in advance of the hearing.

If a witness sets out evidence in writing before the hearing and sends it to the other side this has a number of benefits including:

- all the relevant evidence is brought to the attention of the court and nothing is missed out due to courtroom nerves
- the other side is not "taken by surprise" by the witness' evidence (this also limits the chance of an adjournment)
- reducing the amount of time at the hearing.

The basic "standard" directions, which are routinely used in Small Claims cases, usually "suggest" that witness statements can be used (see table on pages 84 and 85). Only if the District Judge makes an order that witness statements "must" be served, are they obligatory. If the court has not ordered the service of witness statements, then there is nothing to prevent either party from serving a witness statement.

A well prepared witness statement will:

- be in the witness' own words
- describe events in date order, with the earliest events described first
- refer to relevant documents (if possible by the page number in the bundle)
- be set out in short numbered paragraphs
- be legible (typed if possible).

Examples of witness statements appear in Chapter 11.

Note

The person who calls the witness (whether by summons or otherwise) is responsible to pay any expenses and loss of earnings for the witness. The party who wins may recover these sums for expenses from the loser in due course, up to a limit of £50 per day for loss of earnings or loss of leave plus reasonable travel expenses

---

Witness summons

The rules about requiring a witness to attend court are set out in part 34 of the Rules.

If a witness is unwilling to attend court, or requires a witness summons to compel attendance to enable them to get time off work, then the party who wants to call them as a witness can issue a witness summons.

Before issuing the summons consider if the size of the claim and the importance of the matter to the parties merits compelling a witness to attend court – consider carefully if the use of a witness summons is proportionate to the issues in the case with reference to the amount of money involved and the importance of the matter (rule 1.1(2) (c)).

The summons is issued on a form N20 and a fee is payable. The summons must be served no less than seven days before the hearing. The permission of the District Judge is needed to issue a witness summons less than seven days before the hearing. The summons can be served by the court or by the party issuing it.

At the time of service, the witness must be offered a sum reasonably sufficient to cover their expenses for travelling to and from court and compensation for loss of their time. The rates to be offered are equivalent to those offered in the Crown Court. To establish the amount, contact the Crown Court for the details of the current rates. The person in receipt of the summons can apply for the summons to be set aside.

Experts' reports

Basics

- The District Judge has a duty to restrict expert evidence
- The expert has an overriding duty to help the court
- No party can use the written or oral services of an expert without the permission of the court
- If allowed, expert evidence in Small Claims cases is usually by written report rather than by personal attendance

---

Expert evidence shall be restricted to that which is reasonably required to resolve the proceedings (rule 35.1).

No expert may give evidence, whether written or oral, at a hearing without the permission of the court (rule 27.5).

The District Judge will only allow an expert in a Small Claims case if it is necessary. Unless express permission is given to use expert evidence, it cannot be used. If an expert is allowed, the court will want the expert to be jointly instructed by both sides if possible. The duty of the expert is to assist the court impartially and not to promote the interests of one of the parties. The District Judge will specify the specialty of the expert which can be used.

A disincentive for the use of experts is expense. Not only will the expense of an expert often be out of proportion to the amount involved, but the winner cannot recover more than £200 towards the costs of instructing an expert.

The rules recognise that in some cases an expert may be needed and will often allow an expert to be called in disputes about:

- building works
- vehicle repairs
- hardware and software faults in computers.

A **medical report** must be attached to the particulars of the case in claims involving personal injury, *but only* where the claimant relies on medical evidence (PD 16 para 4.2). However, if the injuries are minor and if the claimant does not rely on any future pain and suffering, as may well be the case in a Small Claims case, then a medical report may not be needed. In a Small Claims case the usual format of a "medical report" is an informal general practitioner's letter.

Single joint experts

The joint instruction of an expert can be tricky. Rule 35.8 sets out the ways in which the District Judge can control the instructions to a joint single expert in particular by

- directing who should pay the expert's fees
- saying when (and how) the expert can inspect the subject matter in dispute and carry out experiments.

Before a single joint expert is instructed the District Judge can direct the maximum fee for the expert to charge and make a direction that this money be paid into court in advance by the parties (rule 35.8 (4)).

The usual rule is that the parties are both liable to pay the fees of a single joint expert (rule 35.8 (5)).

What does an expert need to know about preparing a report for a Small Claims hearing?

For a Small Claims case the essential rules that apply are that

- the overriding duty of the expert is to the court and to help the court on matters within his or her expertise (rule 35.3)
- the District Judge can give directions on how to instruct a joint expert (rule 35.7) and
- the court has a power to restrict expert evidence (rule 35.4)
- the winner can recover up to £200 for the cost of an experts report.

The more technical rules about the preparation of experts' reports, which apply in fast track and multi-track cases do not apply to Small Claims cases. However, in addition to the essential rules which do apply (see above) there are commonsense and practical matters to be borne in mind when instructing an expert in a Small Claims case.

The following is a list of the points to make the most of the expert's report. Keep matters in proportion at all times, however – the report need not be unduly formal; if the points are not covered, the District Judge will take a practical approach to the matter (rule 1.1(2)).

In every case the expert should:

- know that the overriding duty of the expert is to the court (rule 35.3)
- understand that the report should not promote the views of one party but inform the court objectively. The purpose of the report is to inform and help the District Judge
- keep any technical language to a minimum
- make sure he or she fully understands exactly what points should be covered in the report
- be clear about the deadline for preparing the report and promise to meet it

- be aware that he or she is unlikely to be given permission to give personal evidence at the hearing, so the written report should be as complete as possible
- know in advance who is paying for the report (he or she can demand payment before releasing the report)
- summarise his or her experience or qualifications.

The parties are 'jointly and severally' responsible for paying the fees of the single joint expert; this means that the expert can look to either party for the full fee or for contributions from both but can only recover the full cost once. Joint experts usually require the fee to be paid by the parties equally.

The District Judge has the power to give directions as to who should pay for the report and may order that a sum of money be paid into court to cover the fees (rule 35.8(4)).

> See also –
> Costs and experts – Chapter 6
> Evidence at the final hearing
> – Chapter 7
> Rules which do not apply to experts in Small Claims cases
> – Chapter 10

Lists of disputed items

In cases involving lists of disputed items the District Judge will sometimes suggest that the parties prepare a schedule of items in dispute. The parties may in some cases actually be ordered to prepare such a schedule, and the schedule may have been explained to the parties at a preliminary hearing. These lists are very useful, and if the facts justify their use should be considered by the parties, even if not suggested or ordered by the court.

The advantages are:

- all the information is summarised in point form before the hearing
- it is convenient for the parties and the District Judge to comment on the individual points

- the lists often highlight whether any items are agreed, thus saving time at the hearing.

An example of such a schedule (sometimes called a 'Scott Schedule') can be found in Chapter 11.

Photographs and sketch plans

The standard directions in road traffic cases and those involving repairs to vehicles and buildings suggest that photographs may be included in the documents. Under the 'no costs' rule, the cost of the photographs will not be recovered from the loser; but photographs are so useful in many types of case the expense should not be spared! The photographs should be of the scene of a road traffic accident and the damage to the vehicles. In this digital age the District Judge might, quite reasonably ask a witness producing photographs to confirm at the hearing that the photographs have not been manipulated or altered on a computer.

A sketch plan of the scene of a traffic accident may also be helpful. The cost of an expert to prepare a plan is unlikely to be justified and permission must be sought before such an expert is instructed (see above under expert evidence). Every effort must be made to produce photographs and plans which relate to the layout of the road at the time of the accident. The problem with satellite images of road layouts is that they are not dated and may be some time out of date.

Inform the court if the case is settled before the hearing

This applies in all cases. Court timetables are very busy and if the hearing slot can be vacated this may release time for the District Judge to do other work.

Time estimate

The notice of allocation informs the parties what time estimate has been placed on the case by the District Judge. If either of the parties thinks that the estimate is too short they should inform the court in writing at once.

It is not easy to give an accurate time estimate for the hearing of a case, even with a properly completed allocation questionnaire to assist. The District Judge uses experience combined with guesswork and the information on the questionnaire to determine how much time must be set aside to hear the case.

However, as a guide, District Judges may give time estimates as follows

Time estimate	Type of case
$\frac{1}{2}$ to $1\frac{1}{2}$ hours	Cases which appear straightforward and where there is to be no expert evidence
1 to $1\frac{1}{2}$ hours	Road traffic accidents – although these cases can take longer if both liability and quantum are at issue
2 to $2\frac{1}{2}$ hours	Apparently complex cases, e.g. building disputes and cases involving expert evidence or a number of lay witnesses

These time estimates are a rough guide only, time estimates will depend on the nature of each case – for example cases take longer if there are more than one or two witnesses on each side, if there are more than about a dozen documents to consult and if either party needs an interpreter.

Special directions

Appendix A to PD 27 contains a battery of special directions that the District Judge can use in addition to, or instead of, the standard directions. These include

- requiring either party to clarify aspects of their case
- requiring the parties to instruct a joint expert (see above under expert evidence)
- making arrangements for a site inspection
- ordering that the item in dispute be brought to court for the hearing.

The list of directions is not limited to those in the practice direction and the District Judge will make whatever directions are sensibly needed to bring the case to a hearing.

The District Judge usually gives special directions and sets a date for the final hearing but may require that the matter is referred back in up to 28 days for further directions (rule 27.4(c)). If the District Judge needs to know more about the case before giving directions or giving a time estimate he or she may order a party to send their documents or witness statements to the court before a hearing date is set. The court may, of its own initiative, order a party to provide further in formation if it considers it appropriate to do so (rule 27.2(3)).

Preliminary hearing

The District Judge will decide whether to list the matter for a preliminary hearing, but only if

- special directions are needed and
- it is necessary for the parties to attend court to understand how to comply with the special directions or
- to dispose of the claim because one side has no real prospect of success or to strike out a hopeless claim or defence.

(Rule 27.6)

The court must "have regard to the desirability of limiting the expense to the parties of attending court" (rule 27.6(2)), and for this reason preliminary hearings are not the norm.

Preliminary hearings are not a formality. The parties must prepare for them and make sure that they are ready to deal with points arising. The parties cannot simply "write in" and say that they have agreed between themselves not to attend.

The notice of the preliminary hearing will give the reason for the hearing. If either side does not understand the reason for the preliminary hearing they should write to the court at once for clarification. The purpose of the hearing may be defeated if its purpose is obscure.

At the preliminary hearing the District Judge may strike out any claim, defence or counterclaim and may give directions as to how the case will progress. After the preliminary hearing, both sides will be given at least 21 days notice of the date for the final hearing and written confirmation of the directions, including the time allowed for the hearing (rule 27.6).

Applications for directions by the parties

In a Small Claims case there should rarely be the need to apply to the court for directions. The standard directions given at allocation or at the preliminary hearing will usually cover all the steps reasonably needed to prepare the case for a hearing. The procedural devices which are used in cases allocated to the fast track and multi-track and which often give rise to pre-hearing applications are excluded in the Small Claims track. This includes applications for further information and applications concerning disclosure and inspection.

There could be some matters of "housekeeping" which need tidying up in a Small Claims case. For example:

- to set aside or vary any order or direction made by the District Judge at the allocation stage or without a hearing
- to change the venue of the hearing
- to request permission to use expert evidence
- an application for the case to be heard in private
- an application to change a hearing date.

If any application is necessary, it should be issued as soon as possible after allocation. Chapter 10 deals with rules about applications; note that, because of the "no costs" rule, any legal fees incurred in connection with the application will not be recoverable (see Chapter 6).

Checklist for preparing for a Small Claims hearing

Step 1   Note the date and time ☐

Step 2   Evaluate and consider settlement ☐

Step 3   Prepare documents for the hearing
(at least 14 days before the hearing) ☐

Step 4   Prepare and serve witness statements
(at least 14 days before the hearing) ☐

Step 5   Prepare schedules of items in dispute
         (if needed or ordered)   ☐

Step 6   Obtain expert evidence
         (but only if permission has been given)   ☐

Step 7   Decide whether to attend the hearing (rule 27.9(1)
         (Do this at least a week before the hearing)   ☐

Step 8   Pay the hearing fee   ☐

Step 1 – Note the date and time

Practitioners must tell their own client and any witnesses of the hearing date. If the date is not convenient for the parties or any witness the other side and the court must be told at once that another date is needed. It is far better for the parties to co-operate with each other and agree in principle for the date to be changed – if the parties do not agree on an adjournment then a formal application must be made on notice for the date to be changed. If the parties agree to the date being changed then the application will be by consent.

Check the directions and note the date before the hearing when documents are to be sent to the other side (usually two weeks before the hearing).

Step 2 – Evaluation, settlement and agreement

The strengths and weaknesses of a case must be considered carefully in response to any defence or counterclaim. The evaluation must be repeated at this stage as well as when the other side have provided their documents and any witness statements.

Litigants in person can get legal advice from solicitors and citizens advice bureaux. Even if they do not get legal advice, they should discuss the case with a friend who, even though not legally qualified, may be able to give an "objective view" of the case. Members of motoring organisations and other clubs may be entitled to advice on consumer or other legal problems, free of charge or upon payment of a modest fee. Some house insurance policies and car insurance policies include legal advice as part of the package.

At all stages, both parties should actively consider settlement. Correspondence which is marked "without prejudice" and which is written with the intention of trying to reach a settlement cannot be shown to the District Judge until after judgment has been given. So, parties can safely write and offer to settle for less than the full amount claimed or offer to make a payment to settle without the fear that the letter will be shown to the District Judge as a sign of weakness.

In some types of case, the directions specifically tell the parties to agree aspects of the claim. In motor claims, the actual cost of repairs can usually be agreed, subject to blame. In cases involving repairs to buildings, including disputes with landlords about deposits, the parties should do their best to agree the cost of works, this will of course be subject to blame.

Make any final checks on the legal position, and if the law is unusual or involves cases or statutory references make copies of the texts and documents which will be used at the hearing to support the case. It is good practice, even if not required by the court, to send copies to the other side in advance of the hearing. Make an additional copy for the use of the District Judge at the hearing.

Step 3 – Prepare documents for the hearing

See the topic "Documents" on page 92

Step 4 – Prepare witness statements

See the topic "Witness statements" on page 94

Step 5 – Prepare a list of items in dispute (if needed or ordered)

> See the topic "list of disputed items" on page 99 and an example of such a list in Chapter 11.

Step 6 – Obtain expert evidence (but only if permission has been given)

> See the topic on experts on page 96

Step 7 – Decide whether to attend the hearing (rule 27.9(1))

Rule 27.9 concerns the non-attendance of parties at a final hearing and states as follows:

27.9
Non-attendance of parties at a final hearing

(1) If a party who does not attend a final hearing—
  (a) has given written notice to the court and the other party at least 7 days before the hearing date that he will not attend;
  (b) has served on the other party at least 7 days before the hearing date any other documents which he has filed with the court; and
  (c) has, in his written notice, requested the court to decide the claim in his absence and has confirmed his compliance with paragraphs (a) and (b) above, the court will take into account that party's statement of case and any other documents he has filed and served when it decides the claim.

If a party does not intend to attend the hearing he should notify the court and the other side in advance, failing which the court may disregard his evidence and strike out his case (rule 27.9(2), (3) and (4). See also the provision about awards of costs for unreasonable behaviour (page [ ]). In other words failure to attend without prior notice is likely to give rise to a bad result.

If a party wishes the court to decide the case in his absence but rely on written evidence alone he can use the procedure in rule 27.9(1) above. Note that to use this procedure a party must inform the other side and the court at least 7 days before the hearing. After the hearing the District judge will set out the reasons for the decision in writing and these will be sent to both parties by the court (PD 27 para 5.4).

Step 8 – pay the hearing fee

In 2007 a new fee was introduced to all civil cases – the hearing fee. The introduction of this fee was accompanied by a modest reduction in the fees payable upon the commencement of the claim. The hearing fee is payable upon demand which will be made within 14 days after the court notifies the parties of a hearing date. In a small claims case this is when the court sends out the allocation directions. This fee is payable on a sliding scale up to a hefty £300 for small claims cases. The claim can be struck out if this fee is not paid. As an incentive to settle, however, this fee will be refunded in full if the court receives notice in writing at least 7 days before the hearing date that the case is settled or discontinued. Small claims cases get special treatment here because cases allocated to the fast track or above only get a full refund if a case settles 28 days before the final hearing. It remains to be seen if this new structure for payment of court fees reduces the number of cases going to a final hearing.

Visiting the court before the hearing date

Small claims hearings are in public and a litigant who wants to get a flavour of what their day in court may be like may wish to visit the court beforehand and watch other cases. The courts do not deal with small claims cases every day so contact the court in advance and find out when there is a small claims list. On arrival, tell the usher that you want to watch some cases. Since people rarely ask to watch other peoples cases your request is likely to be treated as a novelty, and the usher is likely to tell the District Judge in advance that you want to sit in. When watching someone else's case bear in mind that, given the wide range of procedures adopted by different judges and for different cases, the procedure you observe may not be replicated in your own hearing. Even if you don't go in and watch a case it is worthwhile attending the actual court building in advance of your big day – just to check that you know how to get there and to plan your journey time so you arrive on time.

CHAPTER 6

The no costs rule

The no costs rule – basics 111

The no costs rule – in detail 113

Routine awards for costs 113

Unreasonable Behaviour 117

Part 36 and the No Costs Rule 118

The court's discretion on costs 119

Standard basis and indemnity basis 121

Procedure for summary assessment 121

Costs terminology 122

Frequently asked questions about costs on the
   Small claims track 124

The no costs rule

Basics

The basic principle is that in Small Claims cases legal costs are not recovered by the winner.

The rules allow for the winner to be reimbursed for

- court fees paid (starting fee/allocation fees/hearing fees)
- the fixed costs shown on the summons, if a solicitor issued the proceedings, or up to £260 if it is an injunction case
- expert fees up to £200
- expenses incurred by the party and witnesses, including the reasonable cost of staying away from home for attending the hearing
- loss of earnings for the parties and any witnesses (up to £50 per day)
- any costs awarded are assessed by the summary procedure

Any award for costs is discretionary, and the District Judge has the final say on whether costs and expenses are allowed in any particular case.

Further sums may be allowed if the District Judge comes to the conclusion that a party has behaved unreasonably.

The no costs rule extends to appeals against decisions made on the small claims track.

The no costs rule – basics

Definition of costs

The term 'costs' means fees, charges, disbursements and expenses including those paid to a solicitor, barrister or lay representative (rule 43.2(1)(a)).

The rule

Rule 27.14 sets out the costs rules in Small Claims cases.

The court may not order a party to pay a sum to another party in respect of that other party's costs, fees and expenses, including those relating to an appeal, except—

(a) the fixed costs attributable to issuing the claim which—
   i) are payable under Part 45; or
   ii) would be payable under Part 45 if that Part applied to the claim.
(b) in proceedings which included a claim for an injunction or an order for specific performance a sum not exceeding the amount specified in the relevant practice direction for legal advice and assistance relating to that claim;
(c) any court fees paid by that other party;
(d) expenses which a party or witness has reasonably incurred in travelling to and from a hearing or in staying away from home for the purposes of attending a hearing;
(e) a sum not exceeding the amount specified in the relevant practice direction for any for any loss of earnings or loss of leave by a party or witness due to attending a hearing or to staying away from home for the purpose of attending a hearing;
(f) a sum not exceeding the amount specified in the relevant practice direction for an expert's fees; and
(g) such further costs as the court may assess by the summary procedure and order to be paid by a party who has behaved unreasonably.

Rule 27.14(2)

The court may also order a party to pay all or part of –

a. *any court fees paid by another party;*
b. *expenses which a party or witness has reasonably incurred in travelling to and from a hearing or in staying away from home for the purposes of attending a hearing;*
c. *a sum not exceeding [£50*] for any loss of earnings by a party or witness due to attending a hearing or to staying away from home for the purpose of attending a hearing; and*
d. *a sum not exceeding [£200*] for an expert's fees*

Rule 27.14(3)

[*the figures in square brackets are specified by PD 27 para 7 – see page 114]

Electing to use the Small Claims track by agreement

Where –

a. *the financial value of a claim exceeds the limit for the Small Claims track; but*
b. *the claim has been allocated to the Small Claims track in accordance with rule 26.7(3),*

the claim shall be treated, for the purposes of costs, as if it were proceeding on the fast track except that trial costs shall be in the discretion of the court and shall not exceed the amount set out for the value of the claim in rule 46.2 (amount of fast track trial costs).

Rule 27.14(4)

Where the parties elect to use the small claims track for claims of greater financial value than the usual qualifying limit the no costs rule applies unless the parties specifically agree otherwise.

Quantifying the costs

If any costs in Small Claims cases are awarded for 'unreasonable conduct' they will be assessed at the hearing by the summary procedure (rule 27.14(2)(d)). See page 121 for more about the summary procedure. Detailed assessment is not available.

Overall discretion

Subject to the general limitations on costs in a Small Claims case, District Judges have overall discretion on costs (rule 44.3) (see page 119 for more detail on the topic of discretion).

Offers of settlement

Parties are encouraged to try and settle their cases out of court and without a hearing and should therefore make offers to settle. If this is not done or if good offers to settle out of court are rejected this can amount to unreasonable conduct – see page 118 et seq.

The no costs rule – in detail

Routine awards for costs

Court fees

A winner will, almost as a matter of routine, recover the any court fee paid plus the fee paid on allocation (Rule 27.14(3)) (see Appendix 1 and 2 for details of court fees).

Sometimes, if the claimant recovers less than the amount claimed in the claim form, the District Judge will "abate" the fee awarded. An example of abatement is that if a claimant claimed £1750 and paid court fees of £120 but was only awarded £450 the claimant may, at the discretion of the District Judge, be awarded only £50 towards the court fees paid.

Fixed commencement costs

The claimant may recover

(a) the fixed costs attributable to issuing the claim which –
  (i) are payable under Part 45; or
  (ii) would be payable under Part 45 if that Part applied to the claim.

(Rule 27.14 (2))

Fixed costs are only relevant where a solicitor has issued the proceedings; they are not recoverable by a litigant in person (rule 45.1(1)).

Where the claim is for a specified sum, the costs are inserted in the claim form in accordance with the scale set out by the rules (see page 39). The scale of costs is set out in Appendix 1.

Where the claim is not specified, the District Judge will fix the issue costs at the hearing after the claim has been determined; the amount being based on the scale set out in Appendix 1.

The rules do not provide for the reimbursement of any fixed costs on a counterclaim.

Expert fees

The parties must have permission from the District Judge to use an expert at the hearing and will be encouraged to appoint a single joint expert.

The District Judge may award the winner up to £200 towards the cost of employing each expert (rule 27.14 (2)(d) and PD 27 para. 7.3(2)). In practical terms this allowance is less than the expert's fees are likely to be, leaving the person who paid the fees liable to pay the balance out of his or her own pocket.

Witness expenses

The expense of attending court for the parties and any witnesses can be reimbursed under two headings:

Loss of earnings (limited to £50 per witness per day)

The District Judge may award the winner and the winner's witnesses up to £50 per person for loss of earnings, plus the reasonable cost of staying away from home for the purpose of the hearing (rule 27.14(3)(c) and

PD 27 para 7.3(1)). The cost of staying away from home could also include, for example, the cost of a babysitter.

This means that a person who has to pay someone to cover for them at work on the day of the hearing can recover that expense up to the stated maximum. A person who takes leave from work to attend court can recover the lost monetary value of that leave.

The loss must be real and not illusory and is easiest to recover in the case of employed persons working on a daily or hourly rate. Self employed persons can also recover their losses, but a distinction must be drawn between those self employed people who do lose earnings by attending court, and those who do not. For example, self employed people working on flexible hours can usually make up for the "lost" time spent in court, so their earnings have not been "lost" at all. However, if the self employed person can demonstrate that he or she lost the chance to earn a fee for a specific job, up to £50 of those losses will be recoverable.

Travelling expenses (limited to a reasonable amount)

The District Judge may award the winner reasonable travelling expenses plus the reasonable cost of the party or a witness staying away from home for the purposes of the hearing.

The provision for payment of travelling expenses and overnight expenses, if justified, may add a hefty sum to the loser's bill – something which should have been borne in mind when considering which court a case should be heard in. If it is inevitable that one party will have to travel a considerable distance to a hearing, then the parties should consider choosing a court to hear the matter which is half way between the claimant and the defendant (see page 40).

Lay representatives

The limits on costs imposed by this rule also apply to any fee or reward for acting on behalf of a party to the proceedings charged by a person exercising a right of audience by virtue of an order under section 11 of the Courts and Legal Services Act 1990 (a lay representative).

Rule 27.14(4)

In Small Claims cases can a party engage an unqualified 'lay representative' for a fee to act as an advocate. Even if paid, these fees cannot usually be recovered from the loser and they are covered by the 'no costs rule'.

Injunction cases

In proceedings which included a claim for an injunction or for an order for specific performance or similar relief, a sum not exceeding [£260] for legal advice and assistance relating to the claim.

Rule 27.14(2)(b) and PD 27 para 7.2.

[*the figure in square brackets is specified by PD 27 para 7]

Any case involving a claim for an injunction or similar order may qualify for an award of up to £260 for solicitors costs. The award will be in the discretion of the District Judge, and will only be made in any particular case if instructing a solicitor was, in the opinion of the District Judge, justified on the facts of the particular case.

Costs of enforcement

The expense of enforcing a judgment is not protected by the 'no costs rule'.

Costs of appeal

The costs of appeal are assessed by the summary procedure are protected by the no costs rule (rule 27.14(2)(c)).

Photographs and sketch plans

In many types of case photographs and sketch plans are of great assistance at the hearing; they are routinely suggested in the allocation directions for a variety of cases including road traffic accidents, building disputes and holiday claims. The rules do not allow the costs of plans or photographs to be recovered from the loser.

However, if the District Judge gives permission *in advance* to instruct a specialist to prepare sketch plans or take photographs, the fees up to a limit of £200 would be recoverable. For example, it may be reasonable to instruct a specialist to prepare a plan in a boundary dispute, but the court is unlikely to sanction the cost of a specialist takings photographs or drawing a plan for a small claims road traffic case.

Unreasonable behaviour

The court may award

Such further costs as the courts may assess by the summary procedure and ordered to be paid by a party who has behaved unreasonably.

Rule 27.14(2)(d)

There is a two-stage process in dealing with costs based on "unreasonable behaviour".

Stage 1:   deciding whether the behaviour has been unreasonable
Stage 2:   assessing the costs.

Stage 1. What amounts to "unreasonable behaviour?"

District Judges are used to resisting applications for costs by over-enthusiastic practitioners, and are unlikely to make an award for costs unless a losing party has behaved in an exceptional way.

There is no doubt, that from time to time, awards for costs are made, but they are rarely appealed, and in such cases are not often reported. As a result of this, there is a dearth of reported cases on this topic and those cases which are reported are of limited general application because they involve specific facts from which it is difficult to extract any universal principles.

The whole ethic of the Small Claims procedure is to give each party a chance to have a say, and often litigants are not legally represented, and only discover at the hearing that the law is against them. Not knowing the law is not generally interpreted as unreasonable behaviour.

The following sets out some categories of behaviour which district judges may deem to be "unreasonable":

- pulling out of a case at the last minute when there has been no change in the circumstances
- the pursuit of a case which is both speculative and unsupportable *Afzal and Others* v *Ford Motor Co Ltd and other appeals* CA [1994] 4 All ER 720

- making unnecessary or disproportionate applications for procedural orders
- pressing a hopeless case with the ulterior motive of embarrassing or inconveniencing the opposite party
- adjournments – if these are caused by one side not turning up at the hearing without a reasonable excuse then a District Judge may in some cases consider this to be unreasonable behaviour and make an order for costs
- requesting an adjournment at the last moment because the evidence to substantiate a case has not been prepared for a hearing (*Lacey* v *Melford* CC [1999] 12 CL 37)
- Making a claim which is dishonest (*Bashir* v *Hanson* CC [1999] 12 CL 143).
- Ignoring a reasonable offer to settle before the hearing (*Closhey* v *Homes June* [2004] 6 CL 47)

In summary, whether a party has behaved in an unreasonable way is a matter of fact and degree. The behaviour must be quite serious to attract an order for costs.

Note that costs awarded under this category are not "wasted costs" – see page 122 (costs terminology).

Part 36 and the No Costs Rule

Having regard to rule 27.14(2A) the District Judge may also consider offers of settlement (otherwise known as 'Part 36 offers') made before the hearing.

What is a Part 36 offer?

A Part 36 offer is an offer made before the case goes to a final hearing which is intended to settle the claim. It is useful in cases where a defendant accepts that it has some liability to the claimant but not to the extent claimed. The facts of a Part 36 offer is kept secret from the final hearing judge until after the judge has made his or her decision; the making of a Part 36 offer therefore does not influence the judge against the party making the offer. Part 36 offers are made in writing and are made 'without prejudice.' They can be made in money cases or in cases where money is not in issue between the parties.

Part 36 and small claims cases

The basic rule is that Part 36 does not apply to Small Claims cases but the court may make an order otherwise (rule 36.2(5)). In specific cases therefore, and following an order of the District Judge, Part 36 cost consequences can apply in small claims cases.

If a party makes a Part 36 offer which is more generous to the other side than the award made by the judge at the final hearing then, under Part 36, the court may award costs in favour of the party who made the offer out of court. This is a reversal of the usual costs rule which is that usually the successful party is awarded costs.

Is rejection of a Part 36 offer unreasonable conduct?

The answer to this question is 'not automatically.' However, when considering what amounts to unreasonable behaviour, the District Judge may take into account the fact of a Part 36 offer and, if it is more generous to the winner than the awards made after a full hearing, may decide that the claimant was unreasonable to press on with the case to a final hearing. Professional advocates should beware of using 'Part 36' offers to unduly pressurise a litigant in person to settle out of court. If the litigant feels correspondence has been unfair he can bring this to the attention of the District Judge and to the attention of the relevant disciplinary body of the professional concerned.

Stage 2. Assessing the costs for unreasonable behaviour

The amount of the costs will be determined at the hearing and the District Judge will have in mind the discretionary factors set out below. The costs are assessed at the hearing (see page 121 – Procedure for summary assessment).

The court's discretion on costs

The rules set out guidelines for judges to exercise their discretion on costs.

Rule 44 defines the Judges discretion on costs. The District Judge will decide

- **whether** costs should be awarded at all
- the **amount** of the costs and
- **when** they are to be paid.

Rule 44.3 emphasises that the "conduct" of the parties will be taken into account. In a Small Claims cases the "whether" will often involve deciding if one of the parties has behaved unreasonably – this is discussed in more detail below.

When quantifying costs, the District Judge will take into account the factors set out in rule 44.5. This involves looking at whether costs are "proportionate" to the claim and whether the costs are reasonable in amount and have been reasonably incurred.

The concept of proportionality is not a mathematical relationship between the amount of money in dispute and the costs awarded. The court looks at all the circumstances including

- the conduct of the parties
- the amount of money involved
- the importance of the matter to the parties
- any special skill or expertise involved in the case
- time spent in the case
- where the work was done.*

* The rates which are normally awarded to a solicitor for work done vary from area to area and are higher, for example, in London and large cities than in other parts of the country

In a Small Claims case this could mean that the costs awarded (if they are awarded at all) could exceed the amount involved in the dispute. The District Judge will, however, be loath to make an excessive award for costs in a Small Claims case as this could offend the overriding objective, which emphasises that the court must deal with a case that is proportionate

- to the amount of money involved
- to the importance of the case
- to the complexity of the issues and
- to the financial position of each party (rule 1.2).

(see Chapter 10 – the overriding objective).

Standard basis and indemnity basis

Where the District Judge is to assess the amount of costs this will be done on either the 'standard' basis or on the 'indemnity' basis. In either case the costs must be reasonable and proportionate. A discussion as to the difference between standard and indemnity basis of costs is outside the scope of this book – the indemnity basis is more generous to the winner and usually applies when the District Judge wants to impose a penalty on the loser or defaulting party.

Procedure for summary assessment

Summary assessment means that the District Judge will put a value on the costs award at the hearing. This will involve considering the amount claimed and giving the paying party a chance to comment if he or she thinks the claim is excessive. The Small Claims rules do not give the District Judge the option of referring the costs for detailed assessment at a later hearing.

The party who is awarded costs must be prepared to explain the costs incurred and justify these by reference to the hourly rate including the seniority of the fee earner and the time spent. A party who has sought legal advice but is not represented at the hearing should bring the solicitor's bill to court; the solicitor should be asked to set out in the bill the hourly rate applied and the time spent. The District Judge will also consider the costs claimed relative to the amount in dispute and decide if the costs are 'proportionate.' However there is no direct correlation between the amount of the award and the costs recovered and if the work done was necessary and reasonable the costs award may exceed the claim.

The best way to prepare a claim for costs is to prepare a schedule of costs along the lines of that set out at page 123 below. In considering the rate claimed for solicitors' costs the hourly rate for solicitors vary with geographical area. A litigant in person's costs are assessed at the rate of £9.25 per hour. Companies that act without a solicitor and barristers and solicitors who conduct their own cases are treated as litigants in person. (Rule 48.6(6)).

Solicitors acting against unrepresented parties may want to warn the other side of the costs that are building up but of course make it clear that these costs can only be awarded of the District Judge makes a finding of unreasonable conduct. It is best to serve any schedule of costs before the hearing but failure to do so in a small claims case should not be fatal to recovering costs for unreasonable conduct; although the rules require service of a costs schedule in advance the Distrct Judge has the discretion to consider a costs schedule produced at the hearing or even to assess costs where there is no schedule.

Costs terminology

The terms used in court orders to do with costs have specific meanings – those most commonly encountered in Small Claims cases are:

No order for costs means that the question of costs has been determined and neither party will be liable to pay the other side's costs.

Where the order says nothing about costs this is the same as "no order for costs" (rule 44.13 (1)).

Costs reserved means that the costs of that hearing will be dealt with at a later date (often the next hearing date) – but if no later order is made, the costs will be the costs in the case.

Costs in the case means that the party in whose favour the court makes an order for costs at the end of the case will have to pay the costs of the application in question (this is generally a meaningless order in a Small Claims case because there is usually no costs awarded at the end of the case).

Wasted costs refers to a special case for costs where the court considers whether to make an order for costs against a party's lawyer who has behaved in an improper, unreasonable or negligent manner and usually applies where a party is publicly funded (CPR 48.7) it is incorrect to refer to the costs orders made in small claims cases as 'wasted costs' orders.

Schedule of Costs for Summary Assessment

This is a summary of the costs which the claimant/defendant will ask the District Judge to award in this case in the event of an award being made in his favour because of the unreasonable conduct of the defendant/claimant

NAME OF COUNTY COURT   CASE NUMBER

claimant's name

defendant's name

this is the claimants* statement of cost for the hearing on   [give date]

fee earner's name   grade   rate claimed

*Time spent with the claimant**
[   ] hours at £   per hour   £

*Time spent dealing with the defendant**
[   ] hours at £   per hour   £

Time spent dealing with others
[   ] hours at £   per hour   £

Time spent working on documents
[   ] hours at £   per hour   £

Time spent at hearings
[   ] hours at £   per hour   £

Counsel's fees (give name and year of call)

Other expenses – court fees   £   £
Other expenses (describe)   £   £

          Total   £

          Add VAT   £

          GRAND TOTAL   £

TO BE SIGNED BY THE SOLICITOR (if acting) OR BY THE LITIGANT IN PERSON

The costs extimated above do not exceed the costs which the claimant is liable to pay in respect of the work which this estimate covers.

Signed...   Name of solicitor..

*This sample has been prepared for a claimant – the parties' names should be changed round if for a defendant

Frequently asked questions about costs on the Small Claims track

1. What happens if a case is allocated to the fast track or the multi-track and is later reallocated to the small claims track?	Any award for costs already made is not affected (see question 4 below). The judge who is making the decision to reallocate **must** decide whether to make an award of costs and, if so, assess those costs by the summary procedure. If this is not done then costs incurred before the change of track will be subject to the rules of the small claims track (PD 44 section 15) unless the situation set out in question 4 applies.
2. What happens if there is a hearing on a case which qualifies for the Small Claims track before allocation? (for example the hearing of an application for summary judgment).	The District Judge is not restricted by the no costs rule when deciding how to deal with the costs (rule 44.9 and PD 44 para 5.1(1)) but will be conscious of the discretion guidelines (see page 117).
3. What happens if there is an initial hearing on a case after allocation to the Small Claims track? (For example the preliminary appointment hearing of an application for summary judgment).	The no costs rule will apply.
4. What happens if the claim is issued for more than the qualifying limit for the small claims track and is then reduced to within the scope of the small claims track because of the defendant's admission?	The usual rule is that fast track costs will apply for the period before the admission (44 PD 9 15(2) and (3)(i) and (ii)).
5. What about orders for costs made before allocation to the Small Claims track?	The orders are not affected (rule 44.11 and PD44 para 5.1(2)).
6. When do the costs have to be paid?	Although the District Judge can specify when costs are to be paid, if no period is mentioned, the costs are payable within 14 days (rule 44.8).
7. The claim is worth over £5,000 but both parties want to use the Small Claims track – will the "no costs" rule apply?	Yes – unless the parties agree otherwise (see page 80).
8. What about the costs before the allocation to the small claims track?	Except in the circumstances set out in questions 1 and 4 above, the costs of the case from the beginning will be those covered by the small claims rules about costs.

9. Does the no costs rule apply to appeals against decisions on the Small Claims track?	Yes

CHAPTER 7

The hearing

Overview	128
Rights of audience (advocacy)	129
Hearings are in public	131
It is never too late to settle	132
Recording the hearing – tapes and notes	133
Layout of the court and court room etiquette	134
People at the hearing	135
Procedure at Small Claims hearings	138
The organisation of the hearing	139
Evidence and the Small Claims hearing (including the burden of proof)	143
Advocacy skills and the Small Claims hearing	147
Giving judgment	152
Small Claims hearing – frequently asked questions	154

The hearing

Basics

The key elements of the Small Claims hearing are:

- informality
- the strict rules of evidence do not apply
- the District Judge will ensure that the parties are on an equal footing

---

Overview

There is a great deal of flexibility and unpredictability in Small Claims hearings, but the overall objectives are clear: the District Judge will aim to get to the heart of the matter and then to reach a fair decision with the minimum fuss.

Dealing with cases justly

The Small Claims hearing will be conducted with the overriding objective in mind. The amount of money involved, plus the importance of the case and the complexity of the issues will govern a "proportionate" approach to the case (rule 1.1 (2)).

As well as ensuring that the case is dealt with fairly, the District Judge at the hearing will ensure that the parties are on an equal footing (rule 1.1(2)(a)) and will have an eye on saving expense (rule 1.1(2) (b)).

As well as the specific provisions in rule 27 which govern the conduct of a Small Claims hearing, the District Judge will further the overriding objective by the management of the case at the hearing. This is done by:

- encouraging the parties to co-operate with each other and helping them to settle
- identifying the issues at an early stage
- deciding the order in which issues are to be resolved
- ensuring that the trial (final hearing) proceeds quickly and efficiently (rule 1.4).

> See Chapter 10 for more about the overriding objective

Rights of audience (advocacy)

Basics

- Qualified lawyers have full rights of representation in Small Claims hearings
- Parties can be represented by lay representatives at Small Claims hearings
- A company can be represented by any of its employees or officers
- Individuals can represent themselves

A party can present his or her own case at a hearing, or a lawyer or lay representative may present it on their behalf (PD 27 para 3.2(1)). The party must be present with a lay representative but a qualified solicitor or barrister can conduct the case in the absence of the party.

Lawyers

In fast track and multi-track cases advocacy rights can only be exercised by those professionally qualified and permitted to do so. Such advocates have not only studied law and procedure for some years, of course, but are governed by the codes and rules of their professional bodies. See the glossary (Page ix) under the definitions of Barrister, Legal Executive, Advocate, and Solicitor.

The District Judge will not prevent one party using a professional advocate if the other is acting in person. There is a fundamental right of citizens to be represented by counsel or solicitors of their own choice. Rule 1.1, which includes the provision that the parties should be on an equal footing, is not interpreted to reduce or remove that right. Furthermore the unrepresented litigant faced with a big firm of lawyers representing the other side may need concessions to make sure he is not at a disadvantage, for example extra time to provide copy documents: *Dulce Maltez* v *Damien Lewis and Anr* ChD *Times* May 4 1999.

Lay representatives

A lay representative is not the same as the so-called 'McKenzie friend' who is merely assists the litigant in person in court whilst the party presents the case themselves (see page 137 – Friends and observers).

The function of a lay representative is to give individuals confidence to pursue or defend their cases in court. A lay representative does not need to be particularly skilled, and standards of competence vary. Anyone can be a lay representative.

A lay representative may not exercise any right of audience where the client does not attend the hearing *unless* the court gives permission (see PD 27 para (3)).

Although a lay representative can speak in court this right does not extend to conducting the litigation generally; the claim, the defence and all correspondence with the court, must be signed by the litigant in person personally. The right of audience of a lay representative does not extend to any steps after judgment or to any appeal (PD 27 para 3.2(2)).

Companies

A company can be represented in court by any of its officers or employees (PD 27 rule 3.2(4)).

Hearings are in public

Basics

- Small Claims hearings are normally open to the public
- the parties can agree to a private hearing
- in some cases the court can direct a private hearing
- hearings which take place other than at the court are not in public

---

The general rule for all civil cases is that the trial is to be in public, and there is no exception for Small Claims cases (rule 39.2 and PD 27 para 4.1(1)). This is consistent with Article 6 of the European Convention on Human Rights (ECHR).

Anyone contemplating a Small Claims case should not be deterred from pursuing or defending the claim by the fact that the case will be heard "in public". It is rare for any outside observers to turn up to hear a Small Claims case, which almost always involve no more than the parties, the District Judge and perhaps an observer or two invited by the parties themselves. Journalists rarely, if ever, turn up to listen to Small Claims cases.

Rule 39.2 and the accompanying practice direction set out the circumstances under which a hearing can be in private. For example, a hearing may be in private if publicity would defeat the object of a hearing or if a private hearing is necessary to protect the interests of a child. The court can order the hearing to be in private if it is necessary in the interests of justice – but it is difficult to envisage when such circumstances would arise in a Small Claims case.

Even if the hearing is in private, the decision is not. The judgment itself can, with the permission of the District Judge, be available to the public (PD 39 para 1.12).

The fact that the hearing is open to the public does not impose on the court a duty to make special arrangements for accommodating members of the public (rule 39.2 (2)). This probably does not mean that lack of suitable accommodation is a reason for the hearing not being in public. If the public turn up in numbers, and the case is listed for hearing in a small room, then a decision on how to deal with such a situation would obviously be taken carefully by the District Judge having due regard to all relevant provisions of the rules and ECHR. One option would be, for example, to adjourn the case to another day in a larger court room (PD 39 para 1.10).

The District Judge may decide to hold the hearing in private if both parties agree (PD 27 para 4.1(2)).

If the hearing, or part of a hearing, takes place other than at the court, for example at the home or business address of a party, that part of the hearing will not be in public (PD 27 para 4.1(3)). Failure to attend without prior notice is likely to produce an adverse result, and this is definitely not recommended.

It is never too late to settle

Parties attending a final hearing should bear in mind that a negotiated settlement may bring them more satisfaction than the result of a contested hearing. Chapter 9 sets out what could be described as the personal benefit of reaching an agreement in any case – especially in cases where the opposing sides have to work or live in proximity with each other in the future. Parties attending a final hearing should not be surprised if the District Judge invites them to make 'one last attempt' to settle. Bear in mind that if the settlement is reached at the door of the court the District Judge can be asked to set out the terms of settlement in a court order which is then fully enforceable by the court if the terms are not adhered to.

Recording the hearing – tapes and notes

- *The judge may direct that all or any part of the proceedings will be tape recorded by the court. A party may obtain a transcript of such a recording in payment of the proper transcriber's charges.*
- *Attention is drawn to section 9 of the Contempt of Court Act 1981 (which deals with unauthorised use of tape recorders in court) and to the practice direction [1981] 1 WLR 1526 which relates to it.*
- *The judge will make a note of the central points of the oral evidence unless it is tape recorded by the court.*
- *A party is entitled to a copy of any note made by the judge (of the central points of evidence).*
- *Nothing in this practice direction affects the duty of a judge at the request of a party to make a note of the matters referred to in section 80 of the County Courts Act 1984.*

PD 27 para 5.1 to 5.8

All rooms used by District Judges for Small Claims hearings are equipped with sound recording equipment.

The District Judge does not have to write anything down or take notes if the proceedings are recorded, but will probably do so.

The parties must pay for the cost of any transcript. The fee is paid to the court reporter who prepares the note and not to the court. The rate charged is a commercial one, based on the number of words, so the cost is variable. As a guide, a transcript of a judgment of about an hour would be about £150 plus VAT. Note, however, that if a transcript is needed to support an appeal and the appellant is unrepresented and in poor financial circumstances the cost of the transcript may, with the written permission of the judge, be provided at public expense (PD 52 para 5.17).

Professional advocates are under a duty to take notes at the hearing. It is practical and sensible for litigants conducting their own cases to bring pen and paper to the hearing to make notes. The parties cannot, except with the permission of the court, make personal sound recordings of the case – to do so would be a contempt of court.

Layout of the court and court room etiquette

There is no standard size, shape or layout for the room in which the hearing will be held. If the hearing takes place at court it will usually be held in the judge's room (formerly called "chambers") but it may take place in a court room. If the hearing takes place in the judge's room and the door is shut, this does not make the hearing "private"; the hearing is a public hearing.

The District Judge can direct that the hearing can take place outside the court, for example at the home or business premises of a party, in which case the hearing will not be in public.

If the judge's room is used the parties may sit round a table, but some District Judge's rooms are set up in a formal way. Sometimes a District Judge may use a large court room for a small claims hearing.

In formal trials, it is conventional for the claimant to sit to the left (facing the judge) with the defendant to the right. This formality should be adopted unless the District Judge or usher indicates otherwise. Sometimes the question "Where do I sit?" is answered by labels or signs, or the usher or District Judge may say where everyone should sit.

It is usual for the lawyer or representative to sit closest to the District Judge with the client or witnesses behind or to the side. Witnesses and observers should sit at the back.

Advocates and witnesses therefore do not need to stand up when addressing the District Judge. The District Judge and the advocates will not wear wigs or robes.

It is essential that all mobile phones and portable email devices are switched off in court and must not be used.

Individuals who wish to use a laptop to take notes should ask the permission of the District Judge conducting the hearing.

Addressing the Court and the District Judge

A woman District Judge should be addressed as "madam", a man as "sir". There is no need to stand when addressing the District Judge unless the District Judge directs otherwise. When addressing the District Judge it is important that everyone in the room, especially the other side, should be able to hear what is said. Court room microphones are for recording purposes and usually do not amplify sound.

Documents

The District Judge will have the court file, which includes:

- the claim and defence plus any court orders (including directions) and correspondence on the court file
- the allocation questionnaires
- any documents, notes or statements (including experts' reports) lodged at court before the hearing by the parties.

Most District Judges will review the court file before the hearing and, if the file is complete, will be able to start the case with an overall understanding of what the case is about.

Wise practitioners may wish to take a spare copy of the court bundle for use in court by the District Judge – it is not unknown for bundles sent to the court not to be on the judge's desk at the start of a hearing.

Introduction of new documents at the final hearing

Proper preparation for the final hearing will have involved each side sending copies of documents to the other in advance (see chapter 5). Note, however, there is no 'default' rule that if the other side has not complied with the order to send documents before the hearing that the other side automatically wins. The claimant still has to prove the case and the District Judge has discretion to allow the introduction of documents at a late stage. Where a party is ambushed by new documents at the final hearing the District Judge will have to decide whether to press on with the hearing or whether to adjourn the case to another date. An alternative course is for the hearing to proceed without the additional documents.

This is an area of considerable difficulty for both professional advocates and litigants in person. A decision will have to be taken under pressure, and allowing a few moments for reflection will assist the party on the receiving end of the new papers to take a sensible decision. It is good practice for the party who is seeing new documents for the first time to have permission to leave the hearing room to consider the documents in private before deciding what to ask the judge to do. A balance has to be struck between the understandable desire to get on with a case and the inconvenience of adjourning the case to another date. Sometimes the documents are not really 'new' in the sense that their contents will be expected. If however the documents do come as a true surprise and the party seeing them for the first time needs time to reconsider their case or prepare fresh evidence themselves the interests of justice may well require the case be adjourned, or for the case to proceed without them. If an adjournment is requested and refused and that refusal is unfair this would be grounds for appeal. If the documents are truly new and come as a real blow to one party's case then it could be considered unreasonable conduct for them to be produced at such a late stage – in such a case the costs consequences should be considered – see chapter 6.

Interpreters in various languages and hearings in Welsh

Litigants who have difficulty with the English language can usually be assisted at a small claims hearing by friends or family members. In cases where a litigant is unrepresented and cannot understand the language of the court well enough to take part in the hearing and cannot afford to pay for an interpreter the court service will provide one without charge. Enquiries should be made with the court manager well in advance of the hearing so arrangements can be made.

The court service in Wales has adopted the principle that the English and Welsh languages must be treated equally. All court hearings, including small claims hearings may be conducted in Welsh, if this is the choice of the parties. Certain District Judges are able to conduct the hearings in Welsh. Arrangements for co-ordinating the Welsh speaking parties with a suitable District Judge are made by the county court and the parties should have notified the court no later than at the allocation stage that a hearing in Welsh is required.

Witnesses

There are two types of witness namely

- **witnesses as to fact,** who tell the story as it happened but do not give any opinion of a technical nature
- **experts,** who have a special qualification and give a considered opinion on technical aspects of the case. In a Small Claims case experts can only appear to give live evidence with the prior

permission of the District Judge; this may be sought at the allocation stage or at a preliminary hearing (see Chapter 5 and page 74).

All witnesses need to know what the case is about and the procedure to be followed and therefore some judges will invite witnesses in to hear the preliminaries (see below). Witnesses as to fact will sometimes sit in the hearing room and wait until their evidence is needed. In some cases, however, especially where the truthfulness of the parties is in issue, the witnesses may be asked to leave after the preliminaries have been completed and wait outside until they are called. The parties should not hesitate to discuss with the District Judge whether the witnesses should wait outside the room, or not.

Friends and observers

People who are not involved with the case, including reporters, can listen to the hearing because the hearing is in public (see above under the heading "Hearings are in public").

Apart from an advocate or lay representative, a litigant in person may invite a friend into the hearing to "quietly make suggestions, take notes and give advice". This is the so-called "McKenzie friend" (*R v Leicester City Justices ex parte Barrow and another* CA [1991] 3 All ER 935). The McKenzie friend does not address the court.

Parties with special needs or concerns about their personal safety

Parties should contact the court in advance to find out about any special facilities. Courts have special facilities, for example "hearing loops" and special parking spaces for those with disabled badges. Most courts have security staff on duty but parties must tell the court in advance if they are concerned for their personal safety so that suitable arrangements can be made. The courts do not have child-minding facilities and children will not usually be allowed in the hearing room. Some courts have childrens rooms where children and a carer can wait during or before a hearing.

Procedure at Small Claims hearings

(1) The court may adopt any method of proceeding at a hearing that it considers to be fair
(2) Hearings will be informal
(3) The strict rules of evidence do not apply
(4) The court need not take evidence on oath
(5) The court may limit cross-examination
(6) The court must give reasons for its decision.

(Rule 27.8)

A fair hearing method

Rule 27.8 allows the court to adopt any method of proceeding that it considers to be fair and to limit cross-examination.

The judge may in particular:

(1) ask questions of any witnesses himself before allowing any other person to do so
(2) ask questions of all or any of the witnesses himself before allowing any other person to ask questions of any witnesses
(3) refuse to allow cross-examination of any witness until all of the witnesses have given evidence in chief
(4) limit cross examination of a witness to a fixed time or to a particular subject or issue, or both.

(PD 27 para 4.3)

Rule 27.8 and the accompanying practice direction are the key to the flexibility of a Small Claims hearing and allows District Judges to be adaptable in approach. They will decide on the day how the hearing of each case is to be organised, asking the questions, helping the parties and generally adopting a much more interventionist role than at a normal trial.

At the start of the hearing (preliminaries)

When everyone has settled down, and before the start of the case itself, it is usual for the District Judge to:

- check who everyone is and deal with introductions
- explain the procedure to be followed including the order in which everyone will speak
- decide whether the witnesses should listen to the whole hearing or wait until their evidence is to be heard
- summarise what he or she understands to be the apparent issues in the case. If the issues are clear at the outset, the District Judge will explain the relevant law.

All this can take quite a while, and the influx of information from the District Judge may be overwhelming. Questions should be asked to clarify anything said by the District Judge, but if a point is not clear then questions can be asked later. Throughout the hearing the District Judge should ensure that everyone knows what is going on.

At this point in the proceedings the minimum information which the parties should know is:

- who everyone in the room is and why they are there
- in what order everyone is going to speak
- whether the District Judge has a view on what the issues are *and* what that view is.

The organisation of the hearing

Before looking at the possible method of proceeding at any particular Small Claims hearing, it will be useful to look at the sequence that is usually followed in civil trials.

Usual sequence in civil trials

When the claimant and defendant are both going to call evidence, the procedure is as follows.

Step 1   Claimant opens

Step 2   Claimant's witnesses (each witness is cross examined by the defendant's advocate in turn immediately after giving evidence)
Step 3   Defendant opens
Step 4   Defendant's witnesses (each witness is cross examined in turn by the Claimant's advocate immediately after giving evidence)
Step 5   Defendant closes
Step 6   Claimant closes
Step 7   Decision
Step 8   Winner applies for costs
Step 9   Loser may apply for permission to appeal.

The advocates will decide in what order their clients' witnesses are to be called, and nearly all the questions will be asked by the advocates with only minimum interruption from the Judge.

Order of hearing for Small Claims cases

The District Judge may adopt the usual sequence of a civil trial and may have this method in mind as the standard to be applied.

However, different methods may be adopted – entirely at the discretion of the District Judge – in accordance with his or her personal preferences and the circumstances of the particular case. Some District Judges habitually adopt an unstructured approach and will not follow a set routine. The District Judge may interject and make comments, and may take over the questioning at any stage.

Here are some possible methods that may be used.

Method 1

This method is suitable in cases where the District Judge can roughly identify the issues at the start of the case. This method is very similar to that for a traditional trial.

Step 1   The claimant is not asked to "open the case". District Judge summarises issues at the outset and asks the claimant and defendant to comment on whether or not the summary is correct and explains any relevant aspects of the law
Step 2   Claimant's evidence (including any witnesses)
Step 3   Defendant cross-questions claimant's witnesses
Step 4   Defendant's evidence (including any witnesses)

Step 5   Claimant cross-questions defendant's witnesses
Step 6   Defendant says how the District Judge should decide the case
          and why
Step 7   Claimant says how the District Judge should decide the case
          and why
Step 8   District Judge gives decision
Step 9   (If appropriate) Winner asks for costs on grounds of
          "unreasonable behaviour". Loser may ask for permission
          to appeal.
Step 10   (If appropriate) Loser may ask for permission to appeal.

Method 2

This second method differs from the sequence at a traditional trial
mainly because all the cross questioning is dealt with at the end of all
the examination in chief. This considerably lessens the burden of cross
examination and cuts out duplicated questions.

Step 1   District Judge summarises issues at the outset and asks the
          claimant and defendant to comment on whether or not the
          summary is correct and explains law
Step 2   Claimant's evidence (including any witnesses)
Step 3   Defendant's evidence (including any witnesses)
Step 4   Defendant cross-questions claimant's witnesses
Step 5   Claimant cross-questions defendant's witnesses
Step 6   Defendant says how the District Judge should decide the case
          and why
Step 7   Claimant says how the District Judge should decide the case
          and why
Step 8   District Judge gives decision
Step 9   (If appropriate) Winner applies for costs on grounds of
          "unreasonable behaviour".
Step 10   (If appropriate) Loser may ask for permission to appeal.

Method 3

This third method is applicable in cases where most of the evidence is
in writing and the District Judge has had an opportunity of reading the
papers in detail before the hearing.

Step 1   District Judge explains what has been deduced from reading
          the papers and explains any relevant questions of law

Step 2   Claimant gives any additional evidence verbally
Step 3   Defendant gives any additional evidence verbally
Step 4   Claimant and defendant each given opportunity to cross-question the other party and any witnesses
Step 5   Each party addresses the District Judge in turn on how the case should be decided and why
Step 6   District Judge gives decision
Step 7   If appropriate winner may ask for costs and loser may apply for permission to appeal.

Informality

The concept of "informality" is relative to the conduct of fast track and multi-track trials, and thus has very little meaning to litigants who are not accustomed to the conduct of civil cases. The usual television court room drama depicts a criminal trial so is an unhelpful reference point.

A litigant who has been told the hearing is "informal" may well be shocked by how "formal" it actually is. Although some Small Claims hearings may be quite relaxed, they are often quite serious affairs and will feel quite "formal" to most people – perhaps as formal as a job interview!

The District Judge will determine for each individual case how "informal" any particular hearing will be, bearing in mind factors including whether the parties are legally represented and the layout of the hearing room being used.

Contempt of court

The informality of the proceedings should not lull any party or their representatives into forgetting where they are. They are still in court, and insulting or threatening a witness, or the District Judge, either in the hearing room or close by, will amount to contempt. The use of recording equipment in court, including devices which are part of computers and mobile phones, except with the permission of the District Judge will be a contempt.

Members of the public who attend the hearing may be held in contempt if they disrupt the proceedings. The punishment may be a spell in prison (section 118 of the County Courts Act 1984). Professional advocates will be bound by the standards of their professional bodies.

Choosing not to attend the hearing

A party may choose not to attend a hearing and to tell the court seven days in advance that they do not intend to appear. In this case the District Judge will take their written evidence and any documents into account before taking a decision (rule 27.9(1)) (see page 106).

If the party has *not* given notice under rule 27.9(1) then the District Judge can disregard their evidence and documents and decide the case on the basis of the party who turns up at the hearing (rule 27.9(2) and (3)).

If neither party turns up the District Judge can strike out the claim, any counterclaim, or both (rule 27.9(4)).

Evidence and the Small Claims hearing (including the burden of proof)

Basics

- Be practical about evidence – the more important it is, the better it must be
- Witness statements will be useful, but are not always obligatory
- The court must give permission if expert evidence is to be called
- The case must be proved "on balance"

The burden of proof

The burden of proof in a civil case is that the case must be proved "on the balance of probabilities" or whether one explanation of events is more likely than another.

The civil burden of proof will be applied in a Small Claims case and must be discharged. When making the final decision the District Judge will first look at all the evidence and then weigh it in the balance. The District Judge will consider how probable it is that matters occurred as alleged. If, and only if, the District Judge considers the claimant's version to be more probable than not, will the claimant win.

It is said that "he who asserts must prove", it is for the claimant to prove the claim and the defendant the counterclaim, on balance.

Rules of evidence

The strict rules of evidence do not apply (rule 27.8(3))

This part of rule 27, possibly above any other, makes the professional advocate apprehensive of a Small Claims hearing. What exactly are the formal rules that do not apply? What rules do apply?

What follows is a practical summary of how evidence is treated in Small Claims cases.

The usual rules of evidence

In order to understand how evidence is treated at Small Claims hearings it is necessary to note the "strict rules" that usually apply at a civil court hearing.

Documents – the originals must be in court, and unless a document is agreed as being authentic by the other side the person who produced the document will have to appear in court to "prove" it.

Witness evidence is given in person and the witness must attend court to be cross examined.

Expert evidence can only be given with the permission of the court by properly qualified experts; also, only experts and not witnesses as to fact can express technical opinions.

Circumstantial evidence and "similar fact" evidence are not allowed.

The starting point at a Small Claims hearing is that none of these rules applies (rule 27.8(3)); a case will not necessarily fail because these strict rules are not followed.

Documents

Copies of all the documents to be used at the hearing should have been sent to the other side two weeks beforehand, or at such other time as directed by the court. The usual directions remind the parties that the originals should be in court. The "maker" of the document will only be needed to prove that the document itself is authentic if the case is about the authenticity of that particular document. It makes sense to bring the originals to court.

Witness evidence

Witness means any person giving evidence about the case including the parties themselves. Witnesses will give verbal evidence, but probably not on oath (rule 27.8(4)). If the standard directions have been given, then a written summary of the witnesses' evidence in the form of a witness summons will have been sent to or exchanged with the opposite party before the hearing in many cases. The advantages of preparing a good witness statement are clear:–

- The other side will have full notice of the evidence they expect to face; this minimises the risk of an adjournment.
- The witness may be allowed to read out their written statement (helpful for nervous witnesses).
- The District Judge may allow witness statements to "stand", even without being read out (even more helpful for nervous witnesses!)
- In any case where the parties have difficulty with English, then it will certainly help matters and speed up the hearing if written statements can be prepared and translated before the hearing.

One of the parties may have notified the court in advance that they do not intend to attend the hearing under rule 27.9(1). The District Judge will take that person's written evidence and submissions into account.

The weight given to the written evidence will depend on the factors set out below.

Often a witness will not be able to attend a Small Claims case to give evidence in person: witness allowances are not generous and the amount of money at stake may not justify the cost of attending and losing a day off work, or paying a baby sitter. District Judges will take into account a letter or written statement from an absent witness.

However, the regard or weight that is given to that statement or letter may not be as great as the impact of the witness attending in person. An absent witness is not able to answer questions about his evidence being tested by cross-examination.

A commonsense decision will have to be taken for each witness and for every case. The following questions must asked.

- How important is the evidence?
- What will be the expense of the witness attending?
- How effective will the evidence be if it is simply written down?
- Is the evidence likely to be controversial?
- Will the other side be able to complain about not being able to ask the absent witness questions about the evidence?

If a witness does not attend in person, then it makes sense to send a written summary of that evidence to the other side well before the hearing.

Settlement Negotiations

The District Judge must not be told the details of any settlement negotiations before the hearing or outside the court before judgment: this information must not be included in any witness statements or mentioned when the witness gives evidence. If the District Judge hears about these offers he or she may have to adjourn the case to different date for it to be heard by a different judge.

Expert evidence

A party can only call expert evidence with the prior permission of the District Judge which should be sought at the allocation stage or at the preliminary hearing (see Chapter 5).

Other types of prohibited evidence

The District Judge will hesitate to allow "similar-fact" and "circumstantial" evidence into the case. However, if the evidence is introduced, or included in a witness statement, then it may be difficult to ignore completely. Tread carefully, a blatant attempt to poison the mind of the District Judge with statements which cannot be supported by other evidence is only going to make the District Judge slow to accept evidence relating to other parts of the case.

Taking evidence on oath

The District Judge need not take evidence on oath (rule 27.8(4)). However, the parties may well be reminded that the hearing is in a court of law and they are expected to tell the truth. A District Judge can require evidence to be taken on oath and will do so if, for example, it is clear that the conscience of the witness to tell the truth will not be bound unless he or she is put on oath.

Limiting cross-examination

The theme here is that the court is in charge, and will not allow a disproportionate amount of time in questioning witnesses (rule 27.8(5)). Cross examination is considered in detail below under "advocacy skills".

Advocacy skills and the Small Claims hearing; making the most of your time in court

A hearing in the judge's room is meant to be less daunting than a hearing in open court. The District Judge will try and put the parties and their witnesses at ease and will assist inexperienced advocates and litigants alike. The District Judge may adopt an interventionist approach, for example by asking questions, limiting cross-examination and generally assisting the parties.

In practice this means that the District Judge may well sideline the professional advocate but should not do so to such an extent that the advocate takes no part.

How, then, can the chances of winning be improved by effective advocacy?

Opening speech

In a formal trial, the claimant's advocate will probably set the scene for the case at the outset by giving a summary of the apparent issues. In Small Claims cases this is often done by the District Judge.

There is no harm in the claimants or their advocates preparing the points which they would like to be covered in a formal opening. When the District Judge gives the "opening summary" the points can then be ticked off, and if any points are not noted by the District Judge these can then be politely added. It is of course possible that the claimant will be asked to open anyway – it depends on what method of hearing is adopted on the day.

The points which should be covered at the opening (whether by the claimant or by the District Judge) are:

- introductions of all the advocates
- a summary of the facts
- a summary of the apparent issues.

Examination in chief

The District Judge may ask many of the questions and the advocate may be left to fill in the gaps. The advocate should therefore prepare a checklist of the points that need to be covered, and these should be checked off to determine what additional points need to be made.

Here are some hints on how to get the best out of a witness giving verbal evidence.

- Remember where you are (it's not a formal trial).
- Keep your questions short.
- Keep your language simple.
- Make sure the District Judge can hear you and your witness.
- Make sure that the District Judge can keep up with his or her notes (don't let the witness go too fast).
- Let the witness tell the story – don't interrupt; the evidence will be much more convincing if given without prompting.
- Stop your witness if he or she strays from the point.
- Ask questions in a logical order.

- Ask specific questions – avoid 'open' questions which may tempt your witness to stray into irrelevant or unhelpful areas of evidence
- Make sure you know what answers to expect.
- Make your last question your best, and be doubly sure that you are confident that the witness will give a helpful answer.

The key is thoughtful preparation:

- all witnesses should have seen a written statement of their evidence and read it over before the hearing
- prepare a list of questions and use it at the hearing.

Questions put to a witness which suggest a particular answer are called 'leading questions.' An example of this is – "is it correct that you were driving a blue car?" The same question not put in a leading way would be "what was the colour of the car you were driving?". In formal trials, a judge will prevent the use of questions which "lead" a witness, unless the evidence which is "led" is not controversial. Since the strict rules of evidence do not apply, it can be expected that the District Judge at a Small Claims hearing will be fairly tolerant of leading questions – after all, they may well speed up the hearing! However, there is a trap here for the unwary: if a witness's evidence consists of words that have been put into his or her mouth, that evidence may not be convincing. It follows that leading questions should be limited and avoided where key issues are at stake.

Cross examination

The object of cross examination is to:

- put the other side's evidence in doubt if it damages your case
- give the witness a chance to comment on your theory of the case.

It follows that if the witness has not damaged your case there may be no need to cross examine. It can be quite difficult to discredit a witness and the District Judge will intervene to stop an aggressive line of questioning (rule 27.8(4)). In formal trials, "putting the case" ensures that no party is taken by surprise and has a chance to comment on any theory advanced by the other side. In a Small Claims case, it will sometimes be unnecessary to "put the case" to the witness; the order of witnesses can be flexible and if something new does turn up then the witness can easily be recalled and asked about the new point later.

As a rule of thumb, it is useful to limit any questions in cross examination to those where you are fairly sure of the answer that will be given. In cross examination you should never ask the other side's witness to give you their theory about the case – you know it won't be favourable to you! The rules about 'leading questions' are relaxed under cross examination and such questions will be allowed.

Closing speech

At the end of the case, each party will be asked to say how the case should be decided and why – this is where a well prepared litigant or advocate can really shine.

You should emphasise only the evidence which has helped you. If the evidence against you has been unhelpful, this is a chance to put it into context and show that the good evidence in your client's favour outweighs the negative evidence.

You may suspect that the District Judge has sympathy with the other side, for example if the other side is unrepresented or apparently less powerful than your client. If so, the best you can do is to emphasise the objective things which help your case – the relevant law and any independent or expert evidence. You should consider the points that tip the balance in your client's favour – never forget that to succeed, the burden of proof must be discharged (see page 143).

Legal points

The District Judge must and will apply the law in Small Claims cases.

Although the District Judge may be familiar with the relevant law the judge's legal knowledge cannot be taken for granted, and professional advocates must come prepared to set out the law clearly and without using complicated language. If previously decided cases are to be relied on, make copies – enough for yourself, the other side and the District Judge.

Practical tips

For road traffic cases, it is useful to bring toy cars to court so that the scene of the accident can be reconstructed as a tableau on the District Judge's table, plus a copy of the *Highway Code*. Always remember to bring a calculator –if your calculator is on your mobile phone you will not be able to use it in court as your phone will have to remain switched off.

Practice note
EFFECTIVE ADVOCACY AT THE SMALL CLAIMS HEARING

- Remember where you are – be brief and use simple language
- Prepare checklists of what you want to say
- Prepare a checklist of what you hope your witnesses will say
- Bring copies of case reports and relevant legal texts to the hearing

---

Taking a note

Legal professionals are under a duty to take a note of the evidence at the hearing. Even if it is not possible to write everything down as it is said, it is useful to note down the main points of evidence and in particular any points which are likely to be useful when making a final summary of the case to the District Judge.

Litigants in person will find the assistance of a friend or supporter to take notes for them and manage their papers, can be invaluable.

Giving judgment

- The District Judge may give reasons as briefly or simply as the nature of the case allows (PD 27 para 5.5(1))
- Judgment will normally be given orally at the hearing but the decision may be given later, either in writing or at another hearing (PD 27 para 5.5(2))

A reasoned decision

The judgment will contain the result of the case and brief reasons for the decision. The detail in the judgment will be proportionate to the nature of the case, and the reasons given may be brief.

The decision will be reasoned (rule 27.8 (6)) but the judge must produce a written note of the reasons for the decision only if:

- there was no recording, or
- if the case was decided without a hearing under rule 27.10 or if either side notified the court under rule 27.9 (1) that they did not propose to attend the hearing.

The District Judge's reasons will be considered by the Circuit Judge in the event of an appeal – if a reasonable note has been made this may save the cost of a transcript of the judgment.

Costs and witness expenses

Decisions on what expenses and costs are to be allowed are taken after the award has been given, and the District Judge will make a note of the sums awarded. The parties and their representatives should have their calculators ready and be prepared to assist the District Judge with

- interest calculations
- witness expenses
- arithmetical calculations.

Costs and witness expenses are dealt with in detail in Chapter 6.

Any "without prejudice" correspondence between the parties can be disclosed to the District Judge at this stage.

Time to pay

If the loser needs time to pay the sum awarded, the District Judge will consider whether the judgment should be paid by instalments. If the judgment is to be paid in one lump sum, the District Judge will decide when the payment is to be made. If no time period is set the judgment must be paid in full within 14 days (rule 40.11). Note that if the loser is granted time to pay then the instalment order is registered as a judgment in the register of county court judgments (see Chapter 12).

Even if the District Judge does not give the loser time to pay at the hearing, an application can be made at a later date (CCR Order 22 rule 10). The party requesting time to pay contacts the court and the staff will send them a form to complete enabling them to set out their income and liabilities. The court staff then work out an appropriate rate of payment using standard guidelines. The debtor and creditor are both then notified of the rate of payment which has been so determined. If either the judgment debtor or creditor is unhappy with the rate determined by the court the matter is, at their request, referred to the District Judge who can confirm the order or set it aside and make such new order as he or she thinks fit. The judgment creditor does not have to accept a payment by instalments, for example, if the debtor has assets which could be sold to meet the judgment immediately then the District Judge may, at the request of the judgment creditor, set aside the instalment order.

Permission to appeal

The loser can ask the District Judge at the end of the hearing for permission to appeal. No formalities or fee is involved and if the request is refused, this does not affect the loser's right to make an application for permission to appeal to the circuit judge within 21 days of the hearing. Permission to appeal will be given only if the appeal has a real prospect of success. The District Judge will inform the parties that any further request for permission to appeal must be to the Circuit Judge who will hear any appeal.

> See Chapter 8 for more about appeals

Court order

The District Judge makes a note of the decision and the money award on the court file. The file is returned to the court office where the court staff "enter the judgment" and enter the judgment details on the court's computer. A formal order is prepared and sealed and sent to both parties as a record of the result.

Small Claims hearing – frequently asked questions

1. Can I bring a friend to support me?	Yes
2. Will I have to wait?	Probably – contact the court to find out how many cases are listed at the same time – you may have to wait for some time for your case to be called. Hesitate before parking your car on a meter – you may be in court for well over two hours!
3. What do I call the judge?	'Sir' or 'madam' (on an appeal or before a circuit judge 'your honour')
4. How formal is the hearing?	The parties will probably sit around a table but the atmosphere will be about as formal as a job interview
5. What will the courtroom look like?	Hearings are generally held in the judge's room and the parties will sit around a table, but the arrangements in courts vary
6. Will the hearing be in public?	Yes – but strangers or court reporters are unlikely to attend unless invited by the parties themselves
7. Can I take notes?	Yes. It will help you to present your case and a note of the judgment will be needed if there is an appeal.
8. Can I make my own recording of the hearing?	It is a contempt of court to make a tape recording of any part of the hearing without the permission of the District Judge (section 9 of the Contempt of Court Act 1981).
9. If I lose, can I appeal?	Yes – if the appeal has a real prospect of success – see Chapter 8 – Appeals

CHAPTER 8

Appeals and applications to set aside judgment

Appeals and applications to set aside judgment – in detail   157

Appeals flowchart   158

1 Appeals   159
   Grounds for appeal   159
   Permission to appeal   160
   Review and not rehearing   162
   Appeals against case management decisions   163
   Paperwork for the appeal   163
   Respondent's cross appeal   165
   Hearing of the appeal   165
   Second appeals   166

2 Setting judgment aside and re-hearing   166
   Procedure   167

3 Setting aside a judgment in default   168
   The mandatory grounds   168
   The discretionary grounds   168
   Procedure   169
   Credit repair applications   170

Summary table – appeals and applications to set
   aside judgment   171

Appeals and applications to set aside judgment

Basics

- The loser must get permission to appeal, which will be given if the appeal has a real prospect of success
- A party who for good reason fails to attend a hearing may be able to get a rehearing
- A judgment in default (without a hearing) can sometimes be set aside
- In rare cases a case may be reheard if fresh evidence comes to light after the hearing
- The 'no costs' rule does applies to the appeal process for small claims cases

---

A party dissatisfied with the final result of the case can appeal, but only if the appeal has a real prospect of success; the prospective appellant must obtain permission to appeal, either from the District Judge at the hearing or from a Circuit Judge. The rules about appeals are set out in Part 52.

There is also a procedure to set aside a judgment given in the absence of one of the parties: If a party had a good reason for not attending, and their case had a reasonable prospect of success, the District Judge may allow a rehearing (see page 166).

This chapter also deals with situations where there has been a default judgment and the judgment debtor wishes to have the judgment set aside. In such cases the applicant must usually be able to establish that he or she has a real prospect of successfully defending the case or there is some other "good reason" to set aside the judgment.

The loser on the appeal will only be ordered to pay costs on the basis of the usual rules applicable to the small claims track including those governing unreasonable behaviour.

A summary of the options available to set aside judgments and appeals is set out on page 171 and an overview flowchart on page 158.

Appeals and applications to set aside judgment – in detail

Terminology

Appellant The party making the appeal

Appeal court The court which hears the appeal *(not to be confused with the Court of Appeal; appeals from decisions of District Judges are made to a Circuit Judge who sits in the County Court)*

Respondent The party responding to the appeal (the respondent can also lodge an appeal)

Appeals: important time limits	
Within 21 days of the decision	Appellant must lodge notice of appeal (including application for permission to appeal if not granted by the District Judge at the hearing)
Within 7 days of the appellant filing notice of appeal	Appellant must serve a copy of the notice of appeal on the other side (no need to serve the notice until permission to appeal has been given)
Within 14 days of the respondent being notified of the appeal	Respondent may lodge notice of appeal

Appeals flowchart

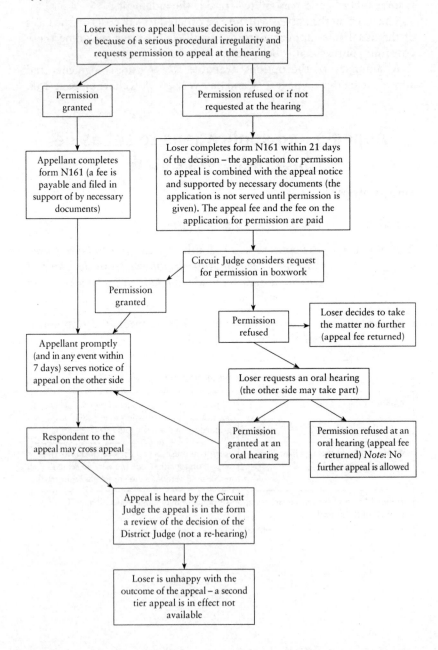

Loser wishes to appeal because decision is wrong or because of a serious procedural irregularity and requests permission to appeal at the hearing

Permission granted

Permission refused or if not requested at the hearing

Appellant completes form N161 (a fee is payable and filed in support of by necessary documents)

Loser completes form N161 within 21 days of the decision – the application for permission to appeal is combined with the appeal notice and supported by necessary documents (the application is not served until permission is given). The appeal fee and the fee on the application for permission are paid

Circuit Judge considers request for permission in boxwork

Permission granted

Permission refused

Loser decides to take the matter no further (appeal fee returned)

Appellant promptly (and in any event within 7 days) serves notice of appeal on the other side

Loser requests an oral hearing (the other side may take part)

Respondent to the appeal may cross appeal

Permission granted at an oral hearing

Permission refused at an oral hearing (appeal fee returned) *Note*: No further appeal is allowed

Appeal is heard by the Circuit Judge the appeal is in the form a review of the decision of the District Judge (not a re-hearing)

Loser is unhappy with the outcome of the appeal – a second tier appeal is in effect not available

1 Appeals

Basics

- The grounds for appeal are limited
- Permission to appeal is required
- The appeal is usually not a rehearing but a review of the decision of the District Judge

---

The Rules which apply to appeals in Small Claims cases are the same as those that apply to appeals from decisions made in cases allocated to the Fast Track and Multi-track; although the paperwork needed on the appeal is slightly reduced for appeals against Small Claims decisions. A full discussion of all the rules relevant to appeals is outside the scope of this book and what follows is a working summary relevant to appeals in Small Claims cases.

Grounds for appeal

The appeal court will allow an appeal where the decision of the lower court was

(a) wrong

(b) unjust because of a serious procedural or other irregularity in the proceedings in the lower court

(Rule 52.11 (3)).

The Circuit Judge will only interfere with decision if it is wrong; this is not the same as a decision with which the loser disagrees!

Ask the following questions when considering an appeal. In making the original decision did the District Judge

1. make a critical finding of fact against the weight of the evidence or
2. make a critical finding of fact which was totally unsupported by evidence or
3. misinterpret a statute and thus come to a wrong decision or
4. get any aspect of law wrong and thus come to a wrong decision
5. fail to give reasons for the decision?

If the answer to any one of these questions is 'Yes' an appeal may be possible. Bear in mind, however, that the District Judge is entitled to take a relatively informal view of what counts as 'evidence' as the strict rules of evidence do not apply (see Chapter 7).

Since the Circuit Judge will not rehear the case but will review the original decision, he or she is interested in the reasons given for the original decision. The Rules require the Circuit Judge to be provided with a suitable record of the District Judge's reasons or judgment (see page 163 – paperwork for the appeal).

A practitioner who is presenting a case at a Small Claims hearing will no doubt have heeded the advice given elsewhere in this book to research the law thoroughly and provide the District Judge with copies of any relevant legal authorities. However, mistakes do happen, not least because litigants in person often present their case in a confusing manner! If the decision is wrong because the District Judge got the law wrong, this should be thoroughly researched before an appeal is mounted and the correct legal analysis set out in the appeal document.

If the ground of the appeal is 'irregularity' it should be noted that this might relate to any part of the proceedings, not just the hearing itself. The irregularity must have been *serious*, but if the irregularity was serious this will make the decision unjust, irrespective of whether the irregularity affected the outcome. In considering a possible procedural irregularity, remember that the Small Claims hearing is, by its nature, a simple affair and that the District Judge can conduct the case in any manner that he or she considers to be fair (rule 27.8(1)). A failure to give reasons is itself grounds for appeal. Reasons are necessary in order for a party to consider if they have grounds for appeal. Justice must be seen to be done *Flannery v Halifax Estate Agencies Limited* [2000] 1 WLR 377.

Permission to appeal

Permission to appeal will only be given where

(a) the court considers that the appeal would have a real prospect of success; or

(b) there is some other compelling reason for the appeal to be heard

(Rule 52.3(6))

There can be no appeal without permission. Permission to appeal will be given if the appeal has a real, not a fanciful, prospect of success.[1] However, in very rare cases, even if the appeal is likely to fail, permission will be given to appeal if the court identifies some other 'compelling reason' why the appeal should be heard. Such reasons may exist in cases of general public importance or where an issue of human rights is involved; circumstances where a weak case is allowed to proceed to appeal will be very rare.

The prospective appellant has two opportunities to apply for permission; at the hearing itself and later to a Circuit Judge.

The loser can ask the District Judge at the hearing for permission to appeal. No formalities or fee is involved, and if the request is refused, this does not affect the right to make a written application to the Circuit Judge after the hearing. The District Judge will consider if the appeal has a real prospect of success and if the request is refused will note his or her reasons on the court file. The failure to apply for permission to appeal at the hearing does not prejudice a party's right to apply later. See Chapter 7.

If an application for an appeal is made after the hearing, the application cannot be made to the District Judge who heard the case but must be to a Circuit Judge. The application is made in writing and must be made within 21 days of the date of decision (Rule 52.4(b) although the District Judge who made the decision may specify a different period. The application is lodged at the County Court where the original decision was made.

If an application for permission to appeal is made over 21 days after the final decision or any extended time granted by the District Judge at the final hearing then a separate application must be made for permission to appeal out of time. These "late" applications will not be granted without good reason and are usually refused if the delay is more than a few days.

The application for permission to appeal is combined with the appeal document (court form N164); If permission to appeal is refused, the fee due on the appeal (£100) is returned to the applicant.

---

1   For more detail on the appellate approach and the appeal courts' powers see *Tanfern Ltd v Cameron-Macdonald* [2000] 2 All ER 801.

The application for permission is reviewed, in the first instance by a Circuit Judge as part of his or her boxwork. Permission to appeal may be given there and then, but if it is refused on paper the prospective appellant has a right to have that reviewed at a hearing (Rule 52.3(4)).

Where the Circuit Judge has refused permission to appeal in writing and had not altered that decision following a hearing the loser can take the case no further. The effect of the refusal of permission to appeal is final: see *Moyse* v *Regal Partnerships Ltd* [2004] EWCA Civ 1269 and s54(4) Administration of Justice Act 1999.

In any case, where permission to appeal is given, the permission may limit the issues to be heard and may be given subject to conditions (Rule 52.3 (7)).

> An outline of the appeal process is set out in the appeal flowchart on page 158

Review and not rehearing

Unless it orders otherwise, the appeal court will not receive

(a) oral evidence
(b) evidence which was not before the lower court

Rule 52.11(2)

The appeal is not a chance for the loser to start again and present the case once more to a fresh judge. The appeal is strictly a review of the original hearing. There is no new evidence and oral evidence is not called. Argument is based solely on whether the original judge reached a decision that was plainly wrong.

In rare cases the Circuit Judge can consider fresh evidence on the appeal, where it could not have been obtained with 'reasonable diligence' for use at the original hearing: see *Ladd* v *Marshall* (1954) 3 All ER 745 CA.

Appeals against case management decisions

A case management decision is a decision made before the final hearing, for example an order refusing permission to call an expert or directions about the timetabling of the case.

The procedure for an appeal is the same as for the appeal against a final decision as described above. However, in considering whether permission to appeal is to be granted, the court will consider not only the points detailed above but also if the issue is of 'sufficient significance' to justify the cost of the appeal and whether the issue would be more conveniently dealt with at the final hearing (PD 52 para 4.5). Given the relatively low value of most Small Claims cases and the high costs of an appeal, permission to appeal against a case management decision in a Small Claims case is rarely given.

Paperwork for the appeal

Where the appeal relates to a claim allocated to the Small Claims track the appellant must file the following documents with the appellant's notice

(1) a sealed copy of the order being appealed
(2) any order giving or refusing permission to appeal, together with reasons for that decision

PD 52 Para 5.8

The form N164 must be properly completed to include all the reasons for the appeal; special permission will be needed to rely on any ground that is not included in the form N164 (Rule 52.11(5)). The form is fairly lengthy, but comes with helpful notes.

The N164 must be supported by a sealed copy of the order appealed against, plus a copy of the order giving permission to appeal (if granted) and a 'suitable record' of the District Judge's reasons for the decision appealed against. The appellant against a Small Claims decision only needs to file a 'suitable record' of the decision of the District Judge if required to do so by the Circuit Judge. It will be required if the Circuit Judge needs to see the judgment to decide whether to grant permission to appeal or to decide the appeal (PD 52 para 5.8); which will be in most cases.

Legal representatives should have made a written note of the original judgment (see page 151) and, if a note was made, the legal representatives must agree the note, if possible. If the appellant is not legally represented and the other party was, the legal representative must make his or her note available for use by the litigant in person free of charge (PD 52 para 5.12).

All Small Claims hearings are now recorded, and the appellant can obtain a transcript of the recording of the judgment. The cost of providing the transcript may be considerable (see page 134). The Rules allow a judge to order that a copy of a note of the judgment is to be supplied at public expense where a litigant in person is in 'poor financial circumstances' (PD 52 Para 5.17 and 5.18). A transcript of the judgment may take several weeks to obtain, and will often not be available to lodge with the N164. In such cases, the N164 should contain a coherent summary of the District Judge's reasons; the form N164 should contain a request that the Circuit Judge allow sufficient time for a full transcript of the judgment to be made.

The documents required to support an appeal from a Small Claims case are slightly fewer in number than the documents needed to support an appeal from a decision made in a case allocated to one of the other case management tracks. However, the Small Claims appellant may, if he or she chooses, add to the documents strictly required, a skeleton argument, a bundle of documents relevant to the appeal and copies of relevant witness statements (PD 52 para 5.6 and 5.8).

The notice of appeal must be served on the other side promptly and in any event no less than seven days after it has been filed at the court. The service is done by the appellant and not by the court.

**Practice Note
– documents needed for a Small Claims appeal**

- Fully completed N164 (and fee)
- Sealed copy of the original order
- Any order giving/refusing permission to appeal
- Suitable record of the original judgment (note or transcript of tape recording)

Plus (optional)

- *Skeleton argument*
- *Witness statements*
- *Documents to support the appeal*

Respondent's Notice and Cross Appeal

The respondent to the appeal who wishes to ask the appeal court to vary the order of the District Judge in any way must also appeal, and permission is needed on the same basis as the appellant. The respondent's notice is prepared on the form N164 and the time limit is 14 days after he or she has notified the the appellant has obtained permission (rule 52.5 and see the Practice Direction at para 7.1).

The respondent does not need to prepare a respondent's notice or cross appeal if he is only wanting to support the original decision of the District Judge.

Hearing of the appeal

The appeal hearing will be before a Circuit Judge. Whereas many District Judges deal with the open court hearings of Small Claims cases in the relatively informal setting of a room (see page 134), the Circuit Judge will hear the case in a traditional court room. Advocates must expect to be robed. The procedure is formal.

A litigant in person may be assisted by a friend at the hearing (see page 138 – the so-called McKenzie Friend) but cannot be assisted by an unqualified lay representative on an appeal (PD 27 para 3.2(2)). The only advocates allowed at an appeal hearing are those formally qualified so to act (see Chapter 7).

Although the appeal papers are lodged in the court where the case was heard by the District Judge, the appeal hearing may be in a different town, in the same 'court group' as the original county court. The reason for this is that smaller county courts do not always have their own facilities for Circuit Judges to hear cases. The staff at the local county court will be able to advise the prospective appellant where the appeal is likely to be heard.

Orders for costs on appeal are restricted by the rules applicable to Small Claims cases under Rule 27.14 the no costs rule applies to appeals (see Chapter 6).

It is usually sensible for the respondent to the appeal to attend the appeal hearing but, even if he does not, the appeal may still be dismissed in his absence. In deciding the merits of the appeal the Circuit Judge will have to be satisfied that the appeal should be granted having regard to the factors previously discussed (see page 159–160).

Second appeals

The Civil Procedure Rules impose severe restrictions on second-tier appeals. The rejection of the appeal itself is the effective end of the appeal process. The Court of Appeal itself must give permission for any second appeal and this will only be given if the appeal would raise an important point of principle or practice, or if there is some other compelling reason for the court to hear it (Rule 52.13).

2 Setting judgment aside and re-hearing

(1) A party –
   a. who was neither present nor represented at the hearing of the claim; and
   b. who has not given written notice to the court under rule 27.9(1), may apply for an order that a judgment under this Part shall be set aside) and the claim re-heard.

(3) The court may grant an application...[to set aside the judgment]...only if the applicant –

a. had a good reason for not attending or being represented at the hearing or giving written notice to the court under rule 27.9(1); and

b. has a reasonable prospect of success at the hearing.

Rule 27.11

An application to set aside a judgment after a hearing is limited to genuine cases where a hearing has been missed, for example by accident, and where the absent party had a "reasonable prospect" of success.

A party who did not attend the final hearing and gave the court notice under rule 27.9(1) in advance should not use this procedure but must make an appeal.

The party must give "good reason'" for not attending. It will be down to the District Judge who hears the application to decide on what is a "good" reason. There are no hard and fast rules – but a District Judge may be sympathetic to reasons relating to sudden illness or unforeseen circumstances.

Having a good reason for not attending is not enough. The party must also show that their case had a reasonable prospect of success so, on the hearing of the application, the strength of the case will be considered. Determining whether a case has a reasonable prospect of success is quite a high test to pass – the District Judge will not order a re-hearing unless the case is reasonably sound. This may involve looking not only at the case as set out in the defence or on the claim form, but also making sure that the party can call suitable evidence to win at a hearing.

Procedure

Any application must be made within 14 days after the party was "served with the notice of judgment"; see the notes in Chapter 10 as to when the court order will be deemed to have been served.

Chapter 10 deals with the general procedure on applications. The party applying must complete a form and pay a court fee. The form must set out the reason for the application in as much detail as possible. The reasons must cover not only the reason for missing the hearing but also why the party has a reasonable prospect of success. The statement of truth on the application should be signed.

The application will be listed for hearing with a time estimate to cover the time needed to deal with the application (typically 15 or 30 minutes). The parties should not expect the court to to hear the whole case again on the day of the application, a further attendance at court will be needed for any re-hearing.

The District Judge may use the court's case management powers to attach conditions to setting a new hearing date. These conditions must be expressed clearly and must be capable of being complied with – for example, making it a condition that the party pays a sum of money into court until the case is re-heard (rule 3.1(3)) – should not be ordered unless it is likely he can raise the necessary funds.

3 Setting aside a judgment in default

The relevant rules are found in Part 13 of the CPR.

A judgment in default means a judgment entered because a defence (including a defence to counterclaim) or acknowledgment has not been filed (rule 12.1). It follows that the case will not have been allocated to the Small Claims track and the application is not protected by the "no costs" rule.

The mandatory grounds

The court *must* set aside a judgment in default if it was wrongly entered (sometimes called an irregular judgment) (Rule 13.2). Examples of irregular judgments are those entered before the time for filing a defence had expired or a judgment entered after an application had been made for summary judgment[2].

The discretionary grounds

The court has discretion to set aside a default judgment if

(a) the defendant has a real prospect of successfully defending the claim or
(b) it appears to the court that there is some other good reason why –
　　(i) the judgment should be set aside or varied or
　　(ii) The defendant should be allowed to defend the claim.

---

2   Once a claimant has made an application for summary judgment the defendant does not need to file a defence before the hearing of the application (rule 24.4(2)).

So, although the *quality* of the proposed defence will usually be the key to success, the District Judge can also set the judgment aside for other "good reason".

The defence must be something more than an illusion. The District Judge will look at the matter in the round, and all the circumstances considered. This may include examining any evidence that the defendant may use to support the defence and considering whether any legal argument has substance.

Procedure

There is no set time limit on making the application – although the rules do specify that the application must be made "promptly". The District Judge will take every case on its own merits. Therefore, if there is a delay of more than a fortnight before issuing the application, there must be a special explanation for the delay. Where a party who did not attend trial but did not apply for a rehearing until 26 days after receiving the adverse judgment the Court of Appeal decided that the application had not been made promptly enough (*Regency Rolls Ltd and Another* v *Carnell* LTL October 16 2000).

Chapter 10 deals with the general procedure on applications. The judgment debtor must complete an application and pay a court fee. The application must set out the reason for the application in as much detail as possible and be supported by evidence (rule 13.4(3)).

A District Judge will hear the application. The judgment debtor must be prepared to show evidence to explain why the original time limits were not adhered to, and any reason for a delay in making the application.

If the judgment is set aside for one of the mandatory grounds, the District Judge will not attach any conditions. If the judgment is set aside on a discretionary ground then the District Judge can attach conditions – for example making the judgment debtor pay a sum of money into court to await the outcome of the case.

The District Judge may use the court's case management powers to attach conditions to setting the judgment aside. These conditions must be expressed clearly and must be capable of being complied with; a party should not be ordered to bring money into court as such a condition unless it is likely he can raise the necessary funds.

Credit repair applications

Registration of County court judgments is discussed in Chapter 10. A judgment debtor may discover years or months after a hearing which he or she did not attend, or after a default judgment, that their credit record is blighted. If the judgment debtor was genuinely unaware of the proceedings and would have had a good prospect of defending, then a valid application can be made to set aside the judgment. The application is made as explained above. However, if the judgment debtor's only motive in applying is to "repair" their credit record, the application will fail.

Summary table – Appeals and applications to set aside judgment

Note – Appeals in bold type are heard by a circuit judge – all other applications are heard by a District Judge

	Circumstances	Complaint	Action	Timescale
Judgment after hearing	Both parties attend the hearing	Decision was wrong and the loser has a real chance of success on appeal	**Apply for permission to appeal. Appeal will be heard by a Circuit Judge**	Apply for permission at the hearing to the District Judge or within 21 days to the Circuit Judge
		Loser unhappy, but the decision was not wrong	No action can be taken	
	One party does not turn up at the hearing having given notice in advance under Rule 27.9 of absence	The absent party considers the decision was wrong and has a real chance of success on appeal	**Apply for permission to appeal. Appeal will be heard by a Circuit Judge**	Within 21 days of the decision to the Circuit Judge
	Loser fails to attend the hearing (no notice having been given under Rule 27.9)	Losers case has a reasonable prospect of success *and* has a good reason for non attendance	Application to set aside (Rule 27.11) – will be heard by the District Judge	No more than 14 days after receipt of the judgment notice
Judgment in default	No acknowledgement or defence	Judgment entered too soon or after the whole of the claim was paid in full (rule 13.2)	Application to set aside or vary default judgment (rule 13)	Promptly (note that the District Judge must set aside the judgment and will not impose a penalty)
	Failure to file defence or acknowledgement	Judgment debtor has *real prospect* of defending or there is other *good reason* why the judgment should be set aside (rule 13.3)	Application to set aside or vary default judgment (rule 13)	Promptly (note that the District Judge must set aside the judgment and will not impose conditions) (rule 13.3(2))

CHAPTER 9
Mediating Small Claims

What is Mediation?   174

The Benefits of Mediation   178

What is the difference between Mediation and Litigation?   180

When Mediation might be inappropriate   181

Is this justice?   183

Who are the Mediators?   183

How does it work   184

What are the possible outcomes of Mediation?   185

What happens if the parties cannot agree a settlement   185

Practical tips for parties to Mediation   186

Mediating Small Claims

What is Mediation?

As long ago as 1996 the Lord Chancellor's Department set up a series of pilot studies in the County court to establish whether the process of mediation could operate as a successful alternative to litigation as a means of resolving people's disputes. Once a claim is issued the court's duty actively to manage cases includes "encouraging the parties to use an alternative dispute resolution procedure if the court considers that appropriate, facilitating the use of such procedure" (Rule 1.4(2)(e)) and "helping the parties to settle the whole or part of their case" (Rule 1.4(2)(f)). Courts now frequently explore the possibility of mediation at an early stage in the proceedings, for example at case management conferences. Increasingly the courts strongly recommend parties to attempt resolving their disputes by mediation. Court annexed mediation schemes exist at Central London County court, The Mayor's and City of London Court and York, Manchester, Birmingham, Exeter, Barnstaple, Torquay, Guildford, Leeds and South-West Wales County courts but each is also run in conjunction with the National Mediation Helpline which coordinates mediation appointments outside the court buildings.

The results were so encouraging that by 2002 the pilot studies began to focus particularly on the suitability of mediation to be offered, or indeed directed, in Small Claims cases. The Ministry of Justice now actively promotes the view that parties should always consider whether mediation is a suitable method by which to dispose of their claim, and outside the Small Claims track, penalty costs may be awarded against parties who fail unreasonably to mediate their cases.

So let us consider what this process is

Mediation is a voluntary, non-binding, and private dispute resolution process in which a neutral person helps the parties try to reach a negotiated settlement. In Small Claims cases this will usually involve a meeting between the parties organised and chaired by a trained and experienced neutral person over a relatively short period in which he or she tries to aid communication between them and explore options for settlement which are not fixed by the court's own powers. Let us consider the key elements:–

Voluntary

In most cases mediation cannot take place unless the parties agree to enter the process, although this may only be after a strong judicial recommendation, with an associated risk of cost sanctions against a party who refuses to mediate. Mediation is not possible without the participation of all parties, and will cease if one party walks out, which they are free to do at any time.

Non–binding

Mediation is also truly voluntary, as entering the process does not bind the parties to reaching a settlement. Settlement can only come about on the authority of the parties concerned. As the mediator has no authority to make a binding determination, nor make any findings of fact or attribute any blame, if the parties cannot agree, there will be no settlement and the case will proceed to the next stage in the litigation process. However, if settlement is reached the agreed terms will form part of an enforceable contract. Mediation is merely a process which acts as a catalyst for settlement: many of those cases that do not settle at the mediation itself in fact settle shortly afterwards.

Private

The mediation process is both "without prejudice" and absolutely confidential. This means that parties can conduct themselves in the mediation, for example by disclosing information, expressing views, making suggestions or offering concessions, safe in the knowledge that this will not preclude them arguing a different position should the matter proceed to trial. Similarly, a party is free to refuse offers made in mediation, or even to walk out, without the risk of this being held against them if, for reasons of behaviour being outside the 'no costs' rule (see Chapter 6) a court determines costs in the future. The confidential nature of mediation negotiations stands in clear contrast to the courtroom, which is in public and potentially extremely embarrassing. Of course, should mediation break down a party is free to repeat formally any offer made during the mediation process.

The terms of any settlement agreed in mediation are usually also confidential. However, this need not necessarily be so. In certain disputes one of the parties may be seeking some kind of public vindication (e.g. in a defamation case) or apology for past conduct and there is no reason why a public declaration cannot form part of a mediated settlement. For example, in the Alder Hey Hospital "retained organs litigation" while the core element of the claim was compensation, the settlement extended to the creation of a garden of remembrance, a public apology by all institutions involved, a public statement by the relevant government minister, and a plaque to be fixed on the wall outside the hospital. These innovative solutions show that mediation can provide a remedy, such as the giving of a formal apology, which a court cannot order.

Neutral mediator

The role of the mediator is key to the success of any mediation, and it is essential that he or she must be a truly neutral person having no association with either of the parties nor any interest in the outcome. Mediation requires all parties to trust and give authority to the mediator. Should any party withdraw that authority, the mediation will come to an end. Likewise, should trust in the mediator be broken for any reason, it is unlikely that a settlement will be reached.

The mediator's role is to assist the parties in their negotiations with each other and help the parties work towards a consensual resolution to the dispute. However, the parties themselves remain responsible for their own decisions and answerable for the terms of any settlement that may be agreed.

A settlement, negotiated by the parties

As highlighted above, a settlement is only possible in mediation with the consent of the parties, and it is they who are responsible for the terms of any agreement. While mediation certainly aims for a resolution that maximises all parties' interests (often called "win-win" outcomes), by its very nature it should never achieve an outcome with which one party cannot live. As the onus of arriving at the terms of settlement rests with the parties, the flexibility of the process allows for more ingenuity and extra-legal solutions than would ever be possible from a determination imposed by a court or other arbitral process.

This is very important if the parties either want to or are obliged to have continuing social or business relations, or if they live together or in close proximity to each other. Litigation tends to fracture relationships because one party wins, or at least is seen as a winner, and the other is not. The court process attributes fault and finds liability; mediation does not. Where parties involved in a dispute have to continue to live together, live near to each other, work together or just to see each other in their day-to-day lives, it is important that they can face each other without the risk of further difficulty.

The role of the mediator is to create a safe, neutral environment where disputants can discuss relevant issues and know that what they say will be listened to and that they will be assisted in trying to find a mutual, positive and constructive way forward for the future. He or she neither judges nor blame the disputants and any agreement reached is their own and not one imposed by the mediator.

Free mediation

Parties without representation who are in receipt of state benefits, are exempted from court fees, or who cannot otherwise afford the NMH mediation fees will be referred by the National Mediation Helpline or Citizens Advice Bureaux to LawWorks Mediation, a project of the Solicitors Pro Bono Group. The LawWorks mediation scheme arranges three hour mediations throughout England and Wales, for which are appointed a panel solicitor mediator and an assistant mediator willing to act on a rota basis without payment. LawWorks considers each case on its own merits whether it will be taken by the scheme. Some more straightforward cases can be resolved by telephone mediation. LawWorks may be contacted direct at *www.lawworks.org.uk*'.

Whether or Not to Mediate

- A high proportion of Claims settle at or as a result of mediation
- The process is relatively quick and inexpensive
- The outcome is flexible – and only what you agree to – and may be confidential
- You can ask for things the Court cannot give e.g. an apology
- There is relatively little risk in mediation failing as the process is itself confidential and entirely without prejudice

BUT

- Mediation is not an adjudicative process
- The Court does not rule on the rights and wrongs of your case
- If mediation fails the Claim will proceed and the time and costs may have been wasted

---

The Benefits of Mediation

Facts and figures for the effectiveness of mediation are limited since by and large the outcome remains confidential, and in some cases the existence of both dispute and mediation is also confidential – one of its benefits. Anecdotal evidence from those involved in mediation suggests that a very high proportion of mediated cases do settle at the mediation appointment, with a further considerable proportion settling soon afterwards. For example, the Centre for Effective Dispute Resolution ("CEDR") reports on its website that over 70% of cases referred to it settle.

The Ministry of Justice and its predecessor, the Department for Constitutional Affairs ("DCA") keeps records on the uptake and success rates of mediations in which the Government is involved, following the Government pledge in March 2001 to refer all cases it considers suitable to mediation where the other side agrees. In 2001/2, 89% of mediated cases settled without a hearing, and the figures for 2002/3 and 2003/4 were 83% and 79% respectively.

Just as striking is the DCA's estimate of the amount of money mediation appears to have saved in this period. Although the number of government disputes going to mediation is still relatively small, (49 in 2001/2; 163 in 2002/3 and 229 in 2003/4) the Government estimates that the use of mediation since March 2001 has made £23 millions of savings (Department for Constitutional Affairs Research Paper 2005).

The initial two-year pilot mediation scheme at the Central London County Court between 1996–8 has been the subject of a detailed evaluation by Professor Hazel Genn of University College, London (DCA Research Papers 1997, No 5/98). This scheme was in operation before the coming into force of the CPR, and parties refusing to participate were not subject to any sanctions.

Professor Genn found that although the take-up of the offer of mediation was only 5%, 62% of the cases that were mediated settled at the mediation appointment. The settlement rate was constant among different case types, indicating the potential for mediation to be used across a wide range of causes of action. Further, Professor Genn found support for the proposition that mediation promotes settlement even when the mediation itself is unsuccessful, as mediated cases had a much higher settlement rate overall than non-mediated cases.

As to time savings, Professor Genn found that "even on a very conservative estimate, mediated settlements occurred *several months earlier* than among non-mediated cases. Most parties whose cases settled at mediation believed that the mediation had saved time, although those whose cases did not settle often felt that the mediation had involved them in extra time. Solicitors felt strongly that mediation saved time."

In addition to its success rate and the scope for potential time and cost savings, mediation has other benefits of which you should be aware. These may best be seen merely by comparing traditional litigation with alternative dispute resolution processes in general, and mediation in particular.

What is the difference between Mediation and Litigation?

Litigation is formal. It imposes a binding solution where inevitably one party or the other is likely to be dissatisfied with the outcome, often highly dissatisfied. The expense and costs regime may make even the winner dissatisfied. It removes control of the dispute from parties, first by vesting it in the lawyers and then in the court's administration and management system. It addresses issues in a purely legal context, in the public eye, with fixed pre-determined remedies that you either obtain or fail to obtain. It is slow, expensive, and destroys relationships.

By contrast mediation is an informal, very flexible procedure with no imposed solutions. It gives better and more supple results because control remains directly in the hands of the parties as decision makers. Win or lose, it is comparatively quick and cheap as a self-contained process. It saves management time. It is private and confidential. And as a dynamic it actively promotes renewal and reconciliation because it is designed to restore relationships. Litigation looks to find fault and attribute blame. Mediation does not. This makes mediation a particularly attractive route where parties are likely to continue to have dealings and to interact in the future, whether in business, as neighbours or within the confines of some close personal relationship or physical proximity.

In *Halsey* v *Milton Keynes General NHS Trust* [2004] EWCA Civ [2004] 1 WLR 3002 Dyson LJ also took the opportunity to promote the advantages of mediation

> "We recognise that mediation has a number of advantages over the court process. It is usually less expensive than litigation which goes all the way to judgment .... Mediation provides litigants with a wider range of solutions than those that are available in litigation: for example, an apology; an explanation; the continuation of an existing professional or business relationship perhaps on new terms; and an agreement by one party to do something without any existing legal obligation to do so."

In particular there is no great risk for the parties in trying it: they can walk away from the process at any time; they are under no obligation to come to an agreement. If parties agree to mediate but are unable to reach a settlement they can still go to court. But they may find a creative solution is suggested which suits them, and avoids the risk of actually losing their case if it comes before the District Judge.

Once a settlement has been reached an agreement can be drawn up. Generally only agreements that relate to disputes already subject to Court proceedings can be enforced. As will be seen (see page 252) the court charges for this and there is no guarantee that the enforcement will be effective. In practice however, parties tend to keep to the mediation agreement because they have prepared the terms themselves. Statistically it has been shown that more people stand by mediated agreements than comply with court judgments.

In July 2003 Mr. Justice Lightman said in *Hurst v Leeming* [2003] 1 Lloyds Rep 37:

> "Litigation is a high risk gamble – and the risks and burden of costs today are so substantial that for any well advised [person] litigation must be the course of last resort if any reasonable alternative is available...The alternative of choice today is mediation. The law today increasingly recognises the value and importance of mediation as a social necessity...Give mediation a chance. Give it a chance at the earliest opportunity. In litigation there is only one winner and that is generally the lawyers. Mediation is not a universal panacea: it has its limitations and is not always applicable. But where it is available in my view no sane or conscientious litigators or party will lightly reject it.."

When Mediation Might Be Inappropriate

Although the Court of Appeal in *Halsey* decided that parties could not be forced to mediate against their will, since the courts are likely now to impose sanctions on a party who unreasonably fails to mediate claims allocated to Fast or Multi-track, this begs the question when is it reasonable to refuse mediation, or in which cases is mediation inappropriate?

In *Halsey* Lord Justice Dyson considered the appropriateness of parties choosing to mediate in the context of whether a party behaved unreasonably by refusing to do so. He concluded that a number of factors should be taken into consideration when assessing whether to mediate, and these included:

- The nature of the dispute;
- The merits of the case;

- The extent to which other settlement methods have been attempted;
- Whether the costs of the mediation would be disproportionately high;
- Whether any delay in setting up and attending the mediation would have been prejudicial; and
- Whether the mediation had a reasonable prospect of success.

Dyson LJ acknowledged that a small number of cases are intrinsically unsuitable for mediation, and gave a number of examples of these:

(1) Where the parties wish the court to determine issues of law or construction which may be essential to the future trading relations of the parties, as under an on-going long term contract, or where the issues are generally important for those participating in a particular trade or market.

(2) Similarly, where a party wants the court to resolve a point of law that arises from time to time, and one or more parties consider that a binding precedent would be useful.

(3) Cases involving allegations of fraud or other disreputable conduct against an individual or group, which are unlikely to be successfully mediated because confidence is lacking in the future conduct of that party.

(4) Cases where injunctive or other relief is essential to protect the position of a party.

The judge went on to consider that where a party actually does have a watertight case, a refusal to mediate can be reasonable, pointing out that otherwise there would be scope for claimants with a weak case to use the threat of a costs sanction to force a party into a mediated settlement even where the claim or defence is without merit. However, the party's belief that his case is watertight must be reasonable.

The Court of Appeal held that the costs of mediation can be a factor of particular importance where the sums at stake in the litigation are small. This is because a mediation can sometimes be as expensive as a day in court, as the parties will often have legal representation and the mediator's fees and other disbursements are usually be borne equally by the parties regardless of the outcome. In addition the possibility of the ultimately successful party being required to incur the costs of an abortive mediation is a relevant factor that a court may take into account in deciding whether the successful party acted unreasonably in refusing to agree to mediate.

This is an important consideration bearing in mind the increasing trend for courts to suggest mediation in Small Claims. Remember, mediation is not a panacea. *For a legally represented client, a Small Claims mediation is likely to cost at least the same as the hearing itself, but with no guarantee of an outcome at the end of it.* An unsuccessful mediation in a small claim will effectively double a legally represented client's costs, whether or not this client is eventually successful, due to the "no costs" rule of the small claims track.

Having said that it is likely that almost all Small Claims cases would ordinarily be suitable for mediation, and parties should consider the benefits to be derived which have been addressed above.

Is this justice?

It is possible for some parties to feel aggrieved that no legal arguments are generally accepted in mediation, except as a guide to the risk of outcome at a trial, and that often the mediators seem not to know anything about their case. Litigants coming to this process with no experience and an uncertainty of expectation may feel that it is not 'fair' if rights and wrongs are not taken into account. It is true that the streamlined nature of this procedure and the apparent lack of internal checks leave litigants with little or no recourse to challenge, appeal or avenue of complaint about procedures or outcomes. In that sense it is entirely questionable whether the mediation process delivers what the litigant may expect to be a form of substantive justice. However mediation is outcome driven, and looks to satisfy both sides insofar as that is possible. It seeks a result that both sides, if not desperately happy, can at least live with.

Who are the Mediators?

The National Mediation Helpline Mediators are all members of the accredited mediation provider organisations listed at www.nationalmediationhelpline.com They come from many different backgrounds and are all trained and experienced in helping people to settle their disputes. Most, but not all, are lawyers. Some specialise in the particular subject matter of the dispute in question.

Contact details are also available on leaflets available at all County court offices or by telephone at 0845 6030809. The Helpline website offers a very useful and comprehensive range of frequently asked questions. It has been set up by the Ministry of Justice (MoJ) in conjunction with the Civil Mediation Council (CMC) to provide information about mediation and access to mediators. It can answer general questions about mediation and put parties and their representative in touch with mediators through the providers supporting this scheme. The Helpline is attended between 8:30am and 6pm, Monday to Friday with the exception of Public Holidays.

How does it work?

A party or his or her lawyer can either complete the hard copy or downloadable application form or call the helpline on 0845 60 30 809 and information will be sought to ascertain how appropriate the dispute is for mediation. Once this information has been obtained, the National Mediation Helpline adviser will refer the request via email to one of the accredited mediation providers supporting the scheme. They in turn will contact the party or their representative by phone within one working day to discuss the dispute; if all parties agree to proceed with mediation they will be put in contact with a local mediator.

If the other party has not yet consented to mediation, the accredited mediation provider will contact them to discuss the possibility of mediation. If they agree to mediate the provider will assign a locally based mediator. If, however, the other parties do not agree to mediate the provider will inform the applicant party and close the file.

Once a mediator has been appointed they will contact the parties to arrange a suitable time and venue for the mediation meeting.

If a claim regarding the dispute has been issued at Court the claimant must at this stage inform the Court, in writing, that the dispute is going to be mediated.

At the agreed place and time all parties will meet. The mediator will usually speak to all parties together to reiterate the process. Parties will then split off into separate rooms so that the mediator can speak on a one to one basis with the parties.

During the mediation process, the mediator will be looking for common ground amongst the parties and will go back and forth between them discussing offers and proposals until an agreement has been reached. Once an agreement has been reached a mediation agreement can be drawn up and signed by all parties.

What are the possible outcomes of Mediation?

The NMH website sets out a number of ways in which disputes may be resolved and all parties must be in agreement on the settlement. This could be:

- paying compensation
- a refund
- an apology
- an explanation
- replacement goods/services
- a change in policy and/or behaviour

The mediator makes no decisions as to the type or value of the settlement – the parties are solely responsible for the outcomes.

If the dispute is settled, the claimant must inform the judge that an agreement has been reached. If the parties are able to inform the court that the case is settled more than a week before the final hearing then the hearing fee will be refunded in full – see page 108.

What happens if the parties cannot agree a settlement?

As is clear from the discussion above, mediation is not suitable for every dispute, but it can still help settle some of the issues even if the matter must proceed to trial.

If a claim has already been issued at Court, the parties must inform the judge that no agreement has been reached and the Court process will then continue.

Costs

The important feature of having a national service is that the fees charged are both fixed and relatively modest, particularly for Small Claims cases:

Amount you are claiming	Fees – per party	Length of session	Extra hours – per party
£5,000 or less – Small Claim*	£50 + VAT £100 + VAT	1 hour 2 hours	£50.00 + VAT per hour
£5,000 to £15,000 – Fast Track	£250 + VAT	3 hours	£84.00 + VAT per hour
£15,000 to £50,000 – Multi Track	£375 + VAT	4 hours	£93.50 + VAT per hour

*The mediator/mediation provider should agree in advance whether the Small Claim should be dealt with in one or two hours. For the one hour rate the option is available to facilitate settlement over the telephone if appropriate, and if the parties agree. See also page 177 – Free Mediation.

Counter Claims

There have been a few cases where the original claim has been in one band but with substantial counter-claims and counter counter-claims. These in theory can push disputes from one cost band to another e.g. original claim for £4,000 but c/c for £30,000 making an aggregate claim of £34,000.

Practical Tips for Parties to Mediation

Deciding to mediate

This raises two questions: should I agree to mediate (or ask the other side to do so); and if so, am I ready to mediate? The first is concerned with balancing the benefits and drawbacks of entering into the process, bearing in mind the court will generally support such a decision.

Much will depend on the value, strength and type of case in question. Other factors may include the type of relief a party is seeking from the court, and whether something more suitable could be negotiated by agreement. Speed, confidentiality and whether it is necessary to have a lawyer are other factors. If a party is in person he or she may have nothing very much to lose by at least trying it.

As to the issue of timing, this really goes to questions of preparation: does each side possess all the relevant facts, understand the contested issues and have had sight of the key documents? The first two are essential, the last only important if it is necessary for the mediator to understand the nature or detail of the dispute.

Preparation

Each party should prepare a short document which tells the mediator in a couple of paragraphs what the claim is about; what are the contested issues; what, if anything, is agreed; and what their case is on the contested issues. It is important that each side should then state what they want to achieve, and how best that might be achieved by a negotiated agreement. If possible the parties should state what they might be prepared to concede or give, even if this is conditional on some movement from the other side. If they have any particular concerns these may be aired.

This document or position statement for the mediation is sent by each side to the mediator in advance, and he or she can telephone the parties and their lawyers to discuss it before the appointment. Usually the parties will exchange their documents at the same time.

Writing the position statement is not a particularly easy task, but it will focus the mind of the writer on what the claim is really about, and what outcome would be acceptable to him or her. It should not be more than a few pages in length; perhaps between 2 and 3. If you consider the fee payable to the mediator for a Small Claims mediation it is obvious that no payment is made for pre-reading, and the less that needs to be considered the better.

For that reason it is usually unnecessary for the parties to prepare an extensive bundle of documents for the mediator. In particular it is usually unhelpful to have bundles of correspondence. If there are vital documents these may be brought, but they must be vital, for example a copy of any relevant contract the performance of which is being argued about.

Before the appointment the parties should prepare what they intend to say at the mediation. If a litigant is nervous he or she can prepare notes or read a prepared statement when invited to speak in any open session.

Preparing to Get the Best out of Mediation

- Work out the best you can hope for as an alternative to a settlement negotiated through mediation: the true cost to you of pursuing your claim to trial in terms of time and aggravation as well as the risk of losing.

- Work out equally your worst case scenario

- Look at the gap between these two positions to judge what offer you might accept or what you might make

- If you have a range of positions in mind work out how to justify the difference to the mediator

---

The Appointment

Attend the mediation hearing promptly. Allow time to travel, park and find where you are going if the venue is unfamiliar. Do not eat into the limited time available.

The mediator should introduce himself or herself and put the parties at their ease, usually in their own rooms, before calling everyone together for the opening session. Here the parties will be offered the opportunity to speak themselves. It should not be wasted. The parties should address each other directly. Do not speak towards the mediator – he or she is not a judge.

The mediation is an opportunity to say things that perhaps a court would not allow. In particular it is an opportunity to express to the other side how you feel about the subject matter of the claim, be it anger, frustration or some other unhappiness. Giving vent to feelings helps clear the air before the negotiations, and you may say something which the other side simply did not know or understand before.

Preparation also involves getting ready to deal with each of the issues, particularly being able to say why the opposing party is wrong. Having confidence in a position should enable you to project that to the other side.

Once each side has had their say the mediator will invite them to retire to separate rooms where he or she will visit each in turn and encourage the parties to speak freely to him in the knowledge that nothing said will be repeated to the other side without express permission.

Preparation for this stage is equally important. Each party should know what they are prepared to take and what to give before attending; they should be able to explain the difference if asked by reference either to the facts of the case or to their own personal interests. Their positions may well change during the mediation, but at the outset each side must have a clear idea of what they would like to achieve and what they could live with, if pushed, if they can not achieve their higher expectation. Remember that, in mediation, money is not necessarily everything, and both the parties and the mediator can come up with an entirely novel solution: this is a problem solving exercise, not one for the attribution of fault.

The mediator will privately discuss with them the parties' respective expectations and pass between them trying to find sufficient common ground to accommodate both. He or she will test parties' cases, test their resolve and look for innovative solutions in which he may draw upon the wider interests of the parties than just those which the court would look at.

The Conclusion

Mediation will either lead to an agreement at the end of the appointment, or fail because one party has walked out, or it may have run out of time. Even if no settlement is reached there may be agreement on some issues, including a reduction of the evidence necessary at trial. The parties should ensure that this agreement should apply in the further course of the litigation. If the mediation fails simply because of the effluxion of time, the parties should consider resuming on another occasion or using the mediation as a catalyst for further direct negotiations. In no case should the parties merely let the event pass without trying to derive some positive benefit from their participation. After all, they have paid for it.

CHAPTER 10

Other parts of the Civil Procedure Rules

Introduction   192

The overriding objective   192

The court's case management powers   193

Applications generally (including telephone hearings)   197

Statement of truth   200

Rules about service of the claim form and
    other documents   201

Summary judgment   204

The slip rule and correcting procedural errors   206

Time for complying with a judgment or order   207

Calculating time limits   207

Rules which are excluded in the Small Claims track   208

Other parts of the Civil Procedure Rules

Introduction

The Small Claims procedure is set out in Part 27, but that part does not exist in isolation from the other Parts of the Civil Procedure Rules. Some rules which would clash with the objectives of Small Claims case management are excluded. Of the other rules, some are of particular significance to Small Claims cases.

This book contains detailed references to various parts of the rules where appropriate. This chapter explains other rules which are most often encountered in the course of a Small Claims case. They are discussed here with reference to the way they are applied in Small Claims cases. This chapter also considers those rules that are specifically excluded in Small Claims cases.

The overriding objective

> The whole of Part 1 is set out in Appendix 6.

The Civil Procedure Rules are a procedural code with the overriding objective of enabling the court to deal with cases justly (rule 1.1).

Part 1 defines and expands on what "dealing with cases justly" means and how the procedural rules achieve this.

Practicality is a central part of case management. Underpinning every aspect of the rules is the emphasis on keeping things in proportion, and making sure that the cost of litigation is in proportion to the matters in dispute. This is achieved by effective case management, for example requiring the parties to set out their case in writing and restricting the hearing to relevant issues, including the limiting of cross examination. However, the disproportionate use of the court's resources is not a basis for a claim to be struck out, and the fact that there may be a larger claim in the background does not prevent parties from using the Small Claims track. For example *Madden* v *Pattini CC* [1999] 12 CL 53.

The Small Claims track itself is a proportionate way of dealing with disputes of limited financial value. The procedures in the rules must be applied by the court "expeditiously and fairly" (rule 1.1(2)(d)) and the parties are required to assist the court to further the overriding objective (rule 1.3).

Rule 1.4 spells out examples of ways in which the court can achieve the overriding objective by use of its case management powers.

The court's case management powers

Rule 3 gives the District Judge the powers to promote the overriding objective and manage cases effectively.

The court may:

(a) *extend or shorten the time for compliance with any rule, practice direction or court order (even if an application for extension is made after the time for compliance has expired);*

(b) *adjourn or bring forward a hearing;*

(c) *require a party or a party's legal representative to attend the court;*

(d) *hold a hearing and receive evidence by telephone or by using any other method of direct oral communication;*

(e) *direct that part of any proceedings (such as a counterclaim) be dealt with as separate proceedings;*

(f) *stay the whole or part of any proceedings or judgment either generally or until a specified date or event;*

(g) *consolidate proceedings;*

(h) *try two or more claims on the same occasion;*

(i) *direct a separate trial of any issue;*

(j) *decide the order in which issues are to be tried;*

(k) *exclude an issue from consideration;*

(l) *dismiss or give judgment on a claim after a decision on a preliminary issue;*

(m) take any other step or make any other order for the purpose of managing the case and furthering the overriding objective.

(rule 3.1(2))

When can the District Judge exercise these case management powers?

The District Judge can intervene and make directions about a Small Claims case at a number of stages including:

- if the papers are referred to the District Judge for comment by the court staff soon after issue (rule 3.2)
- when the District Judge reviews the claim and defence at the allocation stage (rule 26)
- at a preliminary hearing (rule 27.6)
- if any party writes to the court at any stage to bring any matter of procedure to the attention of the District Judge
- at any application hearing
- at the hearing itself.

Striking out

In considering whether to strike out a case the District Judge will consider whether a fair hearing is possible if the case were to continue.[1]

Claims and defences alike are liable to be struck out if they are plainly hopeless or mischievous. Such cases can be struck out at an early stage (rule 3.4 and the accompanying practice direction).

The District Judge will ensure that the management of the case is in proportion to the amount in dispute – if the case is plainly hopeless then to strike it out will save the parties the inconvenience of the hearing.

The practice direction to Part 3 sets out some suggestions for claims that might fall into this category namely:

- a case setting out no facts e.g. 'money owed £5,000'
- a claim or defence which is incoherent and makes no sense

---

1. A case will be struck out only where the default would result in it being unfair for the case to go to trial: *Biguzzi* v *Rank Leisure plc* [1999] 4 All ER 897, CA.

- a claim or defence which sets out facts, which even if true, do not amount to a legally recognisable case against the defendant
- a defence which is a "bare denial".

A poorly drafted claim or defence will attract the attention of the District Judge and may prompt the case to be "struck out". To avoid this, ensure the case is properly drafted from the outset by following the guidance on drafting in this book (see Chapter 11).

If a case is struck out it may be reinstated (see below – Relief against sanctions).

Civil Restraint Orders

A District Judge may strike out a claim on the basis that it is 'totally without merit'. In this event the District Judge will consider whether to make a civil restraint order. The usual rule is that no such order is made unless the claimant has made two claims which are struck out for this reason. The effect of a civil restraint order is to significantly limit the rights of the person from starting fresh claims. Rule 3.4(6) and rule 3.11 and the accompanying practice direction sets out the rules concerning civil restraint orders. These rules also apply to applications and to appeals.

Other sanctions

As well as striking out, the District Judge will consider other options for case management and will apply sanctions that are relevant to the case management problem in hand. For example any directions will be proportionate to the case but may involve

- making an order for costs (see also below under Relief from sanctions)
- if documents are not sent to the other side before the hearing and take the other side by surprise, then the District Judge may prevent them from being used in evidence
- if either party is unprepared at a hearing and as a result requests an adjournment, then the sanction may be that they pay the costs thrown away by the adjournment

- delay in bringing or pursuing a case may result in the party being deprived of interest
- requiring a party to clarify details of their case.

Relief from sanctions

If a party falls foul of the case management powers of the court then they can make an application for relief. The application must be supported by evidence (rule 3.10).

Note, however, that if the sanction is the payment of costs, the party in default may obtain relief *only* by appeal (rule 3.8 (2)).

Rule 3.9 sets out a non-exclusive list of circumstances which the District Judge will take into account when considering what relief, if any, is to be given, namely:

(a) *the interests of the administration of justice;*
(b) *whether the application for relief has been made promptly;*
(c) *whether the failure to comply was intentional;*
(d) *whether there is a good explanation for the failure;*
(e) *the extent to which the party in default has complied with other rules, practice directions, court orders and any relevant pre-action protocol;*
(f) *whether the failure to comply was caused by the party or his legal representative;*
(g) *whether the trial date or the likely trial date can still be met if relief is granted;*
(h) *the effect which the failure to comply had on each party; and*
(i) *the effect which the granting of relief would have on each party.*

Case management orders made on the court's own initiative

At any stage in the case the District Judge can make an order of his or her own initiative without notifying the parties in advance. If such an order is made, it must be accompanied by a statement notifying any party affected by the order that they can have the order varied or set aside. The order will specify when the application to vary or set aside must be made; often the period specified is seven days, but can be a different period (rule 3.3).

Applications generally

Basics

Applications should

- be made in writing and
- give the opposite party three days notice of the hearing

Overview

There should be little need for applications in a Small Claims case. The objective is for all the issues to be dealt with at a full hearing with the minimum of applications. There are, however, a number of situations where applications need to be made in Small Claims cases. For example, an application to transfer a case to another court, or an application for an alternative method of service. A formal application is also needed if a defendant wishes to add another party to the proceedings or if the defendant wishes to add a counterclaim after the defence has already been filed (see page 55).

Rule 23 sets out the general provisions for making applications. The party making the application is called the "applicant" and the party against whom the order is sought is the "respondent" (rule 23.1). The practice direction to Part 23 emphasises the need to make any application promptly (PD 23 para 2.7). In a Small Claims case this is especially important, because if there is delay the application is unlikely to be listed until close to the date of the hearing which may defeat the objective of the application.

The court form for making an application is the N244 (see Appendix 5). The use of the form is not obligatory (see PD 23 Rule 2.1) but is recommended; if the form is filled out fully, the application will be in good order. The court may accept the written application in any format, including a letter; but note the information which the application notice must include (see below).

The application notice must be sent to the other side at least three clear days before the hearing of the application (rule 23.7 (1) (b)) (see page 207 for rules about calculating time limits).

The application notice must set out what the applicant is seeking, plus brief reasons for making the application. If the application notice includes evidence or reasons then a statement of truth must be signed (see page 34). Evidence in support of the application must be served at the same time as the application notice (rule 23.7). A draft of the order sought should accompany the application notice (rule 23.7).

A fee will be payable to the court when issuing an application. The amount will depend on whether or not it is by consent. (For the fees payable, see Appendix.)

The District Judge has a wide discretion in dealing with applications, including:

- an application can be made verbally (Rule 23.3(2))
- applications can be made without giving notice to the other side (see below)
- the applicant can invite the District Judge to make the order without a hearing (see below)
- applications can be dealt with by consent
- the District Judge can reduce (or "abridge") the notice time to under three days.

Consent applications

A consent order will be given to the District Judge for approval but the final decision to grant the order will be made by the District Judge, the parties must tell the District Judge the reason for applying for the order by consent (PD23 para 10). An application made by consent attracts a lower court fee (see page 235).

Costs on applications in Small Claims cases

Any award for costs will be proportionate to the case, but the no costs rule does not apply to hearings that take place before allocation; however it does apply to hearings that take place after allocation (see page 124).

Hearing an application by Telephone

This section does not apply if both parties are unrepresented.

Applications can be heard by telephone and in certain courts most applications are heard in this way. Guidance for telephone hearings may be found on the court service website, based on procedures that have evolved through a pilot scheme. Readers should check for up to date information at www.hmcourts-service.gov.uk. We set out below a practical guide to telephone hearings in Small Claims cases presupposing there is only one claimant and one defendant. Rules about telephone hearings are set out in Part 23 and the accompanying practice direction.

- The court will inform the parties if the hearing is to be by telephone
- Unrepresented parties are not expected to make arrangements for the telephone hearing – these must be made by the party who has legal representation.
- If both parties have legal representation the applicant must make the arrangements for the hearing.
- The hearing takes place as a "three-way call" involving both parties and the District Judge. The telecom provider must be on a list of approved service providers who are identified on the court service website.
- The hearing is recorded by the telecom company.
- The District Judge will have before him or her the court file and must be sent any other documents, including draft orders, in good time for the hearing: **The deadline is 4.00p.m. on the last working day before the hearing.** Documents can be sent in by fax. All documents must clearly indicate the time and date of the hearing and be marked 'for urgent attention'.
- If a party objects to a hearing being conducted by telephone he or she must apply for a personal hearing. This application must be made at least 7 days before the telephone hearing and the usual application fee will apply.
- The court will aim for the hearing to take place at exactly the time notified on the hearing notice.

Applications without notice

In Small Claims cases, applications made without notice are rare, so they will not be discussed in detail here. An example of an application made without notice is one to extend the life of a claim form where service is difficult. An application without notice can be made if there is "exceptional urgency" or where the overriding objective would be furthered by such an application (for more detail see rule PD23 para 3).

A party who has not been told about an application can apply to have it varied or set aside but the application must be made within seven days (rule 23.10).

Orders without a hearing

The applicant can ask the District Judge to make the order without a hearing, and this will be done if appropriate (rule 23.8)(c)).

Statement of truth

> See page 35 which sets out the rules about statement of truth on the claim

> [I believe][the *claimant/defendant* believes] that the facts stated in this [claim][defence][application] [witness statement] are true

A Statement of case (including a defence) and a witness statement must be verified by a statement of truth (rule 22.1). Any **application** which is supported by evidence written on the application form must also be supported by a statement of truth (rule 22.1(3)).

Failure to verify a **witness statement** may result in the statement not being admissible in evidence (rule 22.3). However, a District Judge in a

Small Claims case has a wide discretion about the conduct of a hearing and the strict rules of evidence do not apply (rule 27.8(3)).

Failure to verify a **statement of case** means that it remains effective until it is struck out, but a party may not rely on the contents of a statement of case in evidence until it has been verified by a statement of truth (rule 22.2 and the accompanying practice direction).

The statement must be signed by the party personally, or by the party's legal representative (not a lay representative) (PD 22 para 3.1).

Proceedings for contempt of court may be brought against anyone who makes a false statement without an honest belief in its truth in a document verified by a statement of truth (rule 32.14).

Rules about service of the claim form and other documents

Overview

Basics

- The court will send the claim form by first class post to the address for the defendant which the claimant provides
- The claimant can elect to serve the proceedings instead of the court
- The claim form expires if it is not served within four months of issue

---

Part 6 sets out the provisions relevant to service of the claim form and other documents relevant to a case. What follows is a practical approach to the subject, designed to equip the reader with enough information to cover situations that commonly arise in Small Claims cases.

The court will serve the claim form and any other documents by first class post (for example applications and notices) unless

- the party on whose behalf the document is to be served notifies the court that he wishes to serve it himself (rule 6.3(b))
- the court orders otherwise (rule 6.3(d)).

If the claimant chooses to serve the claim form himself he must file and serve a certificate of service within 7 days (rule 6.14).

Address for service

Step 6 in Chapter 2 considers how to select the address for service on the defendant of the claim form.

When responding to the claim, the defendant may well provide the claimant with a different address for service, and the claimant and the court will then use the address nominated by the defendant.

The claimant must show an address for service on the claim form.

Deemed day of service

Rule 6.7 summarises the methods of service and the deemed date of service: see the Table below.

Method of service	Deemed day of service
First class post (or an alternative service which provides for delivery on the next working day)	The second day after it was posted.
Document exchange	The second day after it was left at the document exchange.
Delivering the document to or leaving it at a permitted address	The day after it was delivered to or left at the permitted address.
Fax	• If it is transmitted on a business day before 4 p.m., on that day; or • in any other case, on the business day after the day on which it is transmitted.
Other electronic method	The second day after the day on which it is transmitted.

Service by an alternative method

What if the claimant has lost touch with the defendant or the only known address is a place of work? In these cases the court can authorise service by other methods (rule 6.8).

The claimant must provide an address for service and persuade the District Judge that the papers will come to the attention of the defendant if they are sent to the alternative address.

Applications are generally made without notice and must be supported by evidence – the most practical way of presenting the evidence is to include all the detail in the application form and sign the statement of truth. The statement should give as much detail as possible about the problems of service, and state why the claimant is sure that by sending the papers to a particular address the defendant will come to know about them.

If the alternative service address is a place of work, the District Judge will probably order that the envelope is marked "private and confidential".

Delay in service of the claim form (extending the life of a claim form)

The claim form must be served within four months after issue, otherwise it expires (rule 7.5). If time is passing and the summons has still not been served, the claimant must apply to the court for an extension (rule 7.6).

Obtaining an extension is not a formality and the District Judge will need good reasons. The application must be supported by evidence, which is most conveniently set out on the application form and supported by a statement of truth. The evidence should state:

(1) all the evidence relied on
(2) the date of issue of the claim
(3) the expiry date of any rule 7.6 extension
(4) a full explanation as to why the claim has not been served.

These applications are made without notice and the District Judge will usually deal with them without a personal attendance being required.

Summary judgment

Overview

Part 24 contains the rules which govern applications for summary judgment namely judgment on an application without a final hearing on the basis that other side's case "has no real prospect of success". The issuing of an application for summary judgment in a Small Claims case may delay the final hearing of a case and may result in unnecessary costs being incurred. Although available in Small Claims cases it is a procedure more suited to more complex claims and those of higher financial value.

Summary judgment in Small Claims cases in detail

An application for summary judgment may offer a chance to get a judgment quicker than waiting for a Small Claims hearing, but also consider the disadvantages before proceeding.

- Once the application for summary judgment has been made the case is delayed because the defendant will not be obliged to serve a defence (rule 24.4(2).
- If the application fails, then the case will have to go to a full hearing, so the final determination will be delayed.
- Costs can only be awarded if the case has not already been allocated to the Small Claims track when the application is heard and then only if the award for costs would be "proportionate".
- The court fee for making the application is £65 – in addition to the fee payable on issue and any allocation fee.
- Whereas the procedural route to a Small Claims hearing is straightforward and the hearing itself relatively informal, an application for summary judgment under Part 24 involves complying with strict procedural formalities.

When considering whether to make an application for summary judgment in a Small Claims case the conclusion will usually be that it is better to get on with the case and have the matter determined at a final hearing.

The court may give summary judgment against a claimant or defendant if:

(a) it considers that –
   (i) the claimant has no real prospect of succeeding on the claim or issue ; or
   (ii) the defendant has no real prospect of successfully defending the claim or issue; and
(b) there is not other reason why the case or issue should be disposed of at a trial.

(Rule 24.2)

A claimant can make an application for summary judgment under this rule as soon as an acknowledgment has been filed, there is no need to wait for the defence. If the application is made before the defence, the defendant does not need to file a defence until the hearing of the application (rule 24.4).

Part 24 and the accompanying practice direction sets out the procedural steps, and these must be followed.

- The application must state that it is made under Part 24 and
- must state why the order is being sought and
- must identify concisely any point of law or any provision relied on and
- state that it is made because the applicant believes that the other side has "no real prospect of success".

In addition, the notice itself should draw to the attention of the other side to the orders that the court can make on the application (see below).

The rule provides that the court will give the parties at least 14 days notice of the hearing, that the person opposing the application should file evidence in response seven days before the hearing; and that the party making the application should file any counter evidence three days before the hearing.

Orders that the court can make on an application for summary judgment

The court can

- award judgment on the claim
- strike out or dismiss the claim
- dismiss the application
- make a conditional order (for example the court can order that a defendant is only allowed to defend on condition that he pays a sum of money into court to abide the event)
- award costs in the case and in the application.

Costs on an application for summary judgment

The "no costs" rule applies if the hearing takes place after allocation to the Small Claims track. If the hearing takes place before allocation note that the District Judge has a general discretion on costs and will consider the conduct of the parties including whether it was reasonable for a party to contest a particular issue (rule 44.3(5)).

If costs are awarded, the costs will be assessed there and then on the day of the application and will normally be payable within 14 days.

The slip rule and correcting procedural errors

(1) the court may at any time correct an accidental slip or omission in a judgment or order
(2) a party may apply for a correction without notice.

Rule 40.12

The correction of errors in judgments and orders is covered by rule 40.12 and the accompanying practice direction. If there is an obvious typing mistake or accidental error in an order then the court will deal with it informally and the matter should be raised initially by letter. If the mistake is somehow contentious or if the order is ambiguous or requires further explanation then an application should be made for the matter to be dealt with "on notice" – ideally before the District Judge who dealt with the original hearing.

In addition, the District Judge may take any steps necessary to remedy any procedural error (rule 3.10).

Time for complying with a judgment or order

The general rule is that any order, including orders for costs, must be complied with within 14 days (rule 40.11) *unless*

- the District Judge specifies a different time
- the proceedings or judgment are stayed
- a default judgment must be complied with immediately unless the judgment provides otherwise (rule 12.5(2))
- a judgment on an admission must be complied with immediately, or at the rate specified on the judgment (rule 14.5(9)).

Calculating time limits

The rules about calculating time periods are refreshingly clear (rule 2). The court will, where possible, put dates and a time of day into the orders rather than leaving the parties to count the number of days for themselves (rule 2.9).

Where the time limit is stated in a number of days this means "clear days".

Examples (taken from rule 2)

Notice of application must be served at least three clear days before the hearing

An application is to be heard on Friday 20th October. The last date for service is Monday 16th October

Particulars of claim must be served within 14 days of service of the claim form

The claim form is served on 2nd October. The last day for service of the particulars of claim is 16th October.

Weekends and bank holidays plus Christmas Day and Good Friday are not counted if the time period specified is five days or less (rule 2.8(4)).

In the case of a claim form posted on a Thursday or Friday, therefore, the deemed date of service will be no sooner than the following Monday or Tuesday; it will be later if a bank holiday intervenes.

> See also table on page 202 – deemed day of service

Rules which are excluded in the Small Claims track

Some parts of the civil procedure rules are specifically excluded from the Small Claims procedure (rule 27.2). If they were to apply, they could promote unnecessary applications and procedures and this would defeat the overall objectives of the Small Claims track.

Please refer to the table below. The notes in the right hand column correspond to the numbered paragraphs in the text that follows the table.

Rule	Details	Notes
Part 18	Further information (subject to the fact that the court may of its own initiative order a party to provide further information if it considers it appropriate to do so)	1
Part 31	Disclosure and inspection	2
Part 32	Evidence – except rule 32.1 (power of the court to control evidence)	3
Part 33	Miscellaneous rules about evidence	4
Part 35	Experts and assessors – except rules 35.1 (duty to restrict expert evidence) 35.3 (experts – overriding duty to the court) and 35.8 (instructions to a single joint expert)	5
Part 25	Interim remedies except as it relates interim injunctions	6
Part 36	Offers to settle and payments into court	7
Part 39	Hearings – except 39.2 – general rule hearing to be in public	8

Note 1 – Further information

Requests for information following the formal procedures set out in Part 18 have no place in the Small Claims track. The District Judge can order the parties to clarify their case by ordering a party to provide further information if it is appropriate to do so (rule 27.2(3). The determination of a case could hardly be fair if one party is taken by surprise by the other's case, or it is otherwise unclear.

Chapter 11 gives examples of possible statements of case and defences in Small Claims cases and suggests cost effective techniques of ensuring that the case is put fully to the other side before the hearing. In many cases, the parties will exchange witness statements before the hearing.

If these processes still leave the parties in the dark about how the other side puts their case then what can be done? Probably the best course will be to write to the opposite party and ask for an explanation of what their case is about. If the matter is then not clarified, turn up at the hearing and – if the case presented by the opposite party is a true "surprise" – then apply for an adjournment and an order for costs on the basis of the other party's "unreasonable behaviour". Parties who wrongly use this procedure against an unrepresented party could be considered as acting unprofessionally.

Note 2 – Disclosure and inspection

The essential matter to bear in mind with documents and the Small Claims track is "proportionality".

In the Small Claims track "documents" can mean any papers relating to a case including witness statements (see Chapter 5 directions). The whole procedure of disclosing documents before a hearing is simplified to sending the other side copies – usually 14 days before the hearing. All the parties need do in a Small Claims case is to produce documents which they "intend to rely on at the hearing". There are no lists of documents in Small Claims cases.

Therefore, a Small Claims case will not be burdened with the expense of the formal disclosure procedure. In the overwhelming majority of cases this works very well. Problems sometimes arise if one side has exclusive access to documents which the other side needs to win the case or if one side suppresses documents which damage their own case.

In this case, the party affected by such a problem has two possible remedies. *Either:*

- anticipate the problem and point out the concern in the allocation questionnaire – this should prompt the District Judge to order the other side to include the problem documents in the papers to be disclosed before the hearing (see Chapter 4) *or*
- If the problem does not emerge until two weeks before the hearing, write firmly to the other side and point out the omission – tell them that if the documents are not sent to you in good time for the hearing then an adjournment may be necessary. If the documents are not produced then this may be good grounds to apply for an adjournment and an award for costs on the basis of that parties unreasonable behaviour.

The District Judge can make an award for costs if the conduct of either side is unreasonable. Bear in mind the court's duty to deal with the case justly which includes managing the case in a way in proportion to the amount in dispute. The District Judge will not permit or require any exercise in disclosure that would put a disproportionate burden on any party. See also page 135 for what to do when documents are introduced at the final hearing.

Note 3 – Evidence

There are a number of formal provisions set out in Part 32 and the accompanying practice direction concerning the format of witness statements and how they are used at a hearing. None of these formalities applies to a case allocated to the Small Claims track. A witness statement will only be required in a Small Claims case if ordered by the District Judge. The statement can be relatively informal, since paragraph numbers and the width of the paragraphs or the size of the paper are not prescribed in a Small Claims case, as they are in other cases. A statement of truth should be added – see page 200 Statements of truth.

Pages 94 and 144 give some practical guidance on how to make the most of the witness statements.

The key with witness evidence, as with disclosure (see above) is "proportionality".

Power of the court to control evidence

(1) the court may control the evidence by giving directions as to –
(a) the issues on which it requires evidence
(b) the nature of the evidence which it requires to decide those issues
(c) the way in which the evidence is to be placed before the court
(2) the court may use its power under this rule to exclude evidence that would otherwise be admissible
(3) the court may limit cross-examination.

(Rule 32.1)

The court's power to restrict the introduction of unnecessary evidence extends to the hearing itself (see Chapter 7).

Note 4 – Miscellaneous rules about evidence

Much of rule 33 has to do with the subject of hearsay evidence. Guidance is given in Chapter 7 on the use of evidence at a Small Claims hearing.

Note 5 – Experts and assessors

Although many of the rules controlling expert evidence are excluded, four key elements are retained:

1. experts will not be allowed unless necessary (rule 35.1)
2. an expert in a Small Claims case must assist the court first and must not be partisan (rule 35.3)
3. the parties should instruct a joint single expert wherever possible (rule 35.8)
4. the District Judge can order the appointment of a single joint expert (rule 35.7).

See Chapters 5 and 7 for more about experts in Small Claims cases

Note 6 – İnterim remedies

Interim remedies can be granted as an emergency and in urgent cases "without notice"

It is important to note the distinction between an "interim" order which is made early in the case and remains in force until the hearing (or further order), and the "final" order which is made at the hearing.

The rules include a variety of interim remedies, including "search" orders "interim payments" and "accounts and enquiries". Each of these remedies can only be obtained if special rules are followed, and it would plainly be disproportionate in a case of limited financial value to get involved in complex legal procedures.

This limitation does not apply to an ordinary injunction that can be obtained in a Small Claims case on an interim basis. (For example, an order that someone removes scaffolding which is hanging over a neighbour's garden without permission). If considering applying for an interim injunction without notice then bear in mind that the injunction will only be granted in cases of real emergency or where there is a true impossibility of giving notice.

Note that in a Small Claims case a "final" order of *any type* can be obtained (rule 27.3).

Note 7 – Offers to settle and payments into court

Part 36 sets out formal rules about offers to settle and payments into court which are relevant to cases allocated to the fast track and multi-track. These rules usually have no place in cases allocated to the Small Claims track, because of the no costs rule, but it should be noted that there is a discretion under rule 36.2(5) for the court to order otherwise; something which is rarely done.

Instead of all the complexities of Part 36 the Small Claims track has its own simple rules for encouraging parties to settle. In brief, a party who unreasonably rejects an offer puts himself at risk of being ordered to pay costs under rule 27.14(3) (see Chapter 6).

Note 8 – Hearings

> Chapter 7 deals with the special rules for hearings in Small Claims cases

Small Claims hearings have a uniquely simplified method for hearings and the rules that apply to hearings in the fast track and multi-track do not apply.

Drafting rules and precedents in Small Claims cases

Introduction		217
1.	Letters before action (with examples)	218
2.	Sample letter to the court manager at the start of a case	220
3.	Brief description of type of claim (Samples)	221
4.	Statements of case including defences and counterclaims	222
	(a) Basic guidelines for preparation of a statement of case and defence	222
	(b) Detailing the claim	222
	(c) Detailing the defence	223
	(d) Reply to defence	224
	(e) Defence to counterclaim	224
	(f) Admission	225
	(g) Amendments	225
	(h) Interest	225
	(i) Statement of truth	225
5	The court's case management powers – a reminder	226
6	Techniques for setting out a Small Claims case (with some examples)	226
7	Calculation of statutory interest	236
8	Interest	237
9	Witness Statements	238
10	Notice of Appeal	239

11 Application to set aside   240

12 List of complaints   241

Drafting rules and precedents in Small Claims cases

Introduction

Modern litigation demands that documents used in the court process are set out clearly and with the minimum of jargon and legal language. Latin must not be used. It is vital that the case is set out clearly from the start. The benefits of the relative simplicity and speed of the Small Claims procedure will be lost if the case is changed or has to be clarified at the last moment. The case management powers of the court can be used to strike out a claim which is imprecise or not properly explained.

This book is a procedural guide and cannot aspire to explaining the legal matters relevant to claims which are heard on the Small Claims track. Litigants in person requiring guidance on whether to make a claim for a specific sum or how to defend a claim must seek legal advice. This can be accessed through solicitors, citizens advice bureaux, specialist books on particular types of claims (for example holiday claims) and consumer forums and specialist websites.

This chapter sets out the basic rules about preparation of statements of case relevant to Small Claims cases. The material which appears in this chapter does not, for example, cover in detail rules relevant to the preparation of personal injury cases, as these are rare in a Small Claims cases.

The examples that follow in the rest of the chapter give the reader an idea of what particular documents may look like. The objective is to give the reader an idea of how a case might be presented rather than setting out strict precedents. The examples cover:

Letters before action
Letter to the court manager at the start of the case
Brief description of type of claim
Statement of case including defences and counterclaims

Witness statements
Calculation of statutory interest
Witness statement
Application to set aside after failure to attend a hearing
List of complaints.

1. Letters before action

A letter before action may

- Prompt settlement before court action
- Be used later on as the statement of case

Letter before action: claiming a debt

Dear Mrs Jones

Re: Our invoice 98 764 for £550.00

I note that you have not yet paid our invoice dated 24 August, a copy of which I enclose for your reference. I have already phoned you about this more than once and although you promised to pay last week, the cheque has not arrived.

Unless I receive payment from you immediately, and in any event no later than close of business on Friday 7 October, I shall start a claim against you in the County Court without giving you any further warning.

When I have started the court action I shall be entitled to claim from you, in addition to the invoice, the court fee (£65) plus interest which is calculated at the rate of 8% per annum.

I do hope I will not be forced to issue proceedings against you and I look forward to receiving your cheque for £550 at once.

Yours truly

Letter before action: complaint to a holiday company

To: The Customer Services Manager
[name of holiday company] Limited

Dear Sir or Madam

Re: Our holiday, reference 34567GRK
Holiday dates 13 March 2007 to 1 April 2008

My wife and I have just returned from a "nightmare" holiday on the Greek island of Claxson with your company.

We were booked to stay in the Dormos holiday apartments (self catering) which was advertised in your 2007 brochure on page 45. The description of the apartments especially attracted us because it says the apartments are well away from the lively nightlife of the village and yet close to the beach. We told the agent when we booked that my wife is a light sleeper and she told us that the apartments would be ideal.

The Greek island is lovely. We have no complaints about that. But here is a list of complaints about the Dormos holiday apartments.

(a) There was a noisy disco by the swimming pool next to our room run by the owner's son. The music was not turned off until 2 o'clock in the morning.
(b) The bedroom was dirty and the tiles in the bathroom were cracked. We found cockroaches in the toilet pan (photos enclosed).
(c) Although the hotel was only about 50 yards from the beach, to get to it we had to cross a building site – in fact it was more of a junk yard because there wasn't much building going on and the half finished buildings were occupied by local teenagers taking drugs who left their mess and dirty bottles everywhere.
(d) Although we complained to your courier, she said she couldn't help, as it was company policy not to deal with customers' complaints until the end of the holiday.

My wife hardly slept a wink at night for the whole holiday and had to catch up with her sleep in the afternoons, this really spoilt the holiday for both of us as we had wanted to go sight-seeing during the days. We were both upset by the state of the room and I was so disgusted by the "building site" that I hardly went to the beach at all.

We spent £878.80 in total for this holiday and I want to claim a refund and compensation.

Please let me have your answer within 14 days otherwise we shall start a claim against you in the county court.

Yours faithfully

2. Letter to the court manager at the start of the case (suitable for any case)

Dear Sir or Madam:

I enclose

1. Form N1 plus copy
2. A cheque for [   ] in favour of H M Paymaster General.

Please issue the proceedings and [arrange for service on the defendant by post in the usual way] [return the summons when issued to me because I want to serve the documents myself].[1]

Yours truly,

---

1 The court will serve the claim form for you – personal service is an option but not usually necessary.

3. Brief description of type of claim

This is the box which has to be completed on form N1, which will be used to give the court staff an "at a glance" idea of what the case is about (see page 29). Here are some suggestions.

Unpaid debt
Holiday claim
Road traffic accident
Claim against tenant for unpaid rent
Claim against landlord for disrepair
Computer of unsatisfactory quality
Damaged goods
Unpaid consultant's fees
Unpaid accountant's fees
Repayment of personal loan
Payment of school fees
Refund of bank charges

4. Statement of case including defences and counterclaims

4(a) Guidelines for preparation of a statement of case and defence

---

Basics

- Failure to set out a claim or defence clearly can result in it being struck out
- The particulars of claim must be a concise statement of the facts relied on and, if possible, should be set out on the claim form
- A copy of any contract on general conditions which are relied on should be attached to the claim form
- The defence must be specific – stating exactly what is admitted/denied and which matters the defendant wants the claimant to prove
- The defence must set out any alternative version of events
- The claim, defence and any counterclaim must be verified by a statement of truth
- A claimant must file a defence to counterclaim to avoid a default judgment on the counterclaim.

4(b) Detailing the claim

The particulars of the claim must

- be a concise statement of the facts on which the claimant relies (rule 16.4(1)(a))
- include details of any interest claimed (rule 16.4(1)(b) and rule 16.4(2))
- include details of any alleged misrepresentation (PD 16 para 10.2(3))
- set out any facts relevant to mitigation of loss or damage (PD 16 para 10.2(8))

- specify any allegations of fraud or illegality (but see note 1 below) (PD 16 para 10.2(1) and (2))
- attach a copy of a contract if the terms are relied on (PD 16 para 9.3(1))
- attach a copy of any relevant conditions of sale (PD 16 para 9.3 (2))
- in a personal injury case include the claimant's date of birth and attach a medical report (PD 16 para 4)(but see note 2 below)
- be verified by a statement of truth (see page 34).

In addition the claimant may use the claim to

- refer to a point of law (PD 16 para 16.3(1))
- give the names of any witnesses (PD 16 para 16.3(2))
- serve any documents to support the claim (PD 16 para 16.3(3)).

Notes
1. See paragraph 4 of the practice direction to Part 16 for more detail of how to set out a claim for personal injury.

4(c) Detailing the defence

The defence must be more than a bare denial or it is liable to be struck out (see above). Every part of the claim must be considered (PD 16 para 11.2). It is practical to follow the same paragraph numbers as the claim so that nothing is missed out. Each separate defendant must file and serve their own defence.

If an allegation is not covered in the defence it will be taken as proved (rule 16.5(3)). However, if the defendant does not admit a money claim the claimant must still prove that the sums due are owing (rule 16.5(4)).

The defence must state precisely which allegations are:

- denied (rule 16.5(1)(a))
- admitted (rule 16.5(1)(c))
- not admitted or denied but the defendant requires the claimant to prove (rule 16.5(1)(b))
- if an allegation is denied, state reasons (rule 16.5(2)(a))
- set out the defendant's own version of events if different from the claimant's (rule 16.5(2)(b))

- if the defendant states that the claim is made outside a limitation period, define this (PD 16 para 16.1)
- note that all defences must be verified by a statement of truth (see Chapter 3).

In addition the defendant *may* use the defence to:

- refer to a point of law (PD 16 para 16.3(1))
- give the names of any witnesses (PD 16 para 16.3(2))
- serve any documents to support the defence (PD 16 para 16.3(3)).

Notes
– Refer to PD16 para 14 for matters which the defendant must deal with when defending a claim for personal injuries.

4(d) Reply to defence

A reply to defence is not usually needed because a claimant who does not file a reply to a defence is not taken to admit the matters raised in the defence (rule 16.7).

4(e) Defence to counterclaim

Counterclaims fall into two categories – each of which needs different treatment when preparing a defence

Type 1

Counterclaims which simply shift the blame for the matter back onto the claimant. In this type of counterclaim there is one set of disputed facts, which relates to the claim and counterclaim. Typically this is the type of counterclaim raised in a road traffic case.

The defence which this type of counterclaim requires is straightforward (see page 230 for an example).

Type 2

Some counterclaims raise a whole new set of facts and matters. An example would be where a plumber sues for unpaid charges and is then met by a counterclaim alleging a range of defects to the work. These cases need a full defence to counterclaim, which should be drafted with all the care of a defence to a claim.

4(f) Admission

The benefit of an admission is that it narrows the amount in dispute and this will reduce the amount of work needed to bring the case to a final conclusion. The terms of the admission should indicate the points that will be raised when the court decides the amount payable to the claimant. For an example, see page 229.

4(g) Amendments

Once a statement of case has been served it can only be amended with the permission of the court or with the consent of the other side (rule 17.1). In a Small Claims case the "no costs" rule means that the amendment will not usually attract a penalty in costs unless the amendment can be classed as "unreasonable behaviour" (rule 27.14(2)(d)). If a case is amended without warning, or close to the hearing date, and the other side is put at a disadvantage as a result, then this may well force an adjournment and the party making the amendment is likely to have to pay the costs of the adjournment. The version of the case before amendment which does not have to be shown, unless the District Judge so orders. The fact that the case has been amended should be written on the amended case (see PD17).

4(h) Interest

Interest must be fully set out, whether it is claimed "pursuant to statute" or under a contract. Page 236 sets out how to calculate statutory interest, and pages 34 and 35 discusses interest on commercial debts. There are special rules about claiming interest in personal injury cases which is outside the scope of this book.

4(i) Statement of truth

This is covered in more detail on page 35 and 200.

5 The court's management powers – a reminder

Attention is drawn to page 193 (The court's management powers) and the power of the court to strike out a case which is vague or poorly explained.

The sort of case which might be struck out, or the proceedings stayed, under the court's management powers, may include the following.

- "Money owed £5,000".
- "The defendant is not liable to the claimant as claimed, or at all".
- A case which is incoherent or makes no sense.
- A case which sets out a coherent set of facts but those facts, even if true, do not disclose any legally recognisable claim against the defendant.
- Claims which are vexatious, scurrilous or ill-founded.

The guidelines for detailing the claim and the defence should be followed to prevent a case being struck out

6 Techniques for setting out a Small Claims case (and some examples)

In many Small Claims cases, the statement of case should be short enough to fit on the claim form. In other cases, a document which is already in existence (for example an invoice) can be attached to the claim form to avoid having to repeat all the details on the claim form.

Three styles of presentation are suggested:

Style 1   keeping the style short and simple to fit on to the forms provided

Style 2   using attachments effectively

Style 3   using clear, informal, specially drafted particulars.

Style 1 – Short and simple

This style is ideal for debt claims, but it can also be used for slightly more complex cases.

Example – claim by landlord for unpaid rent and service charges

Particulars of claim (Form N1).

1. The Defendant is the Claimant's tenant of Flat 3, 23 Green Gardens, London N6 under a long lease.
2. The Claimant's claim is for unpaid rent and other charges due under the lease amounting to £843.58 according to the Claimant's invoice dated 7 June 2007.
3. The Claimant claims in addition interest[2] pursuant to the lease at 4% above the base rate of National Westminster Bank plc which amounts to £14.20 to date and mounts at the daily rate of 25p until judgment or sooner payment.

I believe that the facts stated in this claim are true

Signed *landlord's name*

Defence (Form N9B)

I dispute the claim because I paid all the rent and service charges by cheque last week and I have checked with my bank and the cheque cleared 29 July 2007[3]

I believe that the facts stated in this claim are true

Signed *tenant's name*

---

2   Note: this is an example of pleading interest under a contract.
3   Note: this is an example of a "states paid" defence (see Chapter 3).

Example – claim against garage for negligent repairs

Particulars of Claim (Form N1)

The Claimant took his Renault car registration R95 OYI in for a routine service at the Defendant's garage on 6 May 2008. During the service the wheel hubs were damaged. This was the Defendant's fault.

The Claimant has had an estimate for the repairs in the sum of £800 plus VAT to have the wheel hubs replaced and claims this sum from the Defendant as compensation.

> The claimant believes that the facts stated in this claim are true
>
> Signed *Claimant's solicitor*

Defence (Form N9B)

We discovered the damage to the wheel hubs but we did not cause it. They were already damaged when the car was brought in. Our mechanic Mr Patel will come to court as a witness to confirm this. We deny the claim.[4]

> I believe that the facts stated in this defence are true
>
> Signed *Proprietor of garage*

Style 2 – Using attachments

If the information to set out the case is already prepared it can be used as it is and simply attached to the claim form.

Example – Holiday claim

Particulars of claim

We went to Greece on holiday but it was a disaster because of the Defendant's failure to provide the holiday we paid for.

---

4 The defence, although short, is to the point and quite adequate.

We have written to the Defendant but they ignored our claim.
Our claim is as set out in the letter[5] to the Defendant dated 4 April, a copy of which is attached.
We claim a refund and damages.

> I believe that the facts stated in this claim are true
>
> Signed *Claimant's name*

Admission (on Form N9C)

The defendants accept that they are responsible for the various problems outlined in the case and will not contest liability. However, the claim for the refund and damages is excessive; the claimants still had excellent value for money for their holiday (which was sold to them at budget rates) and enjoyed a lot of the holiday. The defendants will contest the amount claimed at the hearing.

Example – Claim for unpaid professional fees

Particulars of the Claim (Form N1)

The Claimant's claim is for £2,301.94 being the unpaid cost of accountancy services rendered by the Claimant to the Defendant in accordance with the attached statement of account[6] which is dated 19 February 2006.

The Claimant claims interest[7] under Section 69 of the County Court Act 1984 at the rate of 8% per annum calculated from 19 February 2006 to the date of issue, which is £xxx and continuing until payment or the date of judgment at a daily rate of 50p.

---

5 Note: the letter in this example is the "letter before action" which is on page 219.
6 The attachment here is the Claimant's computerised printout, which shows the running state of various unpaid invoices. There is no point having it all typed out again.
7 This is an example of how to claim statutory interest (see page 236 for notes of how to calculate the interest).

> I believe that the facts stated in this claim are true
>
> Signed *claimant's name*

Defence and counterclaim (to claim for unpaid professional charges)

The accountant is not entitled to this money because he did not do our accounts on time. The accountant was negligent. We attach a copy of a letter from our new accountant which confirms the negligence.[8] We had to pay a penalty of £1,000 to the Inland Revenue.[9]

Counterclaim

Reimbursement of the money paid to the Inland Revenue. We paid £1,000 in June 2007.

> We believe that the facts stated in this claim are true
>
> Signed *Defendant's name*

Defence to counterclaim

The claimant denies the defendant's counterclaim because he acted professionally and competently throughout. He was not negligent – the letter attached to the defence gives an incomplete and biased account of the matter.

---

8   Although fairly brief, these particulars are just enough to alert the claimant's accountant to the nature of the negligence claim against him.

9   The defendant will need the permission of the District Judge to call expert evidence in this case but it is likely that the permission will be granted.

Style 3 – Specially drafted particulars

Example – Road traffic case

IN THE HIGHGATE COUNTY COURT   CASE NO HE...

B E T W E E N

Lauren Verdi (female)   Claimant

and

[name of the defendant company]   Defendant

PARTICULARS OF CLAIM[10]

Introduction

1. The accident happened on 5 June 2007 at about 6pm at the junction of Mill Lane and Silver Street in Highgate. The junction is controlled by traffic lights.

2. The claimant was driving her Ford Escort registration H42 DWQ and the Defendant's vehicle was a white Renault van registration R99 RIT. The claimant does not know the name of the man who was driving the defendant's vehicle. It was daylight, and the weather conditions were good.

About the accident

3. The claimant was in the inside lane at the traffic lights in Silver Street and indicated to turn right. There was no vehicle in the other lane. As she was turning right, across the junction, the defendant's van crashed into the driver's side of the claimant's car.

4. A sketch of the scene of the accident follows on the next page.

5. The accident was the defendant driver's fault. He was negligent because he was not looking where he was going and misjudged his turn at the junction.

---

10 There is hardly anything less useful in a Small Claims case than a list of possible "standard" allegations of negligence taken from a precedent book, when only one or two of the paragraphs have any relevance at all the accident in question. Particulars of the type shown should make it plain to the defendant exactly what case will have to be met at the hearing.

6. The claimant needs her car for work and had to hire a car whilst her car was being repaired. The car hire quoted is the cheapest that could be found.

Details of damage

Cost of repairs	£1,092.63
Car rental when car being repaired	£253.60
Total	£1,346.23

The claimant also claims interest [precedent on page 229, statutory interest].

> The claimant believes that the facts stated in this claim are true
>
> Signed *Claimant's solicitor's name*

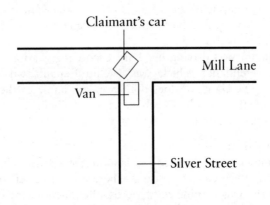

Sketch plan[11]

---

11 The sketch plan is less than perfect, and a lot more information could usefully be included by the addition of traffic lights, arrows and other notes. Two sketches, one showing the position of the vehicles before and the other after the accident could also be helpful. However, despite its shortcomings, a simple sketch is better than nothing at all. Photographs will often provide good information about the scene of the accident and make an elaborate sketch plan unnecessary. Prints of any photographs must be sent to the other side usually two weeks before the hearing in accordance with the directions given by the District Judge when the case was allocated to the Small Claims track.

DEFENCE AND COUNTERCLAIM

1. The defendant agrees with paragraphs 1 and 2 of the defence
2. the claimant's account of the accident is wrong. The claimant pulled out into the defendant's path without warning and she is to blame for the accident.

COUNTERCLAIM

3. The accident was the claimant's fault (see para 2)
4. the defendant has suffered the following losses
   (a) repair to van £576.95
   (b) loss of profit while van is being fixed (3 days at £150 per day) £450.

DEFENCE TO COUNTERCLAIM

The claimant disagrees with all of the defence apart from the admissions. The claimant puts the defendant to strict proof of its losses.

Example – personal injury case

PARTICULARS OF CASE

1 On 15 December 2007, at about 9 o'clock in the morning, the claimant was riding her bicycle along Silver Street in Highgate in an Easterly direction when she was knocked off and fell into the road when the defendants driver opened his door into her path.
2 The accident was the defendant's driver's fault because he should have looked to see if it was safe to open the van door and he failed to do so, or at least failed to take sensible precautions to prevent the accident.
3 The claimant has as a result suffered the following loss and damage.

Particulars of personal injury[12]
The claimant's date of birth is 9th March 1961

She grazed her right knee and had painful bruising on her right arm. The graze healed after about two weeks and the arm was sore for about ten days. Full details are set out in the letter from the claimant's GP which is attached.

---

12 The maximum that can be recovered for an expert's report is £200 in a Small Claims case, so the letter from the GP is a suitable way of providing medical evidence in this small claim.

Particulars of other losses
Ruined jeans and jacket (cost of replacement: £95).
Broken watch (cost of replacement: £29.50).
One day off work (loss of wages: £60).
Repairs to bicycle (£120).

And the claimant claims
Damages for personal injury limited to £1,000 including compensation for the other losses detailed above, plus interest to be assessed.

> I believe that the facts stated in this claim are true
>
> Signed *Claimant's name*

Example – defective goods

PARTICULARS OF CLAIM

1. The defendant's company sells computers; it advertises its goods in newspapers and magazines, and customers buy the computers over the telephone.
2. On 21 February 2007, the claimant called the defendant after seeing an advert in the *Highgate Daily News*. The claimant spoke to a salesman called "Mike" and told him that he wanted a computer which would:

   • enable him to do banking at home on the internet
   • enable him to manipulate photos taken on his digital camera
   • be good for running computer games
   • be supplied ready to use.

3. The salesman told the claimant that their "Top Dog" computer would be suitable for all these things. On this basis the claimant paid the defendant £975 (including VAT and delivery) for a computer and it was delivered to him on 12 March 2007.
4. When the computer arrived it was in eight different boxes and it took the claimant and his son five hours to get it working. The instructions supplied were useless.

5. The computer is not of satisfactory quality and does not match the description given by the salesman, and the salesman misrepresented what the computer would be like because:

- the modem is too slow to make home banking possible
- there is insufficient RAM memory to run the "Photomanipulate" program
- the resolution of the monitor spoils the computer games
- the computer was not supplied ready to use.

6. The claimant therefore claims a refund for the price paid and damages plus interest to be calculated by the court.

I believe that the facts stated in this claim are true

Signed *John Snapper*

Dated

Example – Unpaid school fees

HIGHGATE COUNTY COURT   **CASE NO HE**

B E T W E E N

The Sacred Heart Junior School   Claimant

and

Mrs Maureen Adaya   Defendant

PARTICULARS OF CASE

The claimant claims the sum of £1,542 being one term's school fees. The defendant's son, Darren, was registered at the school in Autumn 2006 and paid one term's school fees in advance. The defendant told the claimant in December 2006 that Darren would be leaving the school and not returning in January 2007.

The claimant's terms and conditions (a copy of which are attached)[13] make it clear that one full term's notice must be given otherwise fees must be paid in lieu.

The claimant's rely on the decided case of *Mount* v *Oldham Corporation CA* [1973] 1 All ER[14].

I believe that the facts stated in this claim are true

Signed *Dawn Jones (School Administrator)*

Dated

7. Calculation of statutory interest

This section offers a guide to calculating interest – this applies to statutory interest only, which is currently simple interest at 8% per annum. A precedent for the wording of the interest claim can be found as part of the precedent on page [   ].

Step 1

Count the number of days (N) between the date when the debt was payable and the date of the preparation of the claim. (Hint: Some diaries conveniently give a number to each day of the year and this number appears discreetly at the bottom of the page – finding this number will save a lot of counting!)

Step 2

Work out the annual interest (A) by multiplying the total debt (D) by 8 and dividing by 100

$$A = D \times 8/100$$

---

13 See page 223 for the requirement to attach terms and conditions to a particulars of case.
14 Case references and law can be set out in a statement of case.

Step 3

Work out the daily interest rate (R) by dividing A by 365

$$R = A/365$$

Write this figure down; (it is needed to put in the claim on the summons).[15]

Step 4

Multiply the daily rate (R) by the number of days (N); the answer is the total interest to the date of drafting the summons

$$\text{Total interest} = R \times N.$$

8. Interest

(a) claim for statutory interest see page 229 for appropriate wording
(b) claim for contractural interest see page 227 for appropriate wording
(c) claim for interest under the Late Payment of Commercial Debts (Interest) Act 1998 see page 33 for when such interest can be claimed.

The claimant claims interest under the Late Payment of Commercial Debts (Interest) Act 1998 at the rate of [*add percentage – official dealing rate of the Bank of England (the Base Rate) + 8%*] from [*the date when interest started to run*] to [*the date you are issuing the claim*] in the sum of £[   ] and continuing at the same rate up to the date of judgment or earlier payment at the daily rate of [*enter the daily rate of interest*]

---

15 Hint: If the daily rate is more than £1.10 then something has gone wrong, because the daily rate of interest on a claim of £5,000 is £1.09.

9. Witness statements

Witness[16] statement (road traffic case)

1. My name is George Green. I work for Verdant Ices and I drive an ice cream van.
2. On 5th June 2007 at about 6pm I was in Highgate village. It was a warm evening and I had been selling ices to people near Kenwood House.
3. The weather was clear and dry.
4. As I came up to the junction with Mill Lane I indicated to turn right. There was a lady in a red car on my right (offside), she was obviously going to turn left
5. Suddenly and without warning the lady cut in front of me, turning right into the path of my van
6. I tried to avoid the crash but could do nothing. She hit the front of my van and damaged it.
7. I took some photos of the damage the day after the crash and they will be produced in court.
8. After the accident the lady was very upset as she would be because it was her fault. She gave me her name and address and I gave her mine.
9. The van has been repaired through my boss' insurance company. I believe that the facts stated in this witness statement are true

I believe that the facts stated in this witness statement are true

Signed *George Green*

Date

Witness statement (contract dispute)

1. My name is Peter Hall. I am a butcher, I specialise in chickens.

---

16 In the context of a court action the term "witness" means anyone who gives a statement at a hearing. This includes the parties themselves plus any bystanders or others who can give evidence about the case.

2. Between 2001 and 2007 I did a lot of business with the defendant. He would sell me chickens and I would sell them in my shop. He is a butcher as well. Sometimes I would let him have meat for sale if I had too much to sell. We helped each other out. We were friends.
3. I kept a note in a book of the chickens I gave to the defendant to sell. I will bring the book to court with me but copies of the pages with the defendant's account on it are at pages 3, 4, 5 and 6 of my bundle of documents.
4. The defendant paid for the chickens he had from me when he had money. I got odd payments. Sometimes weekly, sometimes more often. I kept a note of the money he paid in the book and these notes are on pages 7 and 8.
5. In 2007 the defendant went out of business. He carried on clearing his debt but he still hasn't paid it all.
6. In November 2007 I got tired of waiting for payment and sent him an invoice (page 9). He has not paid the invoice.
7. On 5th December 2007 the defendant wrote me a letter (page 10 and 11). What he says in the letter is rubbish, if he had kept proper records as I have he would know that he still owes me £2,543.00.
8. I had to issue the court case because the defendant would not pay.

I believe that the facts stated in this witness statement are true

Signed *Peter Hall*

Date

10. Appeal

Grounds for appeal to be included in section 7 of form 161

(*Note – the detail to be included in this section must set out fully* each and every *ground of appeal – the example below is brief for illustrative purposes only.*)

The District Judge's decision was wrong because the evidence was that the defendants had inspected the section of road in question every 3 months; the District Judge accepted the defendants evidence on this point and it was therefore irrational of him to conclude that the defendants had failed to discharge their duty to inspect under section 58 of the Highways Act 1980.

> Refer to Chapter 8 for the grounds for appeal and the documents needed in support. The appellant must complete all sections of Form N 161 which includes notes for guidance

11. Application to set aside (rule 27.12)

IN THE HIGHGATE COUNTY COURT   CASE NO HE

B E T W E E N

Ian Hobbs   Claimant

and

Brenda Lythe   Defendant

_____

APPLICATION TO SET ASIDE

_____

The defendant applies for the judgment made by District Judge Faulty on 14 June to be set aside. The defendant went away for a two-week holiday on 13 May with her son. Unfortunately, her son broke his leg and as a result they did not return until 15 June. The defendant then discovered that the case had been heard on 14 June and she had not received the notice of hearing that was posted to her on 14 May. A copy of the tickets and a letter from the tour company confirming the actual dates of travel are attached.

I believe that the facts stated in this application
are true

Signed *Brenda Lythe*

Dated

12. List of complaints[17]

IN THE HIGHGATE COUNTY COURT CASE NUMBER   HE...

Dispute Steven Mishini and Tony Francis (Toni's Car Repairs)

List of complaints

Claimant's complaint	Defendant's comments
Oil leaking from under the car – inconvenience claimed	A nut was loose. We apologised for this and the matter was rectified the next day
Brakes squeaky – for new brake pads including fitting cost will be £60	Not a fault
The clutch is slipping – I have had an estimate of £150 for repair from another garage	This had nothing to do with the service – Mr Mishini needs a new clutch and we would be happy to fit one at his expense
There is a rattle under the bonnet which was not there before the service – I do not know what the fault is so cannot give an estimate	We know nothing about this
The windscreen wiper was damaged by the defendant and I claim £19.96 as the cost of replacement	We accept this and will pay the Mr Mishini £19.96 to cover this

17 In this example both sides have made their comments on the list before the hearing – a useful way of clarifying points in dispute in variety of cases

Claimant's complaint	Defendant's comments
The car was returned dirty with oil on the driver's seat belt which marked my new jacket. I paid £25 to have the car cleaned by a clean-a-car and £5 dry cleaning	We are a garage not a valet service and we deny that the inside of the car was dirty

Signed ....   Signed ....

Claimant   Defendant

Date ....   Date ....

CHAPTER 12
Enforcement of Small Claims Judgments in the County Court

Preliminary	244
– Interest	244
– Finding out about a debtor's assets	245
– Order to obtain information	247
– Register of County Court Judgments	247
– Bankruptcy and company insolvency	248
– Warrant of execution	249
– Third Party Debt proceedings	249
– Attachment of earnings	250
– Charging order on land	250
– Charging order on securities	250
– Order for sale	251
– Timescale for enforcement	251

Enforcement of Small Claims judgments in the County Court

Preliminary

Although this short chapter on enforcement appears at the end of the book there would be a respectable argument for placing it at the beginning. There is no point in pursuing a case through the Small Claims procedure, securing a judgment, and then being frustrated because the defendant has insufficient funds to meet the judgment. A party embarking on litigation should find out in advance if the other side has funds with which to pay.

This chapter offers some practical tips on how to investigate the ability of a company or an individual to meet a judgment – most of which can be done before starting the case. It also offers a simple overview of the most useful methods of securing payment through the court system. The initiative for enforcement comes from the judgment creditor and not from the judge or the court. All the steps for enforcement involve payment of court fees, filling out forms and some delay.

The court service offers leaflets which will assist with the procedural steps to be followed and these are available on line at www.hmcourts-service.gov.uk

This chapter is therefore not a procedural guide, rather an overview of the options available.

Interest

Interest does not run on judgment debts enforced in the County Court for £5,000 or less.

Finding out about a debtor's assets

There are a number of sources of information available to members of the general public. The most important are set out in the table below.

Name of organisation	Information about	Contact details	Fees payable
DVLC Swansea	Registered keeper of vehicle **But note** this may not be the legal owner if the car is on finance (see HPI equifax)	Enquiries in writing only on form V888 – phone 0870 2400010 to request a form	£5.00
Electoral Roll	Discloses current and past residents at a given address	Local town hall and libraries upon personal attendance	Free
HPI Equifax	Will check if a vehicle is stolen, has been written off or is on finance	Enquiries answered over the phone (open daily) on 01722 413434	£39.95 by telephone; £35.95 online – payment by credit card
Land Registry	Provides the name of the registered owner of any house or land and details of any mortgages	Local land registry – contact HM Land registry HQ on 020 7917 8888 for an explanatory leaflet 15 and form 109	£4.00 (to include the cost of obtaining the title number)
Local Bankruptcy County Court	Whether a bankruptcy petition has been issued against a judgment debtor	Contact the bankruptcy County court relevant to the address of the judgment debtor	£5.00
Land Charges Registry	Whether a person is bankrupt	Search Section, Land Charges Registry, Burrington Way, Plymouth PL5 3LP 01752 636666	By post on form K16 – £1 per name (account holders can transact by telephone – £2 per name)

Name of organisation	Information about	Contact details	Fees payable
Companies House	Information about a company, including filed accounts and whether or not a company is in liquidation – free	Crown Way, Cardiff CF14 3UZ 029 2038 0801/ 0870 3333686	Registered office search is without charge; filed accounts and other information, depending on what is required is £9.00 (first set, £2.50 thereafter). Payment can be made by credit card
Registry Trust Limited	Register of county court judgments	Enquiries in person to RTL 173–175 Cleveland Street, London W1P 5PE	Searches may be made in person or on-line or by post using the form accompanied by the appropriate fee. The fee structure is still based on a search against a single name or trading name at an address or against a Limited Company. It now allows a discount where a search is required against the same details on more than one section of the Register of Judgments, Orders and Fines (RJOF) for England and Wales, and/or one of the other registers held by Registry Trust. A search on one RJOF section or any other register is £8.00. Two sections and/or other registers is £16.00. Three sections and/or other registers is £20.00. Four sections and/or other registers is £25.00. Five or more sections and/or other registers is £30.00.

Name of organisation	Information about	Contact details	Fees payable
Local county court (only available after judgment)	Existing attachment of earnings orders	Apply in writing to the County court on Form N336	Free
Local county court (only available after judgment)		Application for order to obtain information	£40.00

Order to obtain information

This is not a direct method of enforcement, but a way in which the court can assist in investigating the assets of the judgment debtor. The judgment debtor is summonsed to court to be questioned by a senior court officer or the District Judge about his or her assets. A manager of a company can be summonsed to answer questions about the company's assets. If the judgment debtor does not cooperate, the matter may be referred to a Circuit Judge, who can make an order for the judgment debtor's committal to prison.

The procedure is effective in investigating the judgment debtor's assets and the inconvenience it can cause is sometimes enough to prompt the judgment debtor into payment.

Register of County Court Judgments

This is not an enforcement method but the system can result in payment to the creditor and use of the system can alert a claimant in advance that the debtor has a history of bad debts (see table at page 246).

The *Register of County Court Judgments* is operated by Registry Trust Limited (for contact details see the table on page 246) which keeps a record of certain judgments against the name of the judgment debtor. The effect of registration is to make it difficult for the judgment debtor to get credit, for example to get a loan to buy a car or to get a mortgage. A judgment debtor may decide to pay a judgment so that it is marked as "satisfied" on the register and to help him or her get credit.

Judgments which are registered include:

- any default judgment (including a judgment on admission)

- a judgment after a hearing which is payable by instalments
- a judgment after a hearing when the money is not paid and the judgment creditor issues enforcement or oral examination.

A registration is cancelled if judgment is set aside (but see page 170 concerning credit repair applications) and is marked as satisfied when it is paid in full. A fee of £10 is payable for a certificate of satisfaction.

Defendants are warned about the possibility of a judgment being registered in the response pack which they receive with the claim form (Form N1C).

Bankruptcy and company insolvency

Although bankruptcy is available for debts of £750 and more, it rarely results in payment to ordinary creditors. A judgment creditor, even the creditor who starts the insolvency action is not a "preferential" creditor and must take a share in any assets with other ordinary creditors, but only after those with security (e.g. mortgagees) have been paid, and after payment of outstanding tax and the fees and expenses of the receiver in bankruptcy.

A statutory demand is the first step to bankruptcy against an individual and this is prepared and served without any court involvement. A statutory demand can be served as soon as the debt is due and a judgment is not necessary. If the debtor who is an individual disputes the claim, he or she can apply for the statutory demand to be set aside. The bankruptcy court will halt the bankruptcy if there is any dispute about the sum outstanding. It can be relatively easy for a debtor to have a statutory demand set aside and the process can result in an order for costs being made against the creditor.

The winding up procedure against companies also starts with a statutory demand. There is no set procedure to set aside a statutory demand against a company, and if the debt is disputed, the case is argued after the presentation of the petition.

The court fees and sums payable to the official receiver by way of deposit are considerable and will deter most creditors pursuing a Small Claims judgment via the bankruptcy or insolvency route.

Warrant of execution

The County Court bailiffs can enforce any judgment up to £5,000 by the seizure and sale of the judgment debtor's goods. Permission to issue a warrant of execution is needed if the judgment debt is more than six years old.

Unless the District Judge orders otherwise the bailiff gives the judgment debtor seven days notice of execution action. Thereafter, the bailiff attends at the judgment debtor's premises and usually invites the judgment debtor to sign a "walking possession" agreement. The judgment debtor promises not to remove the goods in exchange for being given a chance to pay the debt in full. If the debt is then not paid, the goods are removed and sold at auction.

If anyone else claims that the goods seized belong to them and not to the judgment debtor they can issue "interpleader proceedings". The bailiff cannot execute the warrant against items which are on hire purchase, including cars and household furniture. The bailiffs cannot remove any items which the debtor needs, including vehicles, for personal use in his or her employment, or to satisfy the basic domestic needs of the debtor and his or her family.

If the judgment is £1,000 or more the enforcement can be transferred to the High Court for enforcement by the High Court Sheriffs.

Third Party debt order

This is an action to intercept a debt owed to the judgment debtor by someone else and to get the money paid to the judgment creditor direct.

The most usual debts intercepted in this way are credit balances in bank and building society accounts and trade debts owed to the judgment debtor. The method of enforcement is not available against an account or debt due to the judgment debtor jointly with someone else.

The 'order to obtain information' procedure can be used to obtain details about a person's bank and building society accounts. If the judgment debtor has previously paid by a cheque which was not met on presentation this may be a clue that the account does not hold sufficient funds. Any third party holding the debtor's funds can deduct up to £55 for their own expenses before handing the money over to the judgment creditor.

Attachment of earnings

This method of enforcement is available against judgment debtors who are in employment. A sum of money is sent weekly or monthly straight to the judgment creditor direct by the judgment debtor's employer. The procedure is in two parts. The court requires the judgment debtor to fill out a form setting out details of his or her earnings and outgoings (a statement of means). If this is not completed the judgment debtor can be ordered to attend court to give the information. Failure to co-operate completely in this process could result in the judgment debtor being imprisoned.

The second part involves making the order for the employer to deduct a suitable monthly or weekly sum from the judgment debtor's wages. The court sets a "Protected Earnings" threshold, which allows the judgment debtor to cover his or her basic home expenses in priority to any payment to the judgment creditor.

Once an attachment of earnings order is in place, the judgment creditor must bring to the attention of the court the existence of the order before commencing any other enforcement steps.

Overall, this can be an effective, if often slow, method of ensuring that the judgment debt is paid.

Charging order on land

This method of enforcement gives the judgment creditor the equivalent of a mortgage over the judgment debtor's land. The charging order remains on the land registry records and the judgment debtor will have to clear the judgment debt before the land can be sold. Since the judgment does not attract interest and the wait before sale may be several years, the delay in payment may significantly reduce the value of this method to the judgment creditor.

The usual way of proving that the debtor owns the land is to produce a copy of the entry at the Land Registry (see above).

Charging order on securities

The charging order procedure can also be used against stocks and shares including government stock and dividends.

Order for sale

A judgment creditor who has registered a charging order against land may apply to the court for an order for sale. The procedure depends on whether the land is jointly owned or is in the sole name of the judgment debtor. The District Judge has a discretion on whether to make the order and if the judgment debt is small, then the order for sale may not be made.

Timescale for enforcement

A judgment debt can be enforced at any time after judgment. However, a registration of judgment debt runs out after six years, and the permission of the District Judge is required to issue a warrant of execution after six years (CCR Order 26 r 5). Confusingly, if a fresh action is started by way of enforcement (for example an application for an order for sale following a charging order) this must be commenced within six years.

Steps after a Small Claims judgment debt in the County Court – overview

		Available against the following assets	
Enforcement method	Bankruptcy/ company insolvency	An unsecured creditor will share the debtor's assets with all other unsecured creditors	**An uptodate list of court fees can be found at www.hmcourts-service.gov.uk/infoabout/fees/county**
	Warrant of execution (bailiffs seizing goods)	Personal possessions (excluding domestic necessities and possessions needed for the judgment debtor to earn a living)	
	Third party debt proceedings.	Trade debts. Bank and building society accounts which are in credit	
	Attachment of earnings	The wages of an employed (not self employed person) insofar as they exceed the "protected earnings rate"	
	Charging Order	Land. Stocks and Shares. Government securities	
	Order to obtain information	A method of determining the judgment debtor's assets (Not a method of enforcement)	
	Registration of the judgment	Applies to default judgments and judgments after a hearing if payment is made by instalments or enforcement action is taken (Not a method of enforcement)	

Appendices

1 Court fees payable in small claims cases – commencement
  and allocation   255

2 Court fees payable in small claims cases – applications
  and appeals   257

3 Fixed commencement costs   259

4 Fixed costs on entry of judgment   261

5 Forms   263

6 Part 1 of the Civil Procedure Rules   265

7 Part 27 of the Civil Procedure Rules and the Practice Direction   269

Appendices

Court fees payable in Small Claims cases – commencement, allocation and Hearing fees

Amount stated in the claim or counterclaim	Fee payable on commencement Figures in brackets are when the proceedings are issued on-line	Allocation fee	Hearing fee *
Does not exceed £300	£30(25)	0	25*
Exceeds £300 and does not exceed £500	£45(35)	0	50*
Exceeds £500 and does not exceed £1000	£65(60)	0	75*
Exceeds £1000 and does not exceed £1500	£75(70)	0	100*
Exceeds £1500 and does not exceed £3000	£85(80)	35	150*
Exceeds £3000 and does not exceed £5000	£108(100)	35	300*

* There is a refund of 100% of the hearing fee if the court is informed 7 days or more that the hearing is to be vacated.

See notes overleaf.

Notes

No listing fee is applicable on the Small Claims track as there is no pre trial check list.

The fee payable once counterclaim must be paid when the counterclaim is filed.

Court fees payable in Small Claims cases – applications and appeals

Source – County Court Fees Amendment Order 1999 (sch 1)

Any application requiring the attendance of both sides including applications under Part 23 and 24	£75.00
An application for judgment on an admission or application for judgment in default	No fee
Appeal	£100.00
Application by consent	£40.00

Fixed commencement costs

These costs can be awarded only if a solicitor drafted the claim

Value of claim	Where the claim form is served by the court	Where the claim form is served by the claimant personally and there is only one defendant[1]
£25.00 or less	Nothing	Nothing
£25.01 to £500.00	£50	£60
£500.01 to £1000.00	£70	£80
£1000.01 to £5000.00	£80	£90

Source – Rule 45 table 1

Notes
1 Add £15 for each additional defendant personally served.
2 These fixed costs are applicable only where the claim is for a specified sum. If the claim is for the amount to be decided by the court, put the words "to be assessed" on the form N1 next to the words "solicitor's costs". After judgment, the costs which will be fixed at a sum relating to amount awarded (see page 111).

Fixed costs on entry of judgment

These costs are only allowed if the judgment is in default of defence or acknowledgment and do not apply following allocation to the Small Claims track when the "no costs" rule applies.

Different rates apply for claims above £5,000.

Judgment in default of defence	£22
Judgment in default of acknowledgement	£25
Judgment on admission of whole or part and the parties agree on the manner of payment	£40
Judgment on admission of whole or part and the court decides the date or times of payment	£55
Summary judgment or case struck out	£175

Source – Rule 45 table 2

Forms

All forms are downloadable from the Court Service website www.hmcourts-service.gov.uk and follow the links to Forms and Guidance

Readers should download these from the site to ensure the latest version is used. Readers without access to a computer will find their local Reference Library can provide these facilities.

Part 1
of the Civil Procedure Rules

Overriding Objective

Contents of this Part

The overriding objective   Rule 1.1

Application by the court of the overriding objective   Rule 1.2

Duty of the parties   Rule 1.3

Court's duty to manage cases   Rule 1.4

The Overriding Objective

1.1   (1) These Rules are a new procedural code with the overriding objective of enabling the court to deal with cases justly.

     (2) Dealing with a case justly includes, so far as is practicable –

       (a) ensuring that the parties are on an equal footing;

       (b) saving expense;

       (c) dealing with the case in ways which are proportionate –

         (i) to the amount of money involved;

         (ii) to the importance of the case;

         (iii) to the complexity of the issues; and

         (iv) to the financial position of each party;

       (d) ensuring that it is dealt with expeditiously and fairly; and

       (e) allotting to it an appropriate share of the court's resources, while taking into account the need to allot resources to other cases.

Application by the Court of the Overriding Objective

1.2   The court must seek to give effect to the overriding objective when it –

(a) exercises any power given to it by the Rules; or

(b) interprets any rule.

Duty of the Parties

1.3   The parties are required to help the court to further the overriding objective.

Court's Duty to Manage Cases

1.4   (1) The court must further the overriding objective by actively managing cases.

(2) Active case management includes –

(a) encouraging the parties to co-operate with each other in the conduct of the proceedings;

(b) identifying the issues at an early stage;

(c) deciding promptly which issues need full investigation and trial and accordingly disposing summarily of the others;

(d) deciding the order in which issues are to be resolved;

(e) encouraging the parties to use an alternative dispute resolution[GL] procedure if the court considers that appropriate and facilitating the use of such procedure;

(f) helping the parties to settle the whole or part of the case;

(g) fixing timetables or otherwise controlling the progress of the case;

(h) considering whether the likely benefits of taking a particular step justify the cost of taking it;

(i) dealing with as many aspects of the case as it can on the same occasion;

(j) dealing with the case without the parties needing to attend at court;

(k) making use of technology; and

(l) giving directions to ensure that the trial of a case proceeds quickly and efficiently.

Part 27
of the Civil Procedure Rules
and the Practice Direction

The Small Claims track

Contents of this Part

Scope of this Part | Rule 27.1

Extent to which other Parts apply | Rule 27.2

Court's power to grant a final remedy | Rule 27.3

Preparation for the hearing | Rule 27.4

Experts | Rule 27.5

Preliminary hearing | Rule 27.6

Power of court to add to, vary or revoke directions | Rule 27.7

Conduct of the hearing | Rule 27.8

Non-attendance of parties at a final hearing | Rule 27.9

Disposal without a hearing | Rule 27.10

Setting judgment aside and re-hearing | Rule 27.11

Revoked | Rule 27.12

Revoked | Rule 27.13

Costs on the small claims track | Rule 27.14

Claim re-allocated from the small claims track to another track | Rule 27.15

Scope of this part

27.1 (1) This Part –

(a) sets out the special procedure for dealing with claims which have been allocated to the small claims track under Part 26; and

(b) limits the amount of costs that can be recovered in respect of a claim which has been allocated to the small claims track.

(Rule 27.14 deals with costs on the small claims track)

(2) A claim being dealt with under this Part is called a small claim.

(Rule 26.6 provides for the scope of the small claims track. A claim for a remedy for harassment or unlawful eviction relating, in either case, to residential premises shall not be allocated to the small claims track whatever the financial value of the claim. Otherwise, the small claims track will be the normal track for –

• any claim which has a financial value of not more than £5,000 subject to the special provisions about claims for personal injuries and housing disrepair claims;

• any claim for personal injuries which has a financial value of not more than £5,000 where the claim for damages for personal injuries is not more than £1,000; and

• any claim which includes a claim by a tenant of residential premises against his landlord for repairs or other work to the premises where the estimated cost of the repairs or other work is not more than £1000 and the financial value of any other claim for damages is not more than £1,000)

Extent to which other parts apply

27.2 (1) The following Parts of these Rules do not apply to small claims –

(a) Part 25 (interim remedies) except as it relates to interim injunctions$^{(GL)}$;

(b) Part 31 (disclosure and inspection);

(c) Part 32 (evidence) except rule 32.1 (power of court to control evidence);

(d) Part 33 (miscellaneous rules about evidence);

(e) Part 35 (experts and assessors) except rules 35.1 (duty to restrict expert evidence), 35.3 (experts – overriding duty to the court), 35.7 (court's power to direct that evidence is to be given by single joint expert) and 35.8 (instructions to a single joint expert);

(f) Part 18 (further information);

(g) Part 36 (offers to settle and payments into court); and

(h) Part 39 (hearings) except rule 39.2 (general rule – hearing to be in public).

(2) The other Parts of these Rules apply to small claims except to the extent that a rule limits such application.

Court's power to grant a final remedy

27.3 The court may grant any final remedy in relation to a small claim which it could grant if the proceedings were on the fast track or the multi-track.

Preparation for the Hearing

27.4 (1) After allocation the court will –

(a) give standard directions and fix a date for the final hearing;

(b) give special directions and fix a date for the final hearing;

(c) give special directions and direct that the court will consider what further directions are to be given no later than 28 days after the date the special directions were given;

(d) fix a date for a preliminary hearing under rule 27.6; or

(e) give notice that it proposes to deal with the claim without a hearing under rule 27.10 and invite the parties to notify the court by a specified date if they agree the proposal.

(2) The court will –

(a) give the parties at least 21 days' notice of the date fixed for the final hearing, unless the parties agree to accept less notice; and

(b) inform them of the amount of time allowed for the final hearing.

(3) In this rule –

(a) 'standard directions' means –

(i) a direction that each party shall, at least 14 days before the date fixed for the final hearing, file and serve on every other party copies of all documents (including any expert's report) on which he intends to rely at the hearing; and

(ii) any other standard directions set out in the relevant practice direction; and

(b) 'special directions' means directions given in addition to or instead of the standard directions.

Experts

27.5 No expert may give evidence, whether written or oral, at a hearing without the permission of the court.

(Rule 27.14(3)(d) provides for the payment of an expert's fees)

Preliminary Hearing

27.6 (1) The court may hold a preliminary hearing for the consideration of the claim, but only –

(a) where –

(i) it considers that special directions, as defined in rule 27.4, are needed to ensure a fair hearing; and

(ii) it appears necessary for a party to attend at court to ensure that he understands what he must do to comply with the special directions; or

(b) to enable it to dispose of the claim on the basis that one or other of the parties has no real prospect of success at a final hearing; or

(c) to enable it to strike out$^{(GL)}$ a statement of case or part of a statement of case on the basis that the statement of case, or the part to be struck out, discloses no reasonable grounds for bringing or defending the claim.

(2) When considering whether or not to hold a preliminary hearing, the court must have regard to the desirability of limiting the expense to the parties of attending court.

(3) Where the court decides to hold a preliminary hearing, it will give the parties at least 14 days' notice of the date of the hearing.

(4) The court may treat the preliminary hearing as the final hearing of the claim if all the parties agree.

(5) At or after the preliminary hearing the court will –

    (a) fix the date of the final hearing (if it has not been fixed already) and give the parties at least 21 days' notice of the date fixed unless the parties agree to accept less notice;

    (b) inform them of the amount of time allowed for the final hearing; and

    (c) give any appropriate directions.

Power of Court to add to, vary or revoke directions

27.7 The court may add to, vary or revoke directions.

Conduct of the Hearing

27.8 (1) The court may adopt any method of proceeding at a hearing that it considers to be fair.

(2) Hearings will be informal.

(3) The strict rules of evidence do not apply.

(4) The court need not take evidence on oath.

(5) The court may limit cross-examination$^{(GL)}$.

(6) The court must give reasons for its decision.

Non-attendance of parties at a final Hearing

27.9 (1) If a party who does not attend a final hearing –

(a) has given the court written notice at least 7 days before the date of the hearing that he will not attend; and

(b) has, in that notice, requested the court to decide the claim in his absence,

the court will take into account that party's statement of case and any other documents he has filed when it decides the claim.

(2) If a claimant does not –

(a) attend the hearing; and

(b) give the notice referred to in paragraph (1),

the court may strike out[GL] the claim.

(3) If –

(a) a defendant does not –

(i) attend the hearing; or

(ii) give the notice referred to in paragraph (1); and

(b) the claimant either –

(i) does attend the hearing; or

(ii) gives the notice referred to in paragraph (1),

the court may decide the claim on the basis of the evidence of the claimant alone.

(4) If neither party attends or gives the notice referred to in paragraph (1), the court may strike out[GL] the claim and any defence and counterclaim.

Disposal without a Hearing

27.10 The court may, if all parties agree, deal with the claim without a hearing.

Setting Judgment aside and re-hearing

27.11(1) A party –

(a) who was neither present nor represented at the hearing of the claim; and

(b) who has not given written notice to the court under rule 27.9(1),

may apply for an order that a judgment under this Part shall be set aside$^{(GL)}$ and the claim re-heard.

(2) A party who applies for an order setting aside a judgment under this rule must make the application not more than 14 days after the day on which notice of the judgment was served on him.

(3) The court may grant an application under paragraph (2) only if the applicant –

(a) had a good reason for not attending or being represented at the hearing or giving written notice to the court under rule 27.9(1); and

(b) has a reasonable prospect of success at the hearing.

(4) If a judgment is set aside$^{(GL)}$ –

(a) the court must fix a new hearing for the claim; and

(b) the hearing may take place immediately after the hearing of the application to set the judgment aside and may be dealt with by the judge who set aside$^{(GL)}$ the judgment.

(5) A party may not apply to set aside$^{(GL)}$ a judgment under this rule if the court dealt with the claim without a hearing under rule 27.10.

Rules 27.12 and 27.13 are revoked.

Costs on the Small Claims track

27.14(1) This rule applies to any case which has been allocated to the small claims track unless paragraph (5) applies.

(Rules 44.9 and 44.11 make provision in relation to orders for costs made before a claim has been allocated to the small claims track)

(2) The court may not order a party to pay a sum to another party in respect of that other party's costs except –

(a) the fixed costs attributable to issuing the claim which –

(i) are payable under Part 45; or

(ii) would be payable under Part 45 if that Part applied to the claim;

(b) in proceedings which included a claim for an injunction[GL] or an order for specific performance a sum not exceeding the amount specified in the relevant practice direction for legal advice and assistance relating to that claim;

(c) costs assessed by the summary procedure in relation to an appeal and

(d) such further costs as the court may assess by the summary procedure and order to be paid by a party who has behaved unreasonably.

(3) The court may also order a party to pay all or part of –

(a) any court fees paid by another party;

(b) expenses which a party or witness has reasonably incurred in travelling to and from a hearing or in staying away from home for the purposes of attending a hearing;

(c) a sum not exceeding the amount specified in the relevant practice direction for any loss of earnings by a party or witness due to attending a hearing or to staying away from home for the purpose of attending a hearing; and

(d) a sum not exceeding the amount specified in the relevant practice direction for an expert's fees.

(4) The limits on costs imposed by this rule also apply to any fee or reward for acting on behalf of a party to the proceedings charged by a person exercising a right of audience by virtue of an order under section 11 of the Courts and Legal Services Act 1990[44] (a lay representative).

(5) Where –

(a) the financial value of a claim exceeds the limit for the small claims track; but

(b) the claim has been allocated to the small claims track in accordance with rule 26.7(3),

the claim shall be treated, for the purposes of costs, as if it were proceeding on the fast track except that trial costs shall be in the discretion of the court and shall not exceed the amount set out for the value of the claim in rule 46.2 (amount of fast track trial costs).

(Rule 26.7(3) allows the parties to consent to a claim being allocated to a track where the financial value of the claim exceeds the limit for that track)

Claim re-allocated from the Small Claims track to another track

27.15 Where a claim is allocated to the small claims track and subsequently re-allocated to another track, rule 27.14 (costs on the small claims track) will cease to apply after the claim has been re-allocated and the fast track or multi-track costs rules will apply from the date of re-allocation.

Practice Direction – Small Claims track

This Practice Direction Supplements CPR Part 27

Judges

1   The functions of the court described in Part 27 which are to be carried out by a judge will generally be carried out by a district judge but may be carried out by a Circuit Judge.

Case Management Directions

2.1   Rule 27.4 explains how directions will be given, and rule 27.6 contains provisions about the holding of a preliminary hearing and the court's powers at such a hearing.

2.2   Appendix A sets out the Standard Directions which the court may give.

Representation at a Hearing

3.1 In this paragraph:

(1) a lawyer means a barrister, a solicitor or a legal executive employed by a solicitor, and

(2) a lay representative means any other person.

3.2 (1) A party may present his own case at a hearing or a lawyer or lay representative may present it for him.

(2) The Lay Representatives (Right of Audience) Order 1999 provides that a lay representative may not exercise any right of audience:–

(a) where his client does not attend the hearing;

(b) at any stage after judgment; or

(c) on any appeal brought against any decision made by the district judge in the proceedings.

(3) However the court, exercising its general discretion to hear anybody, may hear a lay representative even in circumstances excluded by the Order.

(4) Any of its officers or employees may represent a corporate party.

Small Claim Hearing

4.1 (1) The general rule is that a small claim hearing will be in public.

(2) The judge may decide to hold it in private if:

(a) the parties agree, or

(b) a ground mentioned in rule 39.2(3) applies.

(3) A hearing or part of a hearing which takes place other than at the court, for example at the home or business premises of a party, will not be in public.

4.2 A hearing that takes place at the court will generally be in the judge's room but it may take place in a courtroom.

4.3 Rule 27.8 allows the court to adopt any method of proceeding that it considers to be fair and to limit cross-examination. The judge may in particular:

(1) ask questions of any witness himself before allowing any other person to do so,

(2) ask questions of all or any of the witnesses himself before allowing any other person to ask questions of any witnesses,

(3) refuse to allow cross-examination of any witness until all the witnesses have given evidence in chief,

(4) limit cross-examination of a witness to a fixed time or to a particular subject or issue, or both.

Recording evidence and the giving of reasons

5.1 The judge may direct that all or any part of the proceedings will be tape recorded by the court. A party may obtain a transcript of such a recording on payment of the proper transcriber's charges.

5.2 Attention is drawn to section 9 of the Contempt of Court Act 1981 (which deals with the unauthorised use of tape recorders in court) and to the Practice Direction ([1981] 1 WLR 1526) which relates to it.

5.3 The judge will make a note of the central points of the oral evidence unless it is tape recorded by the court.

5.4 The judge will make a note of the central reasons for his judgment unless it is given orally and tape recorded by the court.

5.5 (1) The judge may give his reasons as briefly and simply as the nature of the case allows.

(2) He will normally do so orally at the hearing, but he may give them later either in writing or at a hearing fixed for him to do so.

5.6 Where the judge decides the case without a hearing under rule 27.10 or a party who has given notice under rule 27.9(1) does not attend the hearing, the judge will prepare a note of his reasons and the court will send a copy to each party.

5.7 A party is entitled to a copy of any note made by the judge under sub-paragraphs 5.3 or 5.4.

5.8 Nothing in this practice direction affects the duty of a judge at the request of a party to make a note of the matters referred to in section 80 of the County Courts Act 1984.

Non-attendance of a party at a Hearing

6.1   Attention is drawn to rule 27.9 (which enables a party to give notice that he will not attend a final hearing and sets out the effect of his giving such notice and of not doing so), and to paragraph 3 above.

6.2   Nothing in those provisions affects the general power of the court to adjourn a hearing, for example where a party who wishes to attend a hearing on the date fixed cannot do so for a good reason.

Costs

7.1   Attention is drawn to Rule 27.14 which contains provisions about the costs which may be ordered to be paid by one party to another.

7.2   The amount which a party may be ordered to pay under rule 27.14(2)(b) (for legal advice and assistance in claims including an injunction or specific performance) is a sum not exceeding £260.

7.3   The amounts which a party may be ordered to pay under rule 27.14(3)(c) (loss of earnings) and (d) (experts' fees) are:

(1) for the loss of earnings of each party or witness due to attending a hearing or staying away from home for the purpose of attending a hearing, a sum not exceeding £50 per day for each person, and

(2) for expert's fees, a sum not exceeding £200 for each expert.

(As to recovery of pre-allocation costs in a case in which an admission by the defendant has reduced the amount in dispute to a figure below £5,000, reference should be made to paragraph 7.4 of the Practice Direction supplementing CPR Part 26 and to paragraph 5.1(3) of the Costs Directions relating to CPR Part 44)

Appeals

8.1   Part 52 deals with appeals and attention is drawn to that Part and the accompanying practice direction.

8.2   Where the court dealt with the claim to which the appellant is a party:

(1) under rule 27.10 without a hearing; or

(2) in his absence because he gave notice under rule 27.9 requesting the court to decide the claim in his absence,

an application for permission to appeal must be made to the appeal court.

8.3   Where an appeal is allowed the appeal court will, if possible, dispose of the case at the same time without referring the claim to the lower court or ordering a new hearing. It may do so without hearing further evidence.

Appendix A

Form A
– The Standard Directions
(for use where the district judge specifies no other directions)

The Court Directs

1.   Each party shall deliver to every other party and to the court office copies of all documents (including any experts' report) on which he intends to rely at the hearing no later than [   ] [14 days before the hearing].

2.   The original documents shall be brought to the hearing.

3.   [Notice of hearing date and time allowed.]

4.   The court must be informed immediately if the case is settled by agreement before the hearing date.

Form B
– Standard Directions
for use in claims arising out of road accidents

The Court directs

1.   Each party shall deliver to every other party and to the court office copies of all documents on which he intends to rely at the hearing. These may include:

- experts' reports (including medical reports where damages for personal injury are claimed),

- witness statements,

- invoices and estimates for repairs,

- documents which relate to other losses, such as loss of earnings,

- sketch plans and photographs.

2. The copies shall be delivered no later than [   ] [14 days before the hearing].

3. The original documents shall be brought to the hearing.

4. Before the date of the hearing the parties shall try to agree the cost of the repairs and any other losses claimed subject to the court's decision about whose fault the accident was.

5. Signed statements setting out the evidence of all witnesses on whom each party intends to rely shall be prepared and copies included in the documents mentioned in paragraph 1. This includes the evidence of the parties themselves and of any other witness, whether or not he is going to come to court to give evidence.

6. The parties should note that:

    (a) In deciding the case the court will find it very helpful to have a sketch plan and photographs of the place where the accident happened,

    (b) The court may decide not to take into account a document or the evidence of a witness if no copy of that document or no copy of a statement or report by that witness has been supplied to the other parties.

7. [Notice of hearing date and time allowed.]

8. The court must be informed immediately if the case is settled by agreement before the hearing date.

Form C
– Standard Directions for use in claims arising out of building disputes, vehicle repairs and similar contractual claims

The Court directs

1. Each party shall deliver to every other party and to the court office copies of all documents on which he intends to rely at the hearing. These may include:

    - the contract,

    - witness statements,

    - experts' reports,

    - photographs,

    - invoices for work done or goods supplied,

    - estimates for work to be done.

2. The copies shall be delivered no later than [   ] [14 days before the hearing].

3. The original documents shall be brought to the hearing.

4. [The   shall deliver to the   and to the court office [no later than   ] [with his copy documents] a list showing all items of work which he complains about and why, and the amount claimed for putting each item right.]

5. [The   shall deliver to the   and to the court office [no later than   ] [with his copy documents] a breakdown of the amount he is claiming showing all work done and materials supplied.]

6. Before the date of the hearing the parties shall try to agree about the nature and cost of any remedial work required, subject to the court's decision about any other issue in the case.

7. [Signed statements setting out the evidence of all witnesses on whom each party intends to rely shall be prepared and included in the documents mentioned in paragraph 1. This includes the evidence of the parties themselves and of any other witness, whether or not he is going to come to court to give evidence.]

8. The parties should note that:

    (a) in deciding the case the judge may find it helpful to have photographs showing the work in question,

    (b) the judge may decide not to take into account a document or the evidence of a witness if no copy of that document or no copy of a statement or report by that witness has been supplied to the other parties.

9. [Notice of hearing date and time allowed.]

10. The court must be informed immediately if the case is settled by agreement before the hearing date.

Form D
– Tenant's claims for the return
of deposits/landlords claims for damage caused

The Court directs

1. Each party shall deliver to every other party and to the court office copies of all documents on which he intends to rely at the hearing. These may include:

    *   the tenancy agreement and any inventory,

    *   the rent book or other evidence of rent and other payments made by the to   the   ,

    *   photographs,

    *   witness statements,

    *   invoices or estimates for work and goods.

2. The copies shall be delivered no later than [   ] [14 days before the hearing].

3. The original documents shall be brought to the hearing.

4. The   shall deliver with his copy documents a list showing each item of loss or damage for which he claims the   ought to pay, and the amount he claims for the replacement or repair.

5.   The parties shall before the hearing date try to agree about the nature and cost of any repairs and replacements needed, subject to the court's decision about any other issue in the case.

6.   [Signed statements setting out the evidence of all witnesses on whom each party intends to rely shall be prepared and included in the documents mentioned in paragraph 1. This includes the evidence of the parties themselves and of any other witness whether or not he is going to come to court to give evidence.]

7.   The parties should note that: a) in deciding the case the judge may find it helpful to have photographs showing the condition of the property, b) the judge may decide not to take into account a document or the evidence of a witness if no copy of that document or no copy of a statement or report by that witness has been supplied to the other parties.

8.   [Notice of hearing date and time allowed.]

9.   The court must be informed immediately if the case is settled by agreement before the hearing date.

Form E
– Holiday and Wedding claims

The Court directs

1.   Each party shall deliver to every other party and to the court office copies of all documents on which he intends to rely at the hearing. These may include:

*   any written contract, brochure or booking form,

*   photographs,

*   documents showing payments made,

*   witness statements,

*   letters.

2.   The copies shall be delivered no later than [   ] [14 days before the hearing].

3.   The original documents shall be brought to the hearing.

4. Signed statements setting out the evidence of all witnesses on whom each party intends to rely shall be prepared and copies included in the documents mentioned in paragraph 1. This includes the evidence of the parties themselves and of any other witness, whether or not he is going to come to court to give evidence.

5. If either party intends to show a video as evidence he must:

    (a) contact the court at once to make arrangements for him to do so, because the court may not have the necessary equipment, and

    (b) provide the other party with a copy of the video or the opportunity to see it (if he asks) at least 2 weeks before the hearing.

6. The parties should note that the court may decide not to take into account a document or the evidence of a witness or a video if these directions have not been complied with.

7. [Notice of hearing date and time allowed.]

8. The court must be told immediately if the case is settled by agreement before the hearing date.

Form F
– Some special directions

The   must clarify his case. He must do this by delivering to the court office and to the no later than

[a list of   ]

[details of   ]

[   ]

The   shall allow the   to   inspect
                by appointment within   days of receiving a
request to do so.

The hearing will not take place at the court but at   .

The   must bring to court at the hearing the   .

Signed statements setting out the evidence of all witnesses on whom each party intends to rely shall be prepared and copies included in the documents mentioned in paragraph 1. This includes the evidence of the parties themselves and of any other witness, whether or not he is going to come to court to give evidence.

The court may decide not to take into account a document [or video] or the evidence of a witness if these directions have not been complied with.

If he does not [do so] [   ] his [Claim] [Defence] [and Counterclaim] and will be struck out and [(specify consequence)]. It appears to the court that expert evidence is necessary on the issue of

[   ]

and that that evidence should be given by a single expert

[   ]

to be instructed by the parties jointly. If the parties cannot agree about who to chose and what arrangements to make about paying his fee, either party may apply to the court for further directions. If either party intends to show a video as evidence he must

(a) contact the court at once to make arrangements for him to do so, because the court may not have the necessary equipment, and

(b) provide the other party with a copy of the video or the opportunity to see it at least [   ] before the hearing.

Tables of Citations

Table of Cases   291
Table of Rules   293
Table of Statutes   297

Table of Citations

Cases

Afzal and Others v Ford Motor Co Ltd and other
Appeals CA (1994) 4 All ER,............................64, 66, 117

Bashir v Hanson CC [1999] 12 CL 143, ...118
Berridge (Paul) (t/a EAB Builders) v RM Bayliss
(1999) Lawtel 23 November, ...67
Biguzzi v Rank Leisure plc [1999] CA 4 All ER 897,.................194

Chellaram v Chellaram (No. 2) [2002] EWHC 632, ...29
Closhey v Homes June [2004] 6 CL 47,....................118
Cranfield & Anor v Bridgegrove Ltd [2003] EWCA
Civ 612, ...29

Dulce Maltez v Damien Lewis and Anr ChD *Times*
4 May 1999, ...130

Flannery v Halifax Estate Agents [2000] 1 WLR 377,................160

Geoffrey Arnold Wheen v Smithmann and another
LTL 25 September 2000, ...68

Halsey v Milton Keynes NHS Trust [2004] EWCA Civ, ...180
Hurst v Leeming [2003] 1 Lloyds Rep 1,.........................181

Lacey v Melford CC [1999] 12 CL 37, ...118
Ladd v Marshall [1954] 3 AER 745 CA, ...162
Lunnun v Hari Singh and others, CA, *Times*
1 July 1999, ...58

Madden v Pattini CC [1999] 12 CL 53,..........................193
Maes Finance and Mac No 1 Ltd v Al Phillips and
Co (A Firm), ChD, *Times* 23 March 1997, ...58
Mersey Docks Property Holdings v Kilgour [2004]
EWHC 1638, ...29
Moyse v Regal Partnerships Ltd [2004] EWCA Civ 1269,............162

R v Leicester City Justices ex parte Barrow and another,
CA [1991] 3 All ER 935, ...137

Regency Rolls Ltd and Another v Carnell LTL
October 16 2000, ...169

Tanfern Ltd v Cameron-Macdonald [2000] 2 All
ER 801, ...161

Rules

Civil Procedure Rules 1998
Part 1, ...2, 7, 265–268
  1.1, ...192
  1.1(1), ...10
  1.1(2), ...91, 98
  1.1(2)(a), ...8
  1.1(2)(c), ...96
  1.1(2)(d), ...193
  1.2, ...121
  1.3, ...193
  1.4, ...193
  1.4(1), ...91
  1.4(2), ...10, 174
Part 2, ...207
  2.3(1), ...24, 37
  2.8(4), ...207
  2.9, ...207
  PD 11.2, ...5
Part 3, ...49, 193
  3.1(2), ...193
  3.1(3), ...168
  3.2, ...194
  3.3, ...196
  3.4, ...194
  3.4(b), ...195
  3.8(2), ...196
  3.10, ...196, 207
  3.11, ...195
Part 6
  6.3(b), ...201
  6.3(d), ...201
  6.5, ...28
  6.5(2), ...24
  6.5(3), ...24
  6.7, ...201
  6.14, ...201
Part 7
  7.4(1), ...47

  7.4(1)(b), ...31
  7.5, ...17, 203
  7.5(2), ...29
  7.6, ...203
  PD, ...20, 31, 36, 90
Part 8, ...22
Part 12
  12.1, ...168
  12.3(2), ...56
  12.4, ...57
  12.4(1), ...57
  12.5(2), ...207
Part 13, ...168, 171
  13.2, ...166, 171
  13.2(c), ...52
  13.3, ...171
  13.3(2), ...171
  13.4, ...169
Part 14
  14.1(4), ...48, 49
  14.2(3), ...52
  14.3, ...49
  14.4, ...50
  14.5, ...51
  14.5(9), ...207
  14.6, ...49, 51
  14.7, ...49, 51
  14.7(9), ...51
  14.7(10), ...51
Part 15
  15.8, ...59
  PD 3.2, ...59
Part 16
  16.2(2), ...31
  16.4(1), ...31, 222
  16.4(2), ...34, 222
  16.5, ...54, 55
  16.5(1), ...223

16.5(2), ...223, 224
16.5(3), ...223
16.5(4), ...223
16.7, ...224
16.7(1), ...59
PD 2.2, ...23
PD 3.1, ...224
PD 3.2, ...224
PD 3.3(3), ...224
PD 3.4, ...31
PD 4, ...223
PD 4.2, ...97
PD 8.1(d), ...223
PD 9.3(1), ...223
PD 9.3(2), ...223
PD 10.2(1), ...223
PD 10.2(2), ...223
PD 10.2(3), ...222
PD 10.2(8), ...222
PD 11.2, ...223
PD 14, ...224
PD 16.1, ...32, 224
PD 16.3, ...223, 224
Part 17
17.1, ...225
PD, ...225
Part 18, ...208, 209
Part 20, ...56
20.2(1), ...55
20.4(2), ...55
20.5(1), ...56
20.6, ...56
PD 6.1, ...56
Part 21
21.1(2)(a), ...23
Part 22
22.1, ...200
22.1(3), ...200
22.1(6), ...37
22.2, ...201

22.2(1), ...38
22.2(2), ...38
22.3, ...200
PD 3.1, ...201
PD, 3.8, ...37
Part 23, ...197
23.1, ...197
23.3(2), ...198
23.7, ...198
23.7(1)(b), ...198
23.8(c), ...200
23.10, ...200
PD 2.1, ...197
PD 2.7, ...197
PD 3, ...200
PD 10, ...198
PD 11.1–11.2, ...58
Part 24, ...204
24.2, 166, ...205
24.4(1)(a), ...53
24.4(2), ...168, 204
Part 25, ...208
Part 26, ...194
26.2, ...72, 88
26.2(1)(c), ...90
26.2(4), ...90
26.2(5), ...90
26.3(6), ...71
26.4 (2), ...73
26.4 (3), ...73
26.4 (5), ...73
26.5(5), ...76
26.6,(1)(a)(iii), ...67
26.6, ...67
26.7(3), ...4, 68, 69, 80
26.7(4), ...67
26.8(1), ...66, 68, 69
26.8 (2), ...66, 68, 80
PD 2.5(1), ...76
PD 6.2, ...78

PD 11.1, ...79
PD 11.2, ...79
PD 12.4, ...58
PD 12.8,(2), ...58
Part 27, ...2, 7, 64,
...................192, 269–287
27.1(2), ...65, 67
27.2, ...92, 208, 209
27.2(3), ...102
27.3, ...212
27.4(2), ...84, 102
27.5, ...97
27.6, ...102, 194
27.6(2), ...102
27.8, ...138
27.8(1), ...160
27.8(3), ...144, 201
27.8(4), ...145, 147, 149
27.8(5), ...147
27.8(6), ...152
27.9(1), ...104, 106, 143,
...................145, 152, 167
27.9(2)–(4), ...143
27.10, ...77, 152
27.11, ...166, 171
27.14, ...111, 166
27.14(2), ...2, 111, 114
27.14A, ...118
27.14(2)(b), ...116
27.14(2)(c), ...116
27.14(2)(d), ...113, 114,
...........................117, 225
27.14(3), ...112, 113, 212
27.14(3)(c), ...114
27.14(4), ...112, 115
27.14(5), ...80
PD, ...85–88, 101
PD 3.2(1), ...129
PD 3.2(2), ...130, 166
PD 3.2(4), ...131

PD 4.1(1), ...131
PD 4.1(2), ...132
PD 4.1(3), ...132
PD 4.3, ...138
PD 5.1–5.8, ...133
PD 5.4, ...106
PD 5.5, ...152
PD 7, ...116
PD 7.2, ...116
PD 7.3(1), ...115
PD 7.3(2), ...114
Part 28, ...64
Part 29, ...64
Part 30,
30.3, ...91
PD 6.1, ...91
Part 31, ...94, 208
31.1(2), ...92
Part 32, ...208, 210
32.1, ...211
32.2, ...94
32.14, ...35, 201
Part 33, ...208
Part 34, ...96
Part 35, ...208
35.1, ...97, 211
35.3, ...98, 211
35.4, ...98
35.7, ...98, 211
35.8, ...97, 98, 199, 211
Part 36, ...208
36.2, ...119
Part 39, ...208
39.2, ...131, 208
Part 40
40.11, ...153, 207
40.12, ...206
Part 43
43.2(1)(a), ...111

Part 44, ...120
44.3, ...113, 120, 206
44.5, ...120
44.8, ...124
44.9, ...124
44.11, ...124
44.13(1), ...122
PD 5.1(1), ...124
PD 5.1(2), ...124
PD 15,.............................124
Part 45, ...259
45.1(1), ...114
Part 48
48.6(6), ...122
48.7.................................122
Part 52, ...4
52.3(6), ...160
52.4(b), ...161
52.5, ...165

52.11(2), ...162
52.11(3), ...159
52.11(5), ...163
52.13, ...166
PD 4.5, ...163
PD 5.6, ...164
PD 5.8, ...163, 164
PD 5.12, ...164
PD 5.17, ...133, 164
PD 5.18, ...164
PD 7.2, ...165

County Court Rules
O5r9, ...27
O5r10, ...26
O19, ...66
O22r10, ...155
O37, ...170

Rules

Administration of Justice Act 1999
s54(4), ...162

Business Names Act 1985, ...25

Contempt of Court Act 1981
s9, ...154

County Courts Act 1984
s118, ...142

Human Rights Act 1998, ...12, 32

Late Payment of Commercial Debts (Interest) Act 1998, ...35, 237

Welsh Language Act 1993
s22(1), ...81

Index

For definitions of the key terms regarding the Small Claims track, see the glossary at the front of the book. Index entries which also appear in the Glossary are in **bold type**.

Access to Justice, 3
Acknowledging the claim, 52
Address of claimant and defendant,
  24, 28
  Individuals, 28
  Limited companies, 28
Admitting the claim, 48, 225
  Summary table, 50
Advocacy, 129, 147
Agents claims against, 26
Agreement see Settlement
Allocation, 63, 64
  After, 84
  Directions, 85, 88
Allocation fee, 12, 71, 255
Allocation hearing, 78
Allocation questionnaires, 61, 70
  Completing, 71–76
  Court dispensing with, 79
  Failure to return, 76
  Time limit, 71
Alternatives to court action, 10
Amending the claim, 225
Amount claimed, 38
  Decided by court, 57
Appeals, 157–171
  Case management, 163
  Costs and, 113
  Credit repair, 170

Fees, 257
Flowchart, 158
Grounds, 159
Hearing, 165
Judgment in default, setting
  aside, 168
Mistake of law, 159
Precedent, 240
Procedure, 167
Re-hearing, 162, 167
Respondent, and, 165
Review, 162
Setting aside judgment, 166
Applications, 197
  Consent applications, 198
  Costs, 198
  Fees, 257
  Orders without hearing, 200
  Overview, 197
  Precedent, 240
  Telephone hearings, 199
  Without notice, 200
Application for directions, 103
Applications to set aside judgments,
  157–171, 240
  Procedure, 169
Applying the law, 8, 150
Attachment of earnings, 250

Attending the hearing
  Whether to, 106

Bankruptcy, 27, 248
Building disputes, 85, 97
Burden of proof, 143
Businesses, claims against, 24

Case management, 192, 193
  Appeals, 163
  Information, 75
Charging orders
  Land, 250
  Securities, 250
Choosing a court, 40, 73
Claim form
  Annotated, 18
  Description, 221
  Extending life of, 203
  Issuing, 41
Closing speech, 150
Commencement costs, 114, 255,
  257, 259
Commercial Debts (interest), 34, 236
Community Legal Service, 13
Company directors, 25
Company representation, 129
Computer claims, 97
Contempt of court, 142
Contractual claims, 85
  Precedent for a witness
    statement, 238
Cost of proceeding, 9
Costs, 109–125
  Court's discretion, 112, 119
  Indemnity basis, 121
  No costs rule basics, 111
  Quantifying, 112
  Questions, 124
  Standard basis, 121

Summary Assessment
  Procedure for, 121
  Schedule for, 123
  Summary judgment and, 206
  Terminology, 122
Counterclaim, 55
  Defence to, 56, 224
Counterclaim fee, 255
County Court
  Choice on issue, 40
  Districts, 89
  Transfer between, 90
Court fees, 39, 113
  Applications and appeals, 257
  Commencement and allocation, 255
Court's management powers, 10, 192
Court order, 154
Court's own initiative, 49, 78
Credit repair applications, 170
Cross-examination, 149
  Limiting, 145

Debtor's assets, assessing, 245
Deemed service, 202
Default Judgment, 57
  Setting aside, 168
Defective goods, 234
Defence to counterclaim, 56, 224
Defending the claim, 53
  Automatic transfer and, 90
  Counterclaim, 55
  Denial, 54
  Full defence, 55
  Precedent, 223
  Reply to, 59, 224
  States paid, 54, 227
Denial, 54
Deputy District Judges, 6
Diarising, need for, 42
Disclosure, 209

Discretionary judgment, 49
Dishonesty allegations, 68
Disposal hearing, 58
Disposal without hearing, 141
Dispute of jurisdiction, 53
Disputed items, 99
District Judges, 6
  Addressing, 134
Documents required, 92
  Frequently asked questions, 94
  From other side, 75
  Inspection, 209
  Judge's copy, 134
  Management of, 94
  Questions, 94
  Rules of evidence, 142

Earnings, witness loss of, 114
Electing to use Small Claims track,
  80, 112
Enforcement, 243–252
  Attachment of earnings, 250
  Bankruptcy and insolvency, 248
  Charging order on land, 250
  Charging order on securities, 250
  Costs and, 116
  Debtor's assets, 245
  Interest and, 244
  Oral examination, 247
  Order for sale, 251
  Register of County Court
    Judgments, 247
  Summary table, 251
  Third party debt proceedings, 249
  Timescale, 251
  Warrant of execution, 249
Estate agents, 26
Etiquette, 134
European Convention of Human
  Rights, 12

Evaluating the case, 7, 22, 47,
  104, 131
Evidence, 8, 74, 143
  Court's control, 210
  Prohibited, 146
  Rules of, 143, 210
  Excluded Rules, 208
Expenses, 114, 152
Expert evidence, 74, 94, 96, 98,
  136, 146
  Fees and, 114
  Single joint experts, 97
Expert reports, 96, 97
Expert witnesses *see* Expert evidence
Extending the life of claim, 203

Fast track, 64
Fees, 9
  Exemption from, 13
Financial limits, 3
Firms claims against, 25
Further information, 208

Hearing, 127–154, 213
  Advocacy tips, 147
  Audience rights of, 129
  Agreeing to do without, 106
  Friends and observers, 135
  Informality, 140
  Judgment, 152
  Layout and etiquette, 134
  Organisation of, 139
  Overview, 128
  People at, 135
  Preparing for, 84–107
  Checklist, 104–107
  Private or public, 131
  Procedure, 137
  Questions, 154
  Recording, 133
  Sequence of, 139

Transcript, 133
Hearing time, 74, 100
Historical background of Small
Claims, 4, 5
Holiday claims, 85
Example letter, 219
Statement of case, 228
Holidays and hearings, 76
Home court, 72, 89
Housing claims, 67
Human Rights Act, 12

Identifying the defendant, 24
Income support (fees remission), 13
Injunctions, 68
Costs and, 116
Insolvency, 248
Inspection of documents, 209
Interest
Calculating, 34
Commercial debts, 35, 236
Contractual, 34, 236
Judgment debts and, 245
Statement of claim and, 237
Statutory, 34, 236
Interim remedies, 212

Judgment, 152
Enforcement, 244–252
Fixed costs on, 261
Setting aside, 166
Steps after (overview), 252
Judgment in default
Appeal, 168
Defence to counterclaim, 56, 224
Not responding in time, 57
Setting aside, 168
Judgment on admission, 48
Judgment on the court's own
initiative, 49

Judicial sanctions, 195
Relief from, 196
Jurisdiction dispute, 53

Landlords' claims, 85
Law, applying, 9
Lawyers, 127
Layout of the court, 134
Lay representatives, 115, 130
Lay witnesses, 94, 135, 145
Expenses and, 114
Loss of earning, 114
Travelling, 115
Getting the best out of, 149
Letters before action, 12, 218
Examples, 218
Letter to the court manager, 220
Letting agents, 26
Limited companies
Claims against, 25
Address of, 28
Directors, 25
In liquidation, 27
List of disputed items, 99, 241
Location of trial, 73 *see also*
Choosing a court, Transfer

Managing agents, 26
McKenzie friend (*see* Lay
Representatives)
Mediation
Appointment, 188
Benefits, 178
Costs, 177, 186
Counterclaims, 186
Definition, 174
Decision to use, 178, 186
Free, 177
Inappropriate, when, 181
Justice, 183
Litigation, comparison, 180

No agreement, 185
Non-binding, 175
Outcomes, 185
Practical tips, 186
Preparation for, 187
Private, 175
Process, 174, 184
Settlement, 176, 189
State benefits, 177
Voluntary, 175
Mediator
Background, 183
Neutrality, 176
Medical reports, 97
Mistake of law, 159
Moneyclaim online, 20
Multi track, 64

Naming claimants and defendants, 22, 28
No costs rule basics, 111
No financial value, 68

Online claims, 20
Opening speech, 147
Oral examinations, 247
Order for sale, 251
Overriding objective, 2, 126, 192

Part 20 Claims, 56, 249
Particulars of claim, 31 *See also* Statement of case
Partnerships, claims against, 26
Payments into court, 212
Permission to appeal, 160
Personal injury claims, 67, 233
Photographs, 100
Costs and, 116
Preliminary hearing, 102
Principals, 26
Private hearings, 131

Procedural errors, correcting, 206
Procedural table overview, xvii
Procedure at hearings, 137
Procedure overview between response and allocation, 44
Prohibited evidence, 145
Public funding of cases, 13
Public hearing, 131

Qualifying for Small Claims track, 65

Reasoned decision, 152
Recording the hearing, 133
Reference materials, 7
Register of County Court Judgments, 247
Re-hearing, 1162, 167, 170, 207
Relief from sanctions, 196
Reply to defence, 59
Representation, 75
Request for further information, 208
Responding to the claim, 46
Time for, 47
Response pack, 46
Review, appeals, 162
Right of the court to determine the dispute, 53
Rights of audience, 129
Road accident claims, 85, 151
Precedent statement of case, 231
Witness statement precedent, 238
Rules excluded in small claims track, 208

Safety, concern for, 137
Sanctions, 196
Second appeal, 166
Sequence of hearing, 139
Serious irregularity, 155
Service, 201–203
Address for service, 202

Alternative method, 203
Deemed service, 202
Delay in service, 203
Methods of service, 202
Overview table, 201
Setting aside judgment, 166
Setting aside judgment in default, 168
Discretionary grounds, 168
Mandatory grounds, 168
Procedure, 169
Settlement, 11, 72, 104
Informing the court, 100
Offers, 212
Shops (Claims against), 24
Sketch plans, 100
Costs and, 116
Slip rule, 206
Small Claims track
Definition, 64
Overview, 3
Qualifying for, 65, 73
Unique features, 7
Solicitors
Address for service and, 24
Costs, 40
Special directions, 101
Special needs and safety, 137
Specified claim, 32
Standard directions, 85
Table, 86
Starting the case
Checklist, 21
Overview, 17
Statement of case, 30, 222
Admission, 205
Amendments, 205
Defence to counterclaim, 204
Detailing the claim, 222
Detailing the defence, 223
Guidelines for preparation, 222

Interest, 205
Reply to the defence, 224
Setting out, techniques for, 206
Statement of truth, 35, 225
Failure to sign, 37
Who can sign, 37
Wording, 36
States paid defence, 54
Stay of Proceedings, 73
Striking out, 194
Summary judgment, 204–206
Costs, 206
Orders, 206
Overview, 204

Tenancy claims, 85
Terminology, 4
Third party proceedings *see* Part 20
Claims
Time to pay, 50, 153
Time estimate for hearing, 74, 100
Time limits, calculating, 207
Tracks, 64
Changing allocated track, 80
Transcript of Judgment, 153, 164
Transfer of hearing, 88
Automatic, 90
Court order, 90
Travel agents, 26
Travelling expenses, 115

Unpaid fees, 235
Unreasonable behaviour, 117
Assessing costs, 118
Unspecified claim, 32
Judgment in default and, 57

Value of claim, 38
Deciding with no hearing, 57
Vehicle repairs, 85, 97
Venue of hearing, 90

Warrant of execution, 249
Wedding claims, 85
Witness of fact, 74 *see also* Lay
   witnesses, Expert witnesses

Witness statements, 92, 94
   Examples, 238
Witness summons, 95

Small Claims flowchart

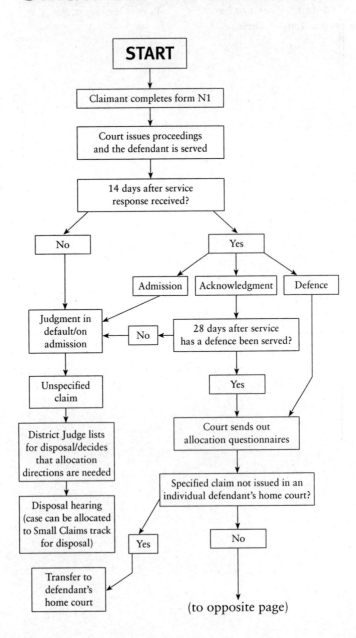

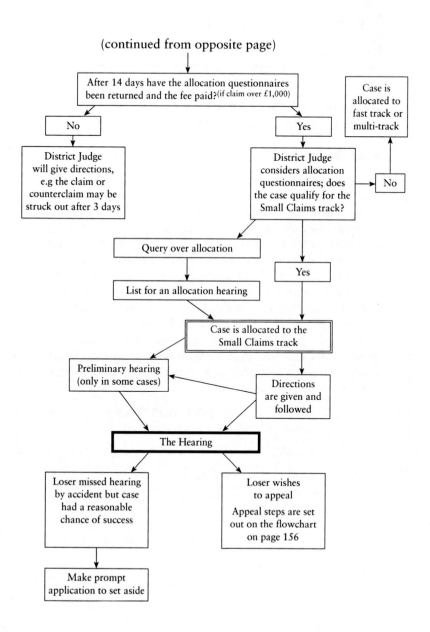

(continued from opposite page)

After 14 days have the allocation questionnaires been returned and the fee paid? (if claim over £1,000)

No

Yes

Case is allocated to fast track or multi-track

District Judge will give directions, e.g the claim or counterclaim may be struck out after 3 days

District Judge considers allocation questionnaires; does the case qualify for the Small Claims track?

No

Query over allocation

Yes

List for an allocation hearing

Case is allocated to the Small Claims track

Preliminary hearing (only in some cases)

Directions are given and followed

The Hearing

Loser missed hearing by accident but case had a reasonable chance of success

Loser wishes to appeal

Appeal steps are set out on the flowchart on page 156

Make prompt application to set aside

Also from XPL

Going Bust? How to Resist and Survive Bankruptcy and Winding Up

Muir Hunter QC

UK citizens have more than a trillion pounds in debt. Many companies are also indebted. Individual bankruptcies, many through debtors' own petitions, are causing considerable alarm, both in banking circles and at Government level. The situation is created more difficult by the decreasing availability of legal aid in insolvency cases (it is prohibited in Winding-up cases). This means an increasing number of determined litigants in person. Any litigant is entitled to conduct his case in person, and this right has at long last been extended, by the Civil Procedure Rules, to the limited company, which may now appear. This book guides individuals and companies through the court process helping them protect themselves and make choices that will work in the long run.

ISBN 1858113687   £19.99

Lightning Source UK Ltd.
Milton Keynes UK
UKOW04f1640090314

227821UK00003B/78/P